High-Performance Building

High-Performance Building

Vidar Lerum

WILEY

John Wiley & Sons, Inc.

Published by John Wiley & Sons, Inc., Hoboken, New Jersey

Published simultaneously in Canada

For general information about our other products and services, please contact our Customer Care Department within the United States at (800) 762–2974, outside the United States at (317) 572–3993 or fax (317) 572–4002.

Wiley also publishes its books in a variety of electronic formats. Some content that appears in print may not be available in electronic books. For more information about Wiley products, visit our Web site at www.wiley.com.

Library of Congress Cataloging-in-Publication Data

Lerum, Vidar.
　High-performance building / Vidar Lerum.
　　p. cm.
　ISBN: 978-0-471-77535-5 (cloth)
　1. Buildings—Performance. 2. Buildings—Energy Conservation. I. Title.
　TH453.L47 2007
　720'.47—dc22

　　　　　　　　　　　　2007015877

Printed in the United States of America

10 9 8 7 6 5 4 3 2 1

Contents

Acknowledgments

Among the many friends and colleagues who have contributed to this book are the School of Architecture directors Ronald McCoy, Catherine Spellman, and Darren Petrucci at Arizona State University and David Chasco at the University of Illinois at Urbana-Champaign. I am grateful for their encouragement and long-lasting support for my research.

Architects, engineers, building managers, users, and owners graciously offered their time and knowledge by accepting my request to sit down for an interview: Klaus H. Nygaard and Ove Neumann (Greenland); Oddvar Hegge (Norway); Jan Søndergaard and Sergio Fox (Denmark); Stefani Reuss and Monika Lauster (Germany); Mario Cucinella (Italy); Gordon R. Beckman, Steven S. Cook, Tim Christ, Will Bruder, and Rosemary Nelson (United States); and Rob Harrison, David Kong, and James Thonger (United Kingdom). Through their insight and enthusiasm about the design of high-performance buildings, they all contributed tremendously to the quality of the research.

Several students assisted with the demanding tasks of processing illustrations and managing databases of images and bibliographical references. Among the many architecture students who provided feedback in the classroom and who worked as research assistants are Melissa Becker, Reid Johnson, and David T. Carroll at Arizona State University and Mike Prohov at the University of Illinois at Urbana-Champaign.

The research leading up to this book involved travels to buildings and sites from the west coast of Greenland—via Scandinavia, Germany, the United Kingdom, Italy, and the Sonoran Desert—to the west coast of the United States. Supporting personnel facilitated travels and provided valuable information. Among the many who made the site visits a welcoming and exciting experience were Peter Barfoed, Tanja Christiansen, Stig Lage, and Emma Kristensen in Nuuk; Knut Johann Jørgensen in Ørsta; Mogens Larsen and Henrik Bo Christiansen in Lyngby; Sanne Hyun Jacobsen in Copenhagen; Dieter Frølich in Bonn; Susanna Quadrelli in Bologna; Catia Giaccaglia in Recanati; Verity Dunn, Rita James, and Simon Grinter in London; and Bill Ruehle in Phoenix.

Research professors Robert W. Jones and James Anderson provided valuable input and encouragement during the many informal but insightful discussions that we had during our meetings in the desert and on the prairie.

I am also indebted to the staff at John Wiley & Sons for their diligent and highly professional work, especially Paul Drougas, acquisitions editor; Raheli

Millman, editorial assistant; Michael Olivo, senior production editor; and Cheryl Ferguson, copyeditor.

This book is dedicated to my late mother, who taught me never to give up, and to my father, who showed me how to go beyond the edge of the village, across the fjord, over the mountains, into the big city, and over to the other side of the ocean.

High-Performance Building

Methods

Introduction

The research leading up to this book is, to a great extent, inspired by the scientific approach that is inherent in the tradition established by Reyner Banham in his environmentalist articles on Frank Lloyd Wright and Sir Joseph Paxton (Banham 1962; Banham 1966). In his 1966 article "Frank Lloyd Wright as Environmentalist," Banham demonstrates how we can investigate the buildings that this great master left behind. This approach to the accumulation of knowledge becomes a necessity because Frank Lloyd Wright did not leave much behind in terms of documentation of his environmental systems design. He did not speak much about this side of his practice, and there is little evidence in his drawings.

Banham explored a claim that Frank Lloyd Wright designed the first *air-conditioned* building. The investigation of this claim led Banham to this conclusion:

> [H]ow easy it might be to miss other innovations which do not produce effects that show up immediately in the printed record. What I have in mind particularly are the environmental innovations which Wright appears to have introduced in his domestic architecture of the Prairie House period (1900–1910), which seem never to have been discussed in the literature and are only likely to be discovered by direct observation, preferably residential, of the houses themselves. (Banham 1966, p. 27)

Banham's examination of Wright's prairie houses began one evening when a group had gathered in the living room of the Baker House in Chicago to rehearse

J. S. Bach's Mass in B Minor. From his position by the fireplace toward the back of the room, Banham noticed that the conductor, who was standing on the window seat near the large bay window, was "perspiring far more freely than the Kyrie would seem to justify." The fireplace was not lit, so there had to be another heat source. Banham discovered that the heat was coming from the grill under the window seat:

> The complete assembly, indoors and out, can be regarded as a single environmental device, controlling heat, light, view, ventilation and (with the help of the overhang of the roof) shade as well. (Banham 1966, p. 28)

In our investigation of the performance of contemporary buildings of great architectural significance, a wealth of information is available in architectural magazines and journals. In addition, the World Wide Web offers a wealth of information for anyone who can operate a networked personal computer. For most contemporary buildings, the architects and engineers behind the design also represent a valuable source of information. So why is it still necessary to investigate the building itself?

Although all these sources may provide valuable input to the process of understanding how great contemporary buildings work, magazine and journal articles tend to miss essential properties of a building—properties or features that do not "produce effects that show up immediately," as Banham stated. Architects and other members of the design team are often the best sources to draw on when seeking knowledge about the properties of the design, since it is the design that is most commonly the focus of architects and engineers. But if there is a discrepancy between the building as designed and the building as built, or a discrepancy between the predicted and the actual performance of the building—and this happens quite often—the ultimate truth can only be found in the building itself.

The seven buildings that are represented in the second part of this book have all been investigated as physical built objects. A site visit to each of the seven buildings, from the west coast of Greenland (shown in Figure 1.1) to the Sonoran Desert in Arizona, was the essential pivot point of the investigation. With one exception, interviews were arranged with the architects for each building. The author also talked to engineers, owners, and users. The interviews generated valuable insight into the design beyond the published sources of information, but at each site visit something unexpected happened. Unknown or hidden features, characteristics, or details about the building were discovered. These features were all relevant to how the actual performance compares to the predicted—or publicized—performance.

Some architects speak volumes about the environmental significance of their building designs. Others are more humble; they quietly let the architecture speak for itself. Does this mean that buildings designed by the most vocal architects are more carefully tuned to the environment than architectural works produced by the silent and the humble? In most cases, the answer to this question can only be found in the built works by the contemporary masters of architecture. If you go ask the building, the built object will provide the answer. As you listen to the building, you will gradually gain the ability to hear it speak!

Fig. 1.1 The Greenland Nature Institute on a winter day with snow.

DESIGN FOR SUSTAINABILITY

The United Nations Conference on Environment and Development (Robinson UNCED, et. al., 1992) defined *sustainability* through the concept of carrying capacity. Earth's population is growing exponentially, placing an ever-increasing demand on nature's capacity to carry the load. As the economic system that serves this population continues to deplete nature's resources and dump the waste into nature's sinks, there are warnings that the economy is about to grow beyond the limits of what nature can carry. One of the most challenging tasks in today's world is, therefore, to reshape the global man-made system of economic development in such a way that it does not extend beyond the limits of the carrying capacity of the natural system.

Sustainability is a serious challenge for the entire economic system, from agriculture to space exploration. In architecture, sustainable design is about developing built forms—buildings and urban spaces—that are tuned to their context, to culture and climate, and to the natural resources of the place; creating designs that are functional; and designing buildings that are aesthetically pleasing. Architectural design for sustainability cannot reach its goals unless the new solutions, the future innovations in building design, are embraced by their owners and users. Design for sustainability must therefore reach toward excellence not only as it is measured against environmental impact, but also in terms of comfort, utility, and beauty.

Approaching building design with a focus on building in harmony with the environment is not an entirely new phenomenon, but it has gained momentum as we enter a new millennium. What started out as a passive solar design movement in the early 1970s has now evolved into a widely accepted interest in sustainable design and green buildings. As these concepts of sustainability in architecture are entering the mainstream, there is a growing concern that the terms *sustainable* and *green* are being co-opted into modern architecture as a style: a new modernism with a touch of green. In the acceptance into the mainstream of environmental concerns and aspirations lies also a possibility that issues that may turn out to be life-threatening on a global scale are treated superficially.

Building rating systems have been developed as a way to formalize and regulate the use of labels for certified green buildings. Many rating systems have initially focused on building design rather than on architectural objects *as built*. In the process of achieving certification, buildings are awarded points for good intentions rather than for evidence of actual postoccupancy performance. In this context, the following questions must be addressed:

- Where do buildings that claim to be green or sustainable rank on a scale relative to benchmark buildings of the same type?
- How do these buildings contribute to sustainable development in terms of their demand for energy and natural materials?
- Do these buildings provide a high level of thermal comfort for their users?

Buildings designed for sustainability in the twenty-first century should draw on natural resources responsibly, and should provide a comfortable environment for their users. Any building that claims to be recognized as *great architecture* should also qualify as a high-performance building in terms of *energy efficiency*. Although energy efficiency is only one of many indicators that may be used to evaluate architectural designs for sustainability, it is still one of the most significant indicators. This position is now recognized by the building sector. In a press release by ASHRAE, the American Society of Heating, Refrigerating and Air-Conditioning Engineers, the main goal of the "Architecture 2030" initiative is stated as "reducing energy use" in buildings:

> The 2030 Challenge, a global initiative officially launched by Architecture 2030 in January 2006, calls for all new buildings and major renovations to reduce their fossil-fuel GHG-emitting energy consumption by 50 percent immediately, increasing this reduction to 60 percent in 2010, 70 percent in 2015, 80 percent in 2020, 90 percent in 2025, and finally, that all new buildings would be carbon neutral by the year 2030. (ASHRAE 2006)

The group recognized, however, that it is meaningless to establish goals if methods of substantiating achievements are lacking or poorly developed:

> A critical component to the success of this effort is the definition of a baseline by which all reductions will be measured. A complete regional database of actual energy use for all building types is not currently available. (ASHRAE 2006)

PERFORMANCE

In this book, performance will be defined mainly as annual specific energy use. This definition, however, needs to be accompanied by a broader view of performance as a form-generating design principle. In addition to their aspiration toward increased energy efficiency, high-performance buildings should provide comfortable and enjoyable work environments for their users, and should be easily maintained within a reasonable budget. In Chapter 13, Tim Christ of Morphosis explains how performance seen as a design parameter becomes a tool that can be used to generate new architectural prototypes.

The rising concern for improved energy performance in buildings has led some countries to consider legislative regulations. The reasoning behind this effort is that higher standards and stricter building codes will lead to more efficient buildings. This assumption has, however, not always proved to be true. There are numerous examples of buildings by highly acclaimed architects that use two to three times more energy than what was predicted during the design phase. This does not mean that attempts to introduce stricter regulations are futile, but demonstrates that the focus needs to be on the actual performance of buildings rather than on the predicted performance.

When evaluating the energy performance of buildings, those making the evaluation should compare the type of building to a baseline. As of the year 2007, no international standards for energy performance have been established, but several countries have introduced stricter standards in their building codes. Figure 1.2 illustrates the new energy performance standards for various types of buildings in Norway. Residential and educational buildings are required to meet a predicted annual specific energy use of between 100 and 140 kilowatt hours per square meter (32 to 44 kBtu/ft^2). Cultural buildings such as performing arts centers, museums, and also physical education buildings and light industrial buildings, should not use more than around 160 kilowatt hours per square meter (52 kBtu/ft^2). Care facilities, hotels, and restaurants are expected to use around 200 kilowatt hours per square meter (63 kBtu/ft^2), with a maximum allowed (predicted) annual energy use of 280 kilowatt hours per square meter (89 kBtu/ft^2) for a hospital.

This new energy-efficiency standard is limited in its impact, since it was just recently signed into law (2007), will not be fully implemented until 2009, and represents a single country where the climate is predominantly cold. The new

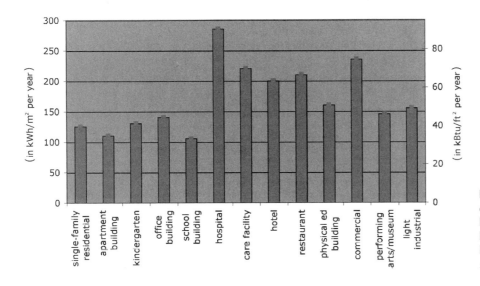

Fig. 1.2 Energy-efficiency standards for buildings in Norway, by building type. Left scale: kWh/m^2 per year, right scale: kBtu/ft^2 per year.

energy standard for Norway, however, still has value as a reference for statistics on the actual energy performance of most buildings today.

Figure 1.3 illustrates the actual energy use of commercial buildings in the United States (ASHRAE 1999). A closer look at the category "office" shows that the annual energy use for a building of this type in the United States averages 320 kWh/m^2 per year. The new proposed standard for Norway is 140 kWh/m^2 per year, which is just above 40 percent of the actual average energy use of a U.S. office building. Many countries in Europe seem to be willing to set even more ambitious goals. There is a trend toward a goal stated as *one quarter*, which means that the goal is to reduce the annual energy use of a new building to 25 percent of the actual energy use of existing buildings of the same type.

When evaluating the specific energy requirement for a building, measured as kWh per square meter per year, we should also take into account the people density inside that same building. The gas mileage of a minivan with seven passengers in it is not directly comparable to that of a small two-seater with one person inside. When evaluating the energy efficiency of people transportation, it is more commonly accepted to use the fuel consumption per passenger mile as a standard. If the same line of thought is applied to building energy efficiency, the annual energy requirement per person occupying and using the building should also be taken into account.

Figure 1.4 shows the annual energy consumption of three houses in Norway designed by the author and built since the year 2000. The graph shows that these three houses use from 47 to 101 kilowatt hours per square meter annually, all included. The figure also shows that each house checks in well below the new energy standard for single-family homes in Norway (125 kWh/m^2 per year).

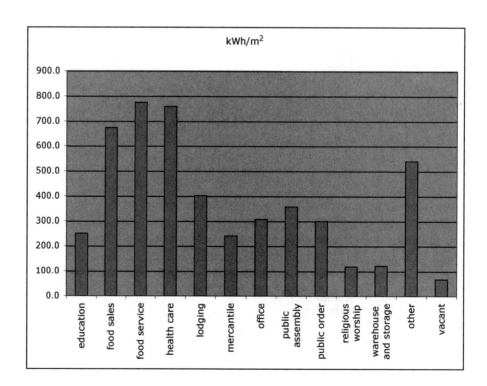

Fig. 1.3 Energy use of U.S. buildings, 1999.

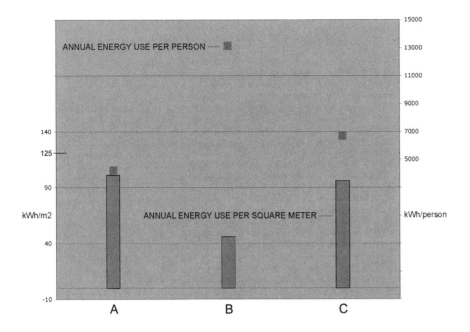

Fig. 1.4A Actual total annual energy use for three houses in Sogndal, Norway.

When the annual energy requirement per person is calculated, however, the three houses rank differently from the picture created by the columns for annual specific energy requirement. The first house (A) is occupied by nine persons: a family with three children and two rental units with two persons in each. The second house (B) had only one person in it during the year when the utility data were acquired. The third house (C) was occupied by three persons: a family with one teenage boy.

The same considerations need to be made when comparing office buildings in Europe and the United States. Due to German legislation concerning labor issues, the Post Tower in Bonn (Chapter 11) has a lower population density on a typical office floor than the San Francisco Federal Building (Chapter 13). If these two buildings were using the same amount of energy per unit of floor area annually, the San Francisco building would use less energy per person on a typical office floor, since the population density in the U.S. building is higher than that of a modern office building in Germany.

A   B   C

Fig. 1.4B Three houses in Sogndal, Norway.

CERTIFICATES

Since the actual performance of many good buildings does not meet the expectation generated by the predicted performance based on codes and standards, there needs to be a way to address this discrepancy. The European Union is now developing legislation that will require that owners of large buildings report the annual energy use of their buildings. These reports will be used to produce statistical information and should be made available to the public. In some countries, such as Switzerland and Germany, it is already required that certificates of annual energy use be issued for any building that is put up for sale. As energy-use certificates become more common, it is likely that the energy efficiency of a building will become a factor that could significantly influence its market value.

The reluctance by many building owners to allow public access to their energy-use data may be seen as a proof of the necessity to introduce legislation that requires energy-use certificates to be issued. Otherwise, it becomes difficult to substantiate the many claims that both building designers and owners have made regarding the energy performance of their recent showcase buildings. One example is the Swiss Re headquarters building in London by Foster and Partners. In an interview with Lord Norman Foster on BBC Radio 4 on April 27, 2004, the designer presented bold claims about how this building would be more eco-friendly by slashing the energy use in half; however, access to actual performance documentation has been limited.

Another example is the Deutsche Post World Net headquarters (the Post Tower) in Bonn, Germany (described in Chapter 11). According to the Deutsche Post Web site (www.deutschepost.de), this newly formed corporation, which used to be the German postal system, places great emphasis on its care for the environment by publishing annual sustainability reports. The reports on the company's efforts to care for the environment address efforts to reduce the total carbon emissions from buildings, ground transportation, and air transportation. At the same time, however, the company has denied requests for documentation on the actual total annual energy use of the Post Tower. It is therefore impossible for the scientific community to generate the analyses necessary to substantiate the claims.

Each new high-performance design carries the potential of becoming a learning tool for new generations of building designers. However, without the ability to generate an energy performance database, quality learning will not take place.

ACCOUNTABILITY

New legislation could potentially demand that documentation of the actual annual energy use for buildings be published. Therefore, new practices and methods must be developed in order to define and account for energy efficiency and, consequently, a building's contribution to carbon emissions and other environmental impact. New legislation could also require auditing the data that will be made available to the public. As energy-use certificates are required, the need for new instruments and methods of energy-use documentation will surface. These methods of instrumentation and data acquisition must address questions about which factors will be accounted for in the numbers and which will be excluded. Only if reliable data are available can comparisons between buildings of the same type bc made and lessons learned.

This new development also presents a tremendous opportunity for developing the science of design improvements through the evolution of virtual iterations based on computer modeling. If data are available on the energy use of various categories of power demand and energy use in buildings, vast opportunities could open up for using computer simulations to develop scenarios for improved building designs. Most computer-based thermal simulation programs available today produce breakdowns of predicted power demand and energy use for categories such as heating, cooling, lights, equipment, and miscellaneous plug loads, by monthly distribution.

These advanced computer models cannot be calibrated effectively, however, if only one accumulated number for the total annual energy use is available. The need for accounting and auditing should therefore be taken as an opportunity to specify instrumentation, metering equipment, data acquisition systems, and systems that can store historic data, with breakdowns on the various energy use categories. The accumulated data produced by these new practices would be a tremendous source of knowledge that, if applied properly in computer models, could lead to improved performance of both existing and future buildings—by design.

LEARNING FROM GREAT BUILDINGS

One purpose of this book is to introduce a systematic approach to energy performance and thermal comfort in existing buildings by proposing a step-by-step procedure for analyzing how great buildings work and how they can act as prototypes for well-designed architectural objects of high performance. The underlying assumption is that a careful investigation of the actual performance of buildings not only is a critical practice relative to the predicted energy use of the design, but will also prove to be the best tool for improving future buildings by reducing and ultimately eliminating the negative impact of designed objects on the environment.

A proposed organization of the process for investigating performance will be described in the next six chapters. This process is organized in 15 steps:

Climate Conditions (Chapter 2)
1 Climate data
2 Climate analysis
3 Design strategies

Documents (Chapter 3)
4 Publications
5 Site analysis
6 Building documentation

Performance by Design (Chapter 4)
    7 Interviews
    8 Transcripts
    9 Claims

As Built (Chapter 5)
  10 Preparing for the site visit
  11 Review utility records, on-site sources of information
  12 Experimental evaluation

What If? (Chapter 6)
  13 Identify scenarios
  14 Run simulations

Summary Report (Chapter 7)
  15 Report content—deliverables

In an educational setting where the investigation is carried out by small teams of students, each step could take one week to complete. This process therefore lends itself to becoming the backbone of a seminar on high-performance buildings.

The same process may be used in analyzing precedent studies as part of the predesign or conceptual design phase in architectural practice. In a group setting, whether in academia or in practice, the investigation could involve several buildings in parallel.

The process described here is designed for analyzing existing buildings. It is possible that the same process, with modifications, could be applied as a method for organizing the schematic design phase, with emphasis on developing several design schemes and analyzing the predicted performance of these schemes as a comparative analysis exercise.

2

Climate Conditions

Our investigation of a high-performance building starts with a thorough examination of the climate at the location. With the use of electric lighting, mechanical heating, and air conditioning, buildings can certainly be designed with disregard for the local climate. Deep cores in buildings can be lit by means of electricity, and sizing up the mechanical systems can compensate for heat loss and heat gain from exterior walls made entirely of glass. But it is now widely recognized that this approach to design leads to buildings that waste energy and contribute to greenhouse gas emissions on a scale that is harmful to the environment and totally undesirable in today's world of climate change and rapid depletion of natural resources.

There is another side to the design of buildings that does not recognize the climate that surrounds them: These buildings also tend to neglect user comfort and satisfaction. Buildings designed for sustainability must address both of these issues. Instead of relying on an increasing extraction rate of nonrenewable resources, buildings should respond to climate and make use of free environmental sources of energy to provide a comfortable environment for human activity. Buildings designed for sustainability must address efficiency in terms of energy and economy, but they cannot succeed in a free market unless they are also built for comfort and beauty. When high-performance building design is seen in this context, we are using the concept of bioclimatic design, where both comfort and climate take prominent positions (Olgyay 1963).

This chapter introduces an analytical approach to a method for understanding the characteristics of the climate at a specific location and how these characteristics may represent challenges and opportunities for the designer. A description of the location and climate is included in the presentation of each case study building in Part Two.

Five computer programs will be explored. Examples from Nuuk, Greenland, and Phoenix, Arizona, will be used to explain the use of the programs. Weather Maker will be used to identify and prepare weather files for locations where TMY (typical meteorological year) data are readily available. Readers will then learn how to use Meteonorm to establish a TMY-formatted weather data file for practically any location on Earth where a TMY file is not available to the general public. We will also learn how programs like Wind Rose and Climate Consultant can use a TMY-type weather file to prepare graphic illustrations of wind conditions (velocity, frequency, and wind direction) at the site. Weather Maker and ENERGY-10 will be used to analyze the seasonal characteristics of the climate. A methodological approach will be explained using the two programs in tandem to arrive at a deeper understanding of challenges and opportunities for a climate-responsive, bioclimatic design.

CLIMATE CLASSIFICATION SYSTEMS

The Köppen system (see Figure 2.1) is one of the most widely used climate classification systems. Dr. Vladimir Köppen of the University of Graz in Austria devised his classification system in 1918 and published several modifications through the next two decades. Köppen was both a climatologist and a plant geographer. His main interest was finding climate boundaries that coincided approximately with boundaries between major vegetation types (McKnight 2000). According to the Köppen classification system, the buildings described in Part Two of this book are located in the following climate zones: subarctic (the coast of Greenland), marine west coast (Norway, Denmark, Germany, northern California), Mediterranean (Italy), and arid (Arizona).

While the Köppen system divides the 48 contiguous states of the United States into six climate zones (Figure 2.1), Olgyay suggests that a classification

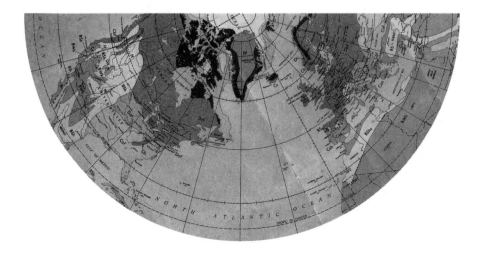

Fig. 2.1 Climate zones for North America and Europe, based on the Köppen climate classification system.

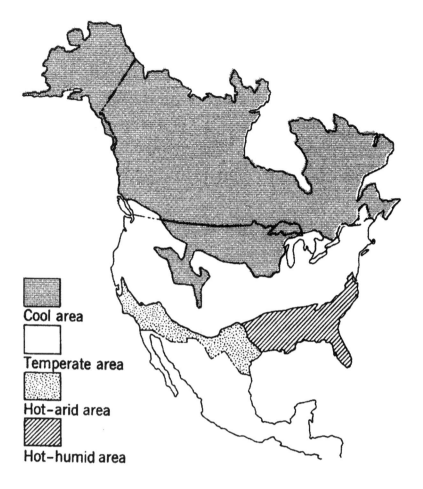

Fig. 2.2 Regional climate zones of the North American continent.

Cool area

Temperate area

Hot-arid area

Hot-humid area

system of four major climate types is more appropriate for bioclimatic design: cool, temperate, hot-arid, and hot-humid (Olgyay 1963). These regions are shown in Figure 2.2. Although a study of these climate zones may be useful as an introduction to understanding the climate at a specific building location, it becomes obvious to the experienced researcher that the climate zones are so broadly defined that a more careful investigation of the local climate is unavoidable. Chicago, Illinois, experiences bitter cold and windy winters, but also copes with hot and humid summers. Summer daytime temperatures in desert cities in Arizona reach 120°F, but ice can form on the roof of a car during clear winter nights when the night sky radiation has a powerful effect on both air temperature and human comfort.

Climate consideration involves three phases:

Step 1: Obtain accurate and valid weather data.
Step 2: Conduct climate analysis: seasons and strategies.
Step 3: Refine design strategies.

The purpose of these three steps is to obtain knowledge and understanding of the climate conditions at the building location. High-performance buildings are characterized by their ability to respond to the local climate by using natural sources of energy to reduce the overall use of energy imported to the site. The general approach that forms the background of this chapter first looks at energy conservation, then looks at how natural sources of energy may be used to create comfortable environments—by design. It next considers how additional energy sources and systems may be used to supplement the basic passive, architecturally integrated systems.

STEP 1: CLIMATE DATA

The first task under step 1 is to establish the best climate data available. In order to find the weather data necessary to analyze the building, we need to know exactly where the building is located in terms of longitude and latitude. Such information is easily obtained from maps, but we may also use Internet tools, such as Google Earth™, to find the exact location of the building.

It is also useful to find and study general descriptions of the climate zone where the building is located. In the United States, four basic climates must be taken into consideration: the hot and dry (arid), the hot and humid, the temperate, and the cold climates. As you study descriptions of each of these climate zones, you will find that some climates are more diverse and complex than others. An example is the previously mentioned city of Chicago, which experiences bitter cold and windy winter days, but also several hot and humid weeks during the summer.

Once the exact location and climate zone are known, we are ready to locate the weather file. TMY (typical meterological year) the most common weather file format. A TMY file is a delimited text file that contains information on a multitude of climate parameters for each of the 8,760 hours in a typical year. The data are usually compiled from 30 years of acquired historical weather data. It is important to understand that a typical meteorological year is not an average year. The typical meteorological year attempts to show weather events and extreme conditions that will typically occur during the various seasons at a specific location.

Another frequently used climate file format is the EnergyPlus weather file (EPW), which is used by the energy simulation program EnergyPlus and also by HEED and Climate Consultant. In this chapter we will look at how the computer programs Weather Maker and Meteonorm may be used to establish and locate an appropriate weather file for your specific location.

Weather Maker takes TMY-type climate files and converts them into a format that can be used by the energy simulation program ENERGY-10. Weather Maker is also a great program for analyzing the various seasons of the climate at a particular location. Weather Maker can convert TMY files into text files, and ENERGY-10 files may be converted back into TMY files.

Weather Maker includes weather files for 239 locations in the United States where TMY weather files are available free of charge. Additional weather files are provided for international locations. These are called *parent locations* in Weather Maker. ENERGY-10 files for the same locations are included with the Weather Maker and ENERGY-10 program package.

If an hour-by-hour weather file for a specific location cannot be found, Weather Maker has a function that lets the user adjust a parent file to create a *child file.* The approach here is to use the nearest or most appropriate weather file constructed from TMY data, and then use typical day or average temperature data for the specific location to create the child file based on the parent file. The process of adjusting a parent weather file to create a weather file for a child location is described in detail in the Weather Maker help files.

As an example, let us look at the analysis of several designs for affordable and energy-efficient housing prototypes for Moenkopi using Weather Maker and ENERGY-10. Moenkopi is a Hopi village located just outside the Navajo town of Tuba City in northern Arizona (see Figure 2.3). In this example, Flagstaff, Arizona, was identified as the most appropriate parent site. The parent site was selected after a study of proximity, elevation, climate, vegetation type, and temperature characteristics for several TMY locations in the region. The Adjust function in Weather Maker was used to create a child weather file for Cameron, a trading post located between Flagstaff and Tuba City. Cameron is included as a child site in Weather Maker. The Adjust function was used a second time to create a child site for Tuba City, using available average-day temperature data for Tuba City to adjust the Cameron file.

The process of establishing accurate and reliable weather data turned out to be crucial in the analysis of the Moenkopi housing prototypes. One of the most significant results from this project was a set of recommendations as to how new housing designs could provide comfort year-round utilizing passive strategies that would require minimal expenditure of energy (see Figure 2.4).

When working with locations outside of the United States where a weather file is not readily available, we may use the computer program Meteonorm to

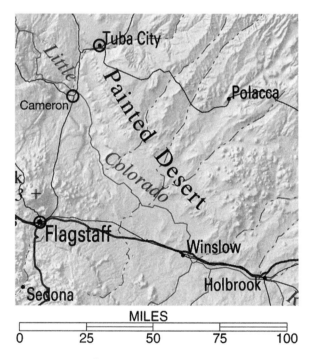

MILES

0   25   50   75   100

Fig. 2.3 Map of northern Arizona, with parent location Flagstaff, first child location Cameron, and second child location Tuba City.

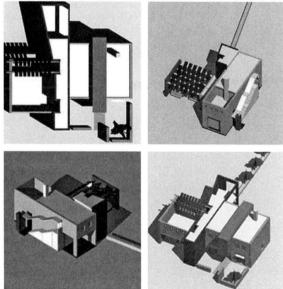

Fig. 2.4 New housing prototypes for the Moenkopi village in northern Arizona. The designs incorporate climate-responsive strategies, such as wind protection, passive solar heating, thermal mass, natural ventilation, and night-vent cooling. A photovoltaic shading structure over the carport provides on-site electric energy.

create a synthetic weather file for that location. The Meteonorm computer program includes weather data from locations all over the world. Based on the latitude and longitude, the characteristics of the location, and other information that the user inputs, Meteonorm will generate a synthetic weather file. These weather files are fairly accurate and sufficiently dependable for the type of building energy analysis being discussed here.

The map feature in Meteonorm was used to establish a weather file for Nuuk, where the Greenland Nature Institute is located. The town of Nuuk, formerly known as Godthab, is on the western coast of Greenland. The location was identified as a station shown on the map in Meteonorm (see Figure 2.5). Average-day temperature data from the Danish Meteorological Institute were used to fine-tune the file, which was then exported from Meteonorm in TMY file format and converted to an ENERGY-10 weather file in Weather Maker.

A specific function in Meteonorm lets the user input information on the horizon shading of the building site. This information is then used to compute a site-specific weather data file from the location-specific file just described. This is particularly important for rural sites with tall mountains or high trees surrounding the building. It is also very useful when analyzing buildings in an urban context, where surrounding buildings could cast shadows onto our site. The solar radiation and daylight information for sites with a skyline above the horizon may vary significantly from the same information in the location-specific file. The procedure of accounting for horizon shading is explained in greater detail in step 5, described in Chapter 3.

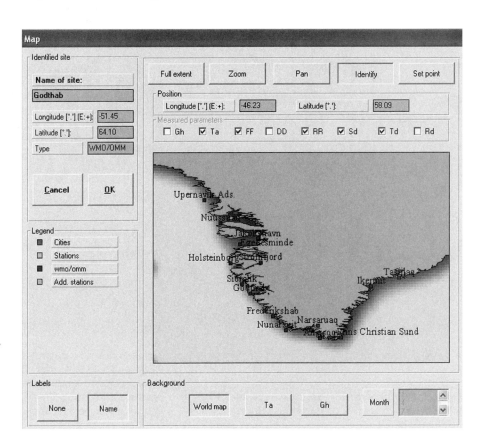

Fig. 2.5 In Meteonorm, weather stations may be located from a world map or by using a name search function. Nuuk was formerly known as Godthab.

STEP 2: CLIMATE ANALYSIS

Most climate data files, such as the TMY or EPW files, include information on hourly values for wind speed, wind direction, and frequency. Wind data are usually displayed graphically as *wind roses*. A wind rose diagram is useful in analyzing the wind conditions at the site, since wind is typically unreliable and elusive. Climate Consultant 3 is a very good computer program to use when analyzing wind data. This program creates diagrams and graphic representations of the wind data, which may be displayed per day, per month, or per season (several months, as specified by the user). The wind data can also be displayed as an animated wind wheel in Climate Consultant 3. The program can be downloaded for free at www2.aud.ucla.edu/energy-design-tools/. It uses the EPW file format from EnergyPlus.

If you do not have an EPW file for your location, there are other programs that can be used to graphically display wind data. One of these programs is Wind Rose, available from Enviroware srl (Italy; www.enviroware.com). A graphic output from Wind Rose is shown in Figure 12.26. Wind Rose can also be used with Google Earth™, as seen in Figure 2.6, where wind information is displayed graphically as an overlay on the satellite image of Bonn, Germany.

Climate Consultant also displays information on temperatures, solar radiation, and other climate data parameters. Temperature data are displayed as average day or typical day per month, and Climate Consultant does not typically generate hour-by-hour representation of the data. However, the program has very good graphing capabilities.

Fig. 2.6 Wind data for Bonn, Germany, displayed graphically as an overlay in Google Earth™. *Source:* Wind Rose image created by Enviroware srl (Italy).

For analyzing climate data hour by hour, Weather Maker is a superior alternative. As mentioned earlier, Weather Maker comes as a component of the ENERGY-10 simulation program. Weather Maker may be used to analyze daily swings, weekly weather events, seasonal temperature data, and solar radiation data. The program even lets the user take a quick look at the entire year. The user can export a summary statistics report as a text file, which gives the user access to important information, such as a design-day for each month of the year. An example described in Chapter 11 uses design day data for Bonn, Germany, to evaluate issues of condensation relative to the fan coil units at the Post Tower.

The most essential part of using Weather Maker for climate analysis is an exercise in which seasons are identified and potential appropriate design strategies are associated with these seasons at the specific location of your building. The reasoning behind this approach is that a seasonal analysis is necessary in order to identify periods of the year when the building may be conditioned predominantly with the use of natural environmental sources of (free) energy, combined with passive design features.

This approach is fundamentally different from the ASHRAE *design day approach,* in which a summer design day and winter design day are used to determine the peak demand on the heating and cooling system. By focusing on one peak heating design day and one peak cooling design day, we can keep the building comfortable all year-round by sealing it up and running mechanical systems appropriately sized to supply heating and cooling under extreme winter and summer conditions. This is, however, not the most energy-efficient approach. The seasonal approach, therefore, becomes a very important alternative method when the energy performance of buildings is examined.

Phoenix, Arizona, will be used as an example to illustrate how this method of seasonal climate analysis may be applied. For more detailed analysis of the Phoenix climate, see Chapter 14.

The first task in applying this method of analysis is to identify three to five periods that represent typical seasonal climate conditions or weather events at the location. Each period representing one season should span 5 to 10 consecutive days. For Phoenix seasonal periods characterized as winter, early spring, early summer, and monsoon will typically cover the climate conditions experienced through an entire year. Using the graphing capabilities of Weather Maker, each of these seasons can be displayed in temperature and solar radiation graphs and analyzed hour by hour or day by day.

The next task is to extract the appropriate passive design strategies from the information displayed seasonally. In order to do this, you need to be familiar with some basic parameters of passive design.

For example, a winter week, even in Phoenix, experiences ambient temperatures well below the comfort zone, particularly at night. Based on the temperature data for a winter week, we may assume that there is a need for heating energy to keep the interior of the building within the comfort zone. A quick look at the solar radiation data for the same week shows that there is an abundance of sunshine available that may be utilized for space heating through passive design features, such as south-facing glazing and internal thermal mass.

Similarly, the analysis of an early spring week will show that many buildings may already experience heat gains that require that heat be removed from the interior. Since the ambient temperatures for most days in a typical early spring week are below the comfort zone, cooling may be achieved in a low-energy fashion by simply opening the windows or pulling in ambient air through a passive or active ventilation system.

In the early summer, daytime temperatures exceed the comfort zone on most days. During this season, outdoor air cannot be used to cool the building simultaneously, but since the nighttime temperatures go well below the comfort zone, cooler night air may be used to subcool thermal mass in the building. This low-energy strategy is commonly called *night-vent cooling with high mass*. Evaporative cooling is another low-energy cooling strategy that works well during the early summer season in Phoenix, since the air is hot and dry. By implementing new innovations combining radiant cooling with the evaporative process, low-energy cooling is available without the discomfort associated with bringing moist air into the building.

As the monsoon season arrives, Phoenix experiences temperatures that are way above the comfort zone during the day as well as during the night. As the dew point temperature approaches 70°F, evaporative cooling cannot be used as a low-energy cooling strategy. This leaves the designer with few alternatives except for mechanical compressor–driven air-conditioning. But again, there is a potential for low-energy solutions that can be tapped through the application of new technologies such as heat-driven adsorption chillers, combined with radiant and desiccant cooling.

STEP 3: DESIGN STRATEGIES

The process of developing design strategies for the location takes the climate analysis one step further, from understanding the climate to understanding how climate response can influence the design of a high-performance building. By going through this process prior to a more detailed study of the building design, and prior to examining the building as built, one can be better informed and prepared to ask the right questions during the interviews and the site visit.

The Phoenix example illustrates how appropriate design strategies can be identified from a careful investigation of the local climate. This process assumes a basic understanding of the meaning and application of strategies for bioclimatic design. The following sources are recommended for further study of the concept of design strategies: *Environmental Control Systems* (Moore 1993), *Sun, Wind, and Light* (Brown and DeKay 2001), *Design with Climate* (Olgyay 1963), *Mechanical and Electrical Equipment for Buildings* (Stein, Reynolds et al. 2006), and the user manual "Mastering ENERGY-10," available for download at <www.sbicouncil.org>.

COMPARING PREDICTED HEAT FLOW TO AMBIENT CONDITIONS

As we develop location-specific strategies for building designs for sustainability, it becomes evident that the analysis needs to go beyond the basic comfort and climate paradigm. This is particularly true for high-performance buildings with sophisticated envelope characteristics. High-performance buildings will often behave differently from what can be expected based on the analysis of the climate data. An example of this phenomenon is described in Chapter 8, where the Greenland Nature Institute is analyzed and discussed.

The air temperature outside the building was at or below freezing for several clear days during the site visit in April 2005. At the same time, some offices inside the building were overheating. Based on the temperature data, this situation may be described as counterintuitive. Without actually experiencing the overheated offices in the building, one would have thought that mechanical heating was required on a spring day in Greenland with freezing temperatures outside.

As it turns out, the offices that were overheating had large windows exposed to the west. At 64°N, the west façade is exposed to solar radiation for several hours in the afternoon in the late spring, when sun angles are still low. The sun path diagram in Figure 8.1 provides an easy-to-read illustration of the solar geometry at 64°N. In mid-April, the sun sets 30 degrees north of west after 7:30 P.M. solar time.

A method for analyzing situations like these is to use ENERGY-10 in tandem with Weather Maker and perform comparative analyses of ambient temperature and solar radiation data with simulation results on heat flow for the same time period. A simple model of the building can be set up fairly quickly in ENERGY-10, and the annual energy use can be simulated using the default settings in the computer program. This exercise will allow the user to create graphs of the same seasonal periods that simultaneously show temperature swings, solar radiation data, and predicted (simulated) heat flow. Quite often, one will find that a building designed according to recent energy standards could easily overheat, even on a cold day. This exercise shows the complexity of designing and analyzing high-performance buildings. It also shows that with a careful analysis and detailed study, we can arrive at a deeper understanding of how buildings work and why some buildings perform better than others.

Figures 8.7 and 8.8 contain two comparative graphs for the same week in early April. It becomes evident from examining these graphs that a conventionally designed and constructed office building will predominantly need heating during this week, but a well-designed, low-energy building will need cooling on any given day in the same week. The good news is that cooling may be provided for free, since the ambient temperatures fluctuate around 0°C, with a minimum at −10°C.

Chapter 8 contains more detailed explanations of how this method may be applied when analyzing a high-performance building. The principal architect of the ENERGY-10 program, Dr. Douglas Balcomb, also created extensive help files. It is recommended that the ENERGY-10 help files be printed and studied carefully before setting up a simplified model of your building and analyzing it and ENERGY-10. Although useful for explaining how to use the many features of the computer program, these help files also function as a study guide to low-energy building design. The software user manual "Mastering ENERGY-10" is available in PDF format from the Sustainable Buildings Industry Council at http://www.sbicouncil.org.

3

Documents

N ow that we are familiar with the environmental (climatic) context for the building in question, the next phase in our investigation is to search for information on the building itself. As an introduction to the analysis of a high-performance building, we set out to learn about the building and its physical context (the site) as documented in publications, site plans, and construction documents.

We often get our first impressions of a building through a journal article, an architectural magazine, or a Web site. Searching for publications is therefore a natural first step in our inquiry into the performance of buildings. We then go on to collect and study representations of the site and the building itself. Along with our analysis of the climate at the building location (Chapter 2), the three steps described here will form the foundation for the interviews with the designers (Chapter 4).

STEP 4: PUBLICATIONS

As the first task in analyzing a building, we seek to know everything that has been published about it. A good place to start is to perform bibliographic searches at university libraries, in public library catalogs, and on the Internet. Some computerized bibliographic search tools and reference database programs, such as End-Note (www.thomsonisiresearchsoft.com), will let the user search for books in library catalogs directly from a personal computer. The EndNote program also makes it possible to create links to PDF (portable document format) versions of each article or (scanned) book chapter. References to journal and magazine articles are most commonly found in bibliographical indexes, such as the *Avery Index to Architectural Periodicals.*

Make it a habit to write a paragraph or two about the content of each article and save it as an abstract of that particular publication. Collecting references in a computerized database makes it easy to create an annotated bibliography. It pays to spend some time on this first task of the building analysis, since we will refer to our sources frequently during our investigation. This time-saving technique enables us to get a quick overview of all the published sources of information that resulted from our search. Since we may need to quickly locate PDF versions of the published articles and book chapters, they should be archived electronically in the same server space or hard drive folder in order to enable easy access.

When referencing information obtained from Web sites, always make a note of the Web address (URL) and the date and time the site was visited. Information posted on the Web is changed and updated at a faster pace than articles are revised and new editions of books are printed. Easy access to Web publishing and the ability to quickly change information posted on the Internet reinforces the need to maintain a critical attitude toward any information obtained from the Web.

The first quick reading through published articles and book chapters is commonly referred to as an *environmental scan.* This scanning process sometimes reveals that the same information is copied and reprinted from one journal or magazine to another. This is not uncommon. One important thing to note here, however, is that if a feature of the building is represented or written up incorrectly the first time, chances are that the same error will be repeated and republished. It is therefore very important to remain critical of what is published, even in the most respected journals and in books published by the most esteemed publishers.

For example, when the Greenland Nature Institute building was first published in the Danish architecture magazine *Arkitektur* (Ahnfeldt-Mollerup 1998), the natural ventilation system was briefly presented as the architect had described it to the journalist. The author of the first article did not critically investigate how the natural ventilation system actually worked. The prevailing wind directions were also described incorrectly as SSE and NNW, while the wind rose for Nuuk shows prevailing winter winds coming from NNE and prevailing summer winds from due south (shown in Figure 8.12).

A shorter version of the first article was later republished by the Canadian architecture magazine *On Site* (Neumann 2004). Since the description of wind patterns and ventilation principles was now published twice in two prominent magazines, one would think that the description was an accurate representation of how the natural ventilation system works in the actual building under normal conditions at the site.

The Nature Institute site experiences frequent strong winds. As it turns out, the natural ventilation of the building *does not* necessarily work in the way it was intended. Rather than exhibiting a simple airflow path based on cross-ventilation and stack effect, air is actually exchanged as it flows in both directions between the individual offices and the atrium, and between the atrium and the ambient air. This example shows how the study of building performance through publications sometimes creates an incomplete or even inaccurate impression of the building. This phenomenon is described in greater detail in Chapter 8.

STEP 5: SITE ANALYSIS

One of the most important tasks in our investigation is to get the site plan right. We should ask the architect or building owner for a detailed site plan, including a correctly oriented north arrow. Likewise, topography, trees, grass areas, roads, parking lots, and other infrastructure elements should be included in a good site plan. The site plan should also show the urban context (footprints and heights of surrounding buildings) in cases where the building is located in a built-up area. If a good site plan cannot be obtained as a scaled architectural drawing, we may need to go back to the journal articles and book chapters, and look for a site plan there. Again, a note of caution is warranted. Site plans are often a missing element in the publication of a building, and when they are published, they sometimes contain errors regarding how the building is positioned and the orientation of north. Research for this book revealed several incorrect or incomplete site plans published in highly respected journals.

A good way to check the building orientation on the site plan is to use Google Earth™, the Web-based computer program found at earth.google.com. In Google Earth™ we can find very good satellite or aerial views of the site for most built-up areas around the world. This is a quick and easy way to check for compliance. It is also an excellent source of information for the actual longitude and latitude of the building in question.

If our building is located in a built-up area, or if tall mountains, trees, or other obstructions surround the site, it may become necessary to create a three-dimensional massing model of the building, including its immediate surroundings, as shown in Figure 3.1 (SketchUp 2006). Such a digital model will allow for a

Fig. 3.1 A three-dimensional model of a city center can be used to analyze sun exposure, view corridors, and observe shading.

quick analysis of the shading effect from nearby objects. A site visit is highly recommended if the building is within reach, but a massing model is still useful because it allows for studies of solar access and shading for any date and time throughout the year.

It is very useful and often necessary to accurately measure the horizon shading (skyline) for buildings that are surrounded by tall objects. The information can then be plotted and imported into programs that can take the horizon shading into account when generating information on solar radiation and daylight. This process will generate a site-specific weather data file from the location-specific data described in step 1.

The process goes as follows: A theodolite or similar instrument can be used at the site to measure the altitude angles by pointing the instrument toward the top of any object that will obstruct the path of the sun's rays. This is most commonly done by measuring the altitude angle of nearby objects at 5- to 15-degree intervals around the horizon. The numerical values of altitude and azimuth angles are then supplied as input to the Meteonorm program in a screen, as shown in Figure 3.2. Meteonorm computes the effect of reduced solar radiation and daylight, including corrected sunrise and sunset times, as a function of the horizon shading at the exact building site.

Horizon shading data for a particular site may also be recorded as a digital picture. The picture is then loaded into Meteonorm and used as a background for tracing the horizon. Pictures of the horizon shading line (skyline) can be imported in JPG file format. The picture must stretch from north over west, south, east, and to north again. The resulting site-specific weather file can be used in building energy-performance simulations with a higher degree of accuracy than would be expected using location-specific data.

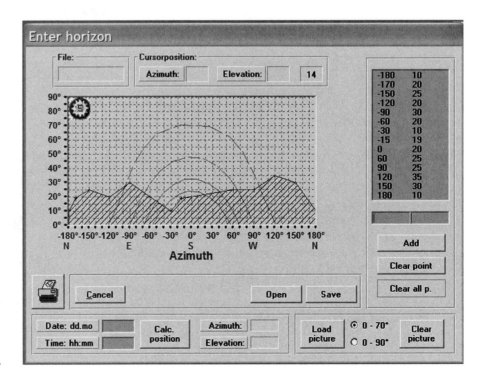

Fig. 3.2 Meteonorm screen shot shows how the horizon shading is entered. The program will adjust the solar radiation data in the weather file accordingly.

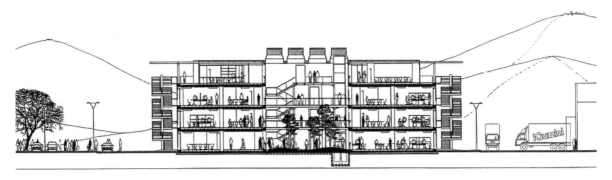

Fig. 3.3 Longitudinal section of the iGuzzini headquarters building.

STEP 6: BUILDING DOCUMENTATION

The next step is to collect documentation on the building that we have started to investigate. Ideally, we would want to obtain copies of construction documents and specifications on the building itself, including structural and mechanical systems. Previously published plans, sections, elevations, and site plans can be obtained with ease (see Figure 3.3), but getting access to detailed drawings and specifications often requires a substantial effort. Finding the information needed to fully understand the building is often a very difficult task, since architects and building owners are sometimes reluctant to provide it. The difficulties in obtaining the requested information are not necessarily based on unwillingness on the part of the designers or the building owners, but are most often a result of the fact that people are busy, and this is just another unpaid service that they are being asked to perform. We should, however, be able to get the information that we need for buildings that are publicly owned and for buildings that do not represent any particular security issue.

Drawings and specifications are now most commonly archived as electronic documents in PDF file formats. This is the format of choice for our investigation, since PDF files are compatible with most computer systems. PDF files are also easy to use. They allow users to zoom in on details in the document and to print at any scale that they prefer.

If we cannot obtain all the documentation that we are asking for, we may need to refer back to the publications of the building and look for plans, sections, elevations, and detailed specifications. Since we are investigating building performance, it is very important to obtain information on properties of the building, such as glazing types, insulation values, and HVAC systems, as well as the general orientation and layout of the building.

It is now time for a careful study of the building documentation. Referring to Chapter 2, we can identify the seasons and develop appropriate design strategies that will guide the analysis of the documents that describe and specify the building. As a start, we should look for obvious building characteristics, elements, and features:

- Window orientation and size
- Glazing properties
- Amount of thermal mass exposed to the interior
- Shading devices
- Insulation values

- Roof types
- Ventilation principles
- User interface

The case study building descriptions in Part Two are a source of information and inspiration as to further things to look for and other questions to ask.

The task of documenting the building and analyzing the construction documents is very demanding. There are often a number of unanswered questions at the end of step 6. It is therefore a good idea to keep a list of outstanding issues that can be formulated as questions during interviews with the architect, the engineer, or the building owner at a later stage in our investigation.

4

Performance by Design

The procedures described in steps 1 to 6 in our investigation of high-performance buildings are based primarily on secondary sources of information in digital or printed form. The literature search, the initial site analysis, the studies of drawings and specifications of the building, the climate analysis, and the development of design strategies are all activities that can be carried out at the library or in the office. Now that these steps are completed, it is time to venture into the field.

This chapter presents a discussion of why the interview with the architect—and other key members of the design team—is so important and why this step in our research can also be insufficient. The nature of an architect's mind is discussed: how intentions and images act as representations of the design, how their mental picture of the building becomes central, and how this mental virtual building in the mind of the architect sometimes is not entirely translated into the actual building. See Figure 4.1 for an example: The design included a light shelf, and during the interview the architect explained in great detail how the light shelf was an integral part of the energy-efficient design. But the actual building does not include this feature. Sometimes the architect continues to focus on how certain things were *intended* to work, even if they were never built.

This chapter also contains practical advice for the arrangement of the interviews, the setup, and the type of equipment that will be useful during this part of our investigation.

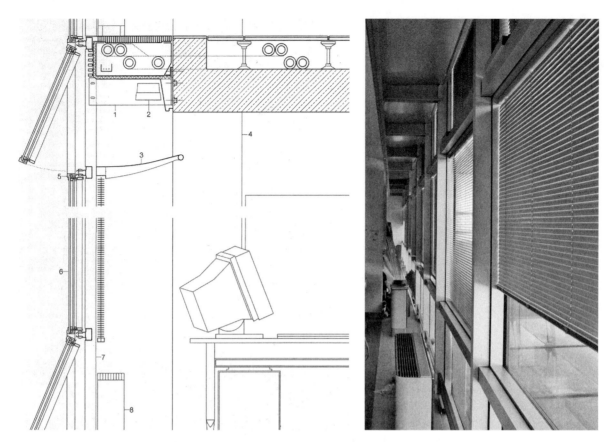

Fig. 4.1 The iGuzzini building: The design shows a light shelf (left). The light shelf was not included as built (right).

STEP 7: INTERVIEWS

It is essential to the investigation of building performance that we understand first the design, then the goals and intentions that formed the base for the design process. For example, computer-based energy simulations are now frequently performed as an integral part of the design process. Information on the predicted performance of a building greatly enhances the analysis of the actual performance, as built. The most efficient way to obtain a broad understanding of the design is to interview the design architect and the most central players in the design process.

Whom to Talk to

When it is time to talk to the architect, it is recommended that you set up an interview with the main architect or the person at the architecture firm who followed the project from beginning to end. Sometimes, if there is a project architect at the site that is different from the design architect, it is recommended that you first talk to the design architect. The purpose here is to get the best description not only of the building, but also of the intentions, concepts, and philosophy behind the design.

If the design architect is not available for an interview, you may opt to speak to another prominent member of the design team, such as the climate engineering firm or mechanical engineering firm. In some cases, it is sufficient to talk only to the architect. There are examples in this book (see Chapter 13 on the San Francisco Federal Building and Chapter 14 on the Burton Barr Central Library) where the architect is so knowledgeable about the building, its construction, and its systems that other follow-up interviews are not necessary. But in some cases, there may be a division of labor between closely cooperating architects and engineers. In such cases, it is recommended that a follow-up interview with an engineer be arranged after talking to the architect. An example of a close and productive collaboration between the main architect and the climate engineer is described in Chapter 10 on the Pihl & Søn headquarters building in Lyngby, Denmark.

Why Talk to the Architect?

The best architects will create a mental, virtual model of the building in all its entirety and complexity. Many architects can see the building in their mind. They can mentally walk through it and study any detail, system, structure, color, material, and other features of the building in its many iterations as the design process evolves. This virtual model of the building takes a strong presence in most architects' minds. Sometimes, this strong presence remains more prominent in its position and weight, even after the building has been constructed. This phenomenon explains both the strength and limitation of the interview with the architect or the information obtained by talking to the architect.

You should come to the interview with the architect prepared with a list of questions generated from a careful study of the documentation and the analyses described in steps 1 to 6. It is a good idea to forward the questions to the architect in advance so that he or she can be well prepared and can provide the information that you are interested in. The list of questions should touch on issues like design philosophy, design intentions, concepts, performance criteria, and main features of the design.

It is important to learn from the architect why he or she thinks that this building stands out, what makes it perform above average, and what qualifies it as a high-performance building. Following up on your analysis of the climate and the location, it is also appropriate to ask questions concerning how the design responds to climate, culture, local building traditions, and available material resources in the region.

It is important to document the interview in its entirety with all its detail. A good way of doing this is to ask permission to record the interview on digital video. The interviews that were organized as part of the research for this book were all recorded on a Canon GL2 digital video recorder (camcorder). Along with a camcorder, you should be equipped with a shotgun microphone and a good-quality tripod. The shotgun microphone is essential for getting good audio quality from the speakers and for avoiding unwanted background noise, such as from fans, traffic, or other people in the office.

STEP 8: TRANSCRIPTS

When the interview has been recorded, a transcript should be made. There are many computer programs that can help you do this. The suggested workflow is to first digitize the content of the videotape and then transfer it to the hard drive of a powerful desktop computer. The interview can then be played back in a program especially made for transcripts, such as Listen and Speak (www.nattaworks .com). This computer program makes it easy to navigate through the content of the interview while you are typing.

Once the interview has been typed up in a word-processing document, it is time to edit the content. The purpose of editing is not to add or subtract any content, but to clarify and organize the content into a flow of information that best describes the building. The edited transcript of the interview should then be sent to the architect or engineer that you interviewed, so that he or she can confirm that your editing is not in violation of what the person you interviewed wanted to communicate.

It is recommended that the video interview be taken through a *first-cut editing* based on the edited transcript. Then it can be recorded onto a digital video disc (DVD). The interviews recorded as part of the research for this book were edited in Final Cut Express (www.apple.com/finalcutexpress/). A DVD was produced for each of the seven buildings, using iDVD software (www.apple.com/ ilife/idvd/). In recognition of the value of their contribution, it is good practice to send a copy of the DVD to all the people who took the time to provide input through an interview.

STEP 9: CLAIMS

Now that you have a good edited transcript of the interview or interviews, you should carefully analyze the content in order to identify any claims that have been made regarding the performance of the building. In addition to the printed and digital sources of information, the interviews form the foundation of your effort to identify claims. These are claims presented by the designer during the interview or claims published in other interviews, in magazine articles, and lectures. As claims are identified, they then need to be substantiated—or discarded.

We will first address how to identify claims and more clearly categorize or characterize claims through follow-up questions. Claims should then be placed in a context of standards and norms, comparing apples to apples. Otherwise, the effort to substantiate claims can end up being futile.

Some architects frequently make bold claims about their designs, while others are more humble and let the built product speak for itself. In any case, the claims need to be identified clearly, since one purpose of our investigation is to find out whether the claims can be substantiated.

Claims are often related to predicted performance, which sometimes may vary greatly from the actual performance of the building. It is important to identify any conditions that are established along with the claims. The design team will often list a number of qualifications that need to be met in order for the predicted performance goals to be achieved or realized. Keep in mind that when predictions are generated from modeling the building in an energy performance simulation program on a computer, assumptions are made regarding the occupancy schedules of the building, the number of people using the building, and how the building systems are managed. Likewise, the energy efficiency (mileage) of two identical cars of the same make, model, and production year may vary greatly, depending on the driving habits of the owner, how often the air conditioning is run, and so on.

When examining the claims, it is important to ask follow-up questions to clarify the extent of the claims. A statement like "This building is predicted to use only half of the energy used annually by a standard office building" certainly needs further examination. What is the annual energy use of a standard office building? What is included in the predicted (reduced) annual energy use? You may find the claim specifically relates only to the heating, cooling, ventilation, and lighting of an office environment, while other significant end-use categories, such as elevators, exterior lighting, cooking equipment, office equipment (plug loads), and other major energy-use categories are excluded.

The business of substantiating claims is one of the most difficult tasks of the investigation of high-performance buildings. It is nonetheless the most important task, since unsubstantiated claims are frequently published. It is only through critical investigation and hard work to substantiate claims that a deeper understanding of high-performance designs can be developed.

An interview with Lord Norman Foster, broadcast on BBC Radio 4, may serve as an example. In this interview, the architect claims that the Swiss Re headquarters building (the Gherkin) is the first ecological skyscraper in London (see Figure 4.2).

Talking to Mark Lawson on BBC Radio 4 on April 27, 2004, Lord Norman Foster explained how the Swiss Re building is an example of "how you can reduce the energy that a building consumes, how you can make the building more eco-friendly if you like, greener. That's been sort of a lifelong quest, and it goes on into the future buildings that consume half the energy in an industrialized society and that is directly linked to issues of pollution, global warming—so anything that in a building like this can slash that in half has to be good news" (Lawson 2004).

However, Rob Harrison, the project architect at the Foster and Partners London office, discussed the green agenda of the Swiss Re design in an interview on July 1, 2004:

> The environmental agenda was never defined precisely—and Swiss Re's brief to us was for an environmentally progressive design. Now, that was never defined—what "environmentally progressive" meant. There was quite a bit of negotiation between all the parties of the design team, the project managers, and Swiss Re themselves. The project management team were all North American based—U.S. and Canada—and they brought with them I suppose a more North American mindset regarding the environmental aspects of a building, whereas Swiss Re themselves—being a Swiss company—had a different agenda (as if they were comparing it to one of the buildings that they had developed in Switzerland). So I think that the building that was produced sits somewhere between the two. It is not going to have the same levels of environmental criteria it would have had if we had designed the building for Switzerland, but it's got rather better environmental standards than if we would have been doing it in North America. So it sits midway between the two. But this definition of what "environmentally progressive" is, was something we all had to work

Fig. 4.2 The London City Hall and the Gherkin.

through during the course of the design process. It was not actually laid down at the beginning, saying "it needs to stay at such and such a target." It was more an approach as we were looking for what we might be able to achieve after looking into the details of what we actually could get out of it. (Lerum and Harrison 2004)

As long as the architect issues vaguely defined performance goals, and as long as the owner of the building is reluctant to publish any actual energy performance data, a conclusion cannot be reached pertaining to how a building actually checks in as an ecological skyscraper or a high-performance building. But the claim is still out there, and the architect has been honored with the Sterling Award by RIBA for this building (Powell, Dawson, et al. 2004).

The Greater London Authority (GLA) may serve as another example of the role of claims in the debate about environmentally friendly designs. In a brochure about the City Hall building, the GLA proudly points out that the door-mats are made from recycled car tires. It turns out that there are two doormats in the building at perhaps 10 square feet each. Although making doormats from recycled car tires is good for the environment, these two doormats represent a drop in the ocean as compared to the environmental impact of the tons of steel, concrete, and glass that were used to construct the building.

chapter 5

As Built

The approach taken in this chapter is inspired by Tapfuma Gutsa's sculpture "Listening to the Baby Kick." Tapfuma Gutsa quotes the pregnant woman, who says, "I am so proud and so full of hope for my first child. I love to feel her kick. She calms me, and my concern for the birth disappears" (Gutsa 1998). The drawing shown in Figure 5.1 was inspired by Tapfuma Gutsa's sculpture.

When you set out to listen to a building, it is a process that in some ways exhibits similarities with attempting to communicate with an unborn baby. Since the subject (baby) or object (building) does not communicate verbally, one needs to find other methods of acquisition, analysis, and interpretation of information. In this context, it becomes evident that communicating with the building from a long-distance perspective is virtually impossible. Those attempting to analyze the performance of great buildings should therefore make it a rule for themselves not to write about any building until they have visited the site.

Although the architect's or the design team's description of the design concepts, the intentions, and the predicted performance of a building and its features are by nature subjective, other sources (such as magazine articles) are also subjective, and sometimes less reliable as they pertain to the designed object as built. The designed object (building) must become the primary source of knowledge. It is the author's belief that anyone who attempts to write about the performance of a contemporary or historical building without listening to the building as it is located in its own environment may not be producing reliable information. In this sense, one can find inspiration in Michel Foucault's writings on the archaeology of knowledge (Foucault 1982).

Fig. 5.1 "Listen to the Baby," drawing by Vidar Lerum, based on the sculpture by Tapfuma Gutsa, "Listening to the Baby Kick, 1998—Opal Stone," image available at: http://www.artthrob .co.za/01mar/news.html.

Archaeology can be defined as "the careful, scientific examination of material remains from [past] cultures." The word *past* is here placed between brackets because more and more archaeologists no longer remove themselves from examining remains from contemporary cultures. The method applied in the research leading up to this book may therefore be described as "the archaeology of contemporary buildings." Foucault writes:

> Archaeology tries to define not the thoughts, the representations, images, themes, preoccupations that are concealed or revealed in discourses; but those discourses themselves, those discourses as practices obeying certain rules. It does not treat discourse as document, as a sign of something else, as an element that ought to be transparent, but whose unfortunate opacity must often be pierced if one is to reach at last the depth of the essential in the place in which it is held in reserve; it is concerned with discourse in its own volume, as a monument. (Foucault 1982, pp. 138–139)

Foucault said that the aim of archaeology was not to recreate the vision that inspired a particular discourse, but to clearly describe that discourse itself.

> Archaeology does not try to restore what has been thought, wished, aimed at, experienced, desired by men in the very moment at which they

expressed it in discourse; it does not set out to recapture that elusive nucleus in which the author and the oeuvre exchange identities; in which thought still remains nearest to oneself, in the as yet unaltered form of the same, and in which language has not yet been deployed in the spatial, successive dispersion of discourse. In other words, it does not try to repeat what has been said by reaching it in its very identity. It does not claim to efface itself in the ambiguous modesty of reading that would bring back, in all its purity, the distant, precarious, almost effaced light of the origin. . . . It is not a return to the innermost secret of the origin; it is the systematic description of a discourse-object. (Foucault 1982, pp. 139–140)

TRANSPARENCY ISSUES

Foucault's thoughts on the archaeology of language are used as an inspiration to develop an archaeology of contemporary buildings, so it becomes necessary to address the use of the term *transparency*. Transparency is used in writings on contemporary (modern) buildings as a way to describe a visual transparency, linking the interior with the exterior space by the use of glass elements in the building envelope. The term *transparency* is also quite commonly used by architects as a metaphor for democracy: an open society. These are not the meanings of transparency that we are after here. As one sets out to investigate the characteristics and achievements of high-performance buildings, it is often necessary to look behind the surface. Heat flow, energy use, airflow patterns, and light distribution are phenomena that are hidden from the naked eye—features that "do not produce effects that show up immediately" (Banham 1966). In the context of investigating high-performance buildings, these features are still integral parts of the built object "in its own volume, as a monument," as Foucault characterized language. In this context, transparency therefore refers to the intentions behind the design, the design concepts—"it does not set out to recapture that elusive nucleus in which the author and the oeuvre exchange identities" (Foucault 1982).

The Norwegian architect Sverre Fehn elaborated on the use of language as a metaphor for building (built object) in interviews published in the architecture magazines *A+U* and *Living Architecture*:

I see materials as letters we use to write our poetic thoughts. We work with letters, an alphabet, we write a story. The story and its structure are inseparable. The poetic idea needs the support of structures to exist. (Fehn 1999).

If the narration we here call architecture does not possess a structure, it is meaningless. Architecture is also irrational, but an irrational idea must be based on a rational structure. (Møller and Fehn 1997)

This chapter will further describe the method of investigating high performance in three additional steps:

Step 10: Prepare for the site visit.
Step 11: Review utility records.
Step 12: Conduct experiments.

STEP 10: PREPARING FOR THE SITE VISIT

It is important to prepare for the site visit in detail, especially if the building is at a remote location such as Nuuk, Greenland, or Ørsta, Norway. You should now have a number of questions about claims, about energy use, about materials and details, about systems, and other issues to which the site visit may turn out to be essential to finding an answer. In addition to putting an itinerary together and locating funds to pay for the travel, the two most important things are to prepare the list of unanswered questions and to create a plan for how you could possibly find the answers. This includes a plan for experiments that may turn out to be helpful in getting to the truth about special features.

Travels to remote and exotic locations are always exciting, but getting to see the building inside out is the most valuable part of your investigation. It is therefore very important that you arrive prepared, not only with the questions, but also with the necessary equipment and, in some cases, the permit to execute a particular test or experiment.

STEP 11: REVIEW UTILITY RECORDS, ON-SITE SOURCES OF INFORMATION

Some of the first pieces of information to look for are the utility records. If possible, ask in advance for permission to obtain records from the utility company on the annual energy use. There are no international standards in place for how to keep energy records. In most cases, the most reliable data will be in the form of utility bills. Usually, data are broken down by time interval (monthly summaries) and by energy source (typically gas and electric). In very few cases, there may be data available that will provide breakdowns on end use, such as heating, light, or plug loads, but this is the exception to the rule. It is also surprising to find that as the technology of building systems controls and automation advances, it is still very difficult to find systems that actually store historical data broken down into increments in terms of time and end use. Here follows a summary of the energy use data obtained for the seven buildings that serves to describe the disparity in the situation:

1. *The Greenland Nature Institute building* (Chapter 8) is publicly owned and all electric, but the local competition between the district heating provider and a utility company that delivers electric energy from hydroelectric power plants forced the electric utility to price energy used for heating separately from electricity for other end uses. This required submetering in the building. The owner provided monthly values for these two categories of electric energy for several years. Despite some difficulties related to the replacement of faulty meters, these records proved to be a valuable source of information.
2. *The Aasen Centre* (Chapter 9) is also a publicly owned, all-electric building. In this case, a permit was issued for the researcher to access the building owners' account through the utility company Tussa's Web site. Monthly energy use data were obtained for two years 2004 to 2005, with projected monthly energy use for 2006. In this case, only one summary number was

displayed. This made it impossible to assess the relative importance of electricity used for heating, lights, plug load, ventilation, and cooling (yes, the building is air-conditioned).

3. *The Pihl & Søn headquarters building* (Chapter 10) is privately owned, but the owner generously offered information on annual energy use, with monthly breakdowns and separate subtotals for natural gas and electricity. Since gas is only used for heating and domestic hot water, it was possible to make a fairly accurate assessment of the relative significance of the energy associated with heating and hot water supply, as measured against the remaining end-use categories. This building is not air-conditioned.

4. *The Post Tower* (Chapter 11) is privately owned. The climate engineers Transsolar presented a summary graph of the specific annual energy use for the Post Tower as compared to a conventional building of the same type. Although it is noted on the energy graph that the findings are based on actual energy use data for 2003, it turns out that only a few end-use categories are included (heating, cooling, lights, ventilation), and that the numbers are actually estimates. The building owner (previously the German Postal Agency, now organized as an independent corporation) refuses to provide access to any energy use data.

5. *The iGuzzini building* (Chapter 12) is privately owned. The building owner was in principle willing to provide energy use data, but since the building is an addition to an older office building, accurate energy-use data are not available. According to the owner, no submeter was installed for the new addition.

6. *The San Francisco Federal Building* (Chapter 13) was not occupied until early 2007, so no actual performance data were available for 2006. The U.S. General Services Administration (GSA), representing the building owner, has been reluctant to provide access to the predicted energy use, citing issues of security as the reason. The upper twelve floors of this building are not air-conditioned. Its reliance on a passive, natural ventilation system for cooling is innovative and exceptional for a contemporary building at this location. It is therefore of great importance to the research community that actual performance data be made public.

7. *The Burton Barr Central Library* (Chapter 14) is owned by the city of Phoenix. The city has provided annual energy use data for two years, with monthly breakdowns and breakdowns on the use of natural gas versus electricity. Since this building is equipped with gas-fired absorption chillers, the variations in the monthly gas usage may be used to assess the relative significance of the energy use for cooling relative to other end uses.

This brief summary leads to the conclusion that three issues need to be addressed:

1. There is a need for submetering so that data can be provided with breakdowns on end-use categories, in addition to time and energy source breakdowns.
2. Building energy management systems must be equipped with the sensors, the software, and the hardware necessary to store historical performance

data (including comfort parameters). With today's technology, this is more a question of creativity and implementation than a budget issue.

3. Owners of nonresidential buildings must be required to permit access to the energy use data for their buildings, if necessary by new legislation.

The site visit is also a good opportunity to talk to owners and users. Information may be obtained by arranging formal interviews, or through informal discussion with users of the building.

STEP 12: EXPERIMENTAL EVALUATION

Sometimes it becomes necessary to conduct tests and other experiments as a method of listening to the building. The type of experiments, and the quantity and quality of information produced by the experiments, depend greatly on the time available, the instruments that you brought to the site, and the permissions you may obtain. A smoke test, for example, is a quick and easy experiment to set up, but it is difficult to get permission to do it because the smoke may interfere with the fire alarm system and also violate no-smoking policies. Here follows a summary of experiments conducted at the seven buildings described in Part Two:

1. Three smoke tests were conducted at the Greenland Nature Institute building in Nuuk. The test results provided insight into issues of airflow patterns inside the building and generated new knowledge about how the natural ventilation system actually works. A handheld infrared temperature meter was used to record comfort parameters, such as surface temperatures. Temperature sensors connected to HOBO data loggers were used to record air and surface temperatures. This instrument setup was also used to probe the performance of a Fresh 100 wall vent.

2. At the Aasen Centre in Ørsta, Norway, a handheld infrared temperature meter was used to record surface and air temperature differences throughout the building. This simple test generated new knowledge about the temperature controls. Although constant air temperature (and relative humidity) was an important design parameter, the building experienced significant interior temperature differences on a summer day.

3. Experimental data from secondary sources were used in the investigation of the Pihl & Søn building in Lyngby, Denmark. The Danish Research Institute (SBI) published reports that included experimental data on airflow rates, light levels, air temperatures, and other comfort parameters.

4. Light transmission, view, and glare related to the perforated blinds in the Post Tower in Bonn, Germany, were tested by digital video recording. This quick and simple test shows that the perforated blinds provide shading while maintaining a sufficient daylight level inside the office. In closed position, the blinds control glare while maintaining a view to the surrounding landscape. Experimental data from secondary sources was also used in the analysis. The climate-engineering firm Transsolar had conducted smoke tests to evaluate the airflow patterns in a typical office resulting from air supplied through the fan coil units (see Figure 5.2).

Fig. 5.2 Testing displacement ventilation with smoke in a mock-up of a typical Post Tower office. Test conducted by Transsolar, climate engineers.

5. Smoke tests, air temperature acquisition, and surface temperature recordings were again conducted at the iGuzzini building in Recanati, Italy. A smoke test was conducted during lunch hour when most of the occupants had left the building. Light levels were recorded by the use of a handheld light meter. New knowledge was generated. The test results show that the performance of the natural ventilation system is multimodal (stack and cross-ventilation), while the literature describes the system as driven by stack ventilation only. Digital photography was used to test the shading effect of the louvered shading canopy on the south-facing glass wall. Since this data represent one day only (May 12), a three-dimensional digital model was built in SketchUp in order to investigate the seasonal performance of the shading structure; see Chapter 12.

6. At the San Francisco Federal Building, which was still unoccupied at the time of the site visit, digital photography was used to evaluate the performance of the perforated screen on the south side (light transmission, views, glare) and the vertical glass fins (shading effect).

7. A year-long experiment was conducted at the Burton Barr Central Library in Phoenix, Arizona. HOBO data loggers and temperature sensors were used to investigate the performance of the 12-inch-thick uninsulated concrete walls. Stratification in the Great Reading Room was also investigated. The concrete wall was instrumented with temperature sensors placed at the surface of both sides of the wall, as well as one sensor that was placed at the core 6 inches from the surfaces. Two HOBO data loggers, placed on each side of the wall, recorded air temperatures and relative humidity. The results from these experiments are described in greater detail in Chapter 14.

Experimental evaluation is a method of investigation that can often generate new knowledge and insight from tests that sometimes are quick and easy and do not require extensive instrumentation. A useful, but not too expensive, kit of instruments should include data loggers and sensors, a handheld infrared thermometer, smoke candles, soap bubbles, a handheld light meter, a digital camera, a digital video camera (camcorder) with tripod and shotgun microphone, and a log book.

6

What If?

What-if scenarios are fascinating. Aided by computer simulations, they become a tool to test-drive multiple virtual models of the building design before wasting any resources on materials.

This chapter discusses how building science and building performance analysis can borrow from the approach taken in the what-if genre of science fiction writing. An example of a great book in this genre is *The Years of Rice and Salt* (Robinson 2002), which deals with an alternative history of mankind as it would have evolved if 98 percent of the population in Europe had been wiped out by the Black Plague (as opposed to two-thirds, which actually happened). We will discuss how to construct meaningful what-if scenarios that can aid in arriving at a deeper understanding of how a building works and how its performance could be improved even further.

METHODOLOGY

As a research topic, *building energy performance* is placed within the field of engineering or at the scientific end of the *art and science* concept of architecture. Consequently, experimental methods are predominantly used when investigating building energy performance. It is still useful, and sometimes necessary, to speculate at some length about the application and appropriateness of methods borrowed from other disciplines, such as methods frequently used in the social sciences.

Modeling in the social sciences can be used as analogies to modeling in the natural sciences. The causal relations model is one type of model that can be adapted in a productive way to explain and to understand problems that belong to architecture and engineering as well.

METHOD TRIANGULATION

Method has been defined as a procedure or way of doing something. *Methodology* is the body of methods used in a particular branch of activity. Since methods may be seen as tools that we need to do the job more efficiently, a toolbox of methods should be selected depending on what we want to do, or what we want to achieve. Only the simplest research problems are solved by the application of one method only.

EXPLANATORY STUDIES (MODELING)

A model is a simplified representation of the real world (Lave and March 1993). Halvorsen adds that models may act as intermediaries between theory and hypotheses (Halvorsen 1987). The usefulness of models can be evaluated from how well they perform in these areas:

- Formulating hypotheses
- Explaining phenomena and data
- Making predictions
- Pointing to conditions for change

The use of physical scale models in architectural design is often an integral part of an experimental or *exploratory* approach. It is also important to see modeling as an *explanatory* activity that will be helpful in creating visual images in the process of conceptualizing the problem. Modeling can be used to arrive at a clearer understanding of the problem. It is often said that a clear description of the problem brings you more than halfway to its solution. For architects, modeling may be used as a visual tool of explanation.

EXPLORATORY STUDIES

One mode of exploration in the field of architecture is to develop a novel design, find a client or donor who will pay for it, build it in full scale, and have a user move into it and use it. We can then measure the performance of the building and the well-being of the occupants as they start using it. This is learning the hard way. If the novelty of the design is substantial, this *real-world exploratory method* is often painful.

This method of learning by doing was traditionally (i.e., in the premodern world) the most common method of improving designs. When only a small incremental change to a traditional design was introduced at a time, the design could develop and be refined over the time span of generations. A study of incremental improvements in the design of traditional Norwegian wooden

Fig. 6.1 Norlands-baaden: A wooden boat type frequently used by fishermen in northern Norway.

fishing boats (see Figure 6.1) is a fine example of how this method was used (Sundt 1865). Indigenous architectural design is another example of the same approach.

The humanist and social scientist Eilert Sundt traveled along the coast of northern Norway during the second half of the nineteenth century. In his report on the development of the design for the Norlandsbaaden fishing boat, he explains how a boat builder would make a modification, an incremental change, to a feature of the boat design. The fishermen then took the new boat out on the ocean for the season. Upon arriving back at their hometown, they would report to the boat builder how the boat had performed. If they approved of the new design, the incremental change would be incorporated in future designs. If not, it would be discarded. Sometimes a design change would come from necessity rather than curiosity. What the boat builder saw as the best quality or the best dimensions of wood for the boat might not be available, so the design would change accordingly. Whether intentional or introduced by necessity or accident, each change would be incorporated or discarded after it was tested in all kinds of weather.

Today, exploratory methods that are analogous to these methods can be adapted in a laboratory-like environment made possible by the personal computer. The power of the personal computer can be utilized by software that lets the user walk through a series of designs and design improvements in virtual reality. Development and testing of what-if scenarios can be a powerful approach to implementing this methodology. What-if scenarios can significantly improve the quality of the design process and consequently contribute to improvements in the built environment by developing new prototypes based on existing high-performance buildings.

An advantage of the incremental design change method is that by testing one small design change at a time and analyzing the effect of changing the value of one specific variable, step by step, the relative significance of each step can be evaluated. Recommendations can then be made on the range of variables that are useful for a specific design. The relative usefulness, productivity, or cost/benefit ratio of each step value of a specific variable can also be evaluated.

What-if scenarios are not different from a method frequently used in architectural design, where several iterations of the project are developed. Architects quite often work with design iterations as an intuitive process. Alternative arrangements and plan layouts may be explored by sketching out new ideas.

Iterations of a project design are usually tested in the mind of the architect, since the architect has the ability to instantly evaluate the various consequences of the new iteration as it influences other parts of the design. In a design process that uses sketching, iterations are tested in a virtual model of the building that resides in the architect's brain. This basically intuitive process is now taken into the digital age by the use of three-dimensional (3-D) computer modeling.

The 3-D model has several advantages over the intuitive sketching approach. Some 3-D computer modeling programs are now capable of analyzing shading effects of the design instantly. This provides a type of feedback on the intuitive sketching process that has a higher degree of scientific reliability.

STEP 13: IDENTIFY SCENARIOS

At this stage in the investigation of high-performance buildings, the student or researcher now has enough information, insight, and understanding of the building to start forming a set of what-if scenarios. It is important to understand that creating a program for what-if scenarios to be investigated involves more than identifying scenarios that may cast new light on significant performance parameters. Once a list of scenarios has been established, a plan for the execution of the scenarios must be made, including the types of computer models to be created and tested. Ideally, any computer model set up to test the performance parameters of a what-if scenario should also be plugged into, or be communicating with, the 3-D building model, thus becoming an integral part of the building information management system.

STEP 14: RUN SIMULATIONS

The process of exploring iterations can now be taken one step further by investigating the energy-performance consequences of various schemes. This new generation of what-if scenarios has been made possible by the energy simulation programs that run on personal computers and perform multiple 8,760-hour calculations. One such program is ENERGY-10.

ENERGY-10 has been used in data analyses of the case studies included in Part Two of this book. In ENERGY-10, the user may explore what-if scenarios by comparing two buildings that are basically similar but have a few parameters that are altered. The first two variants of the building energy model are automatically built by ENERGY-10 by default and named *reference case* and *low-energy (low-E) case*.

By comparing two versions of a building, it is possible to generate output that illustrates the relative advantage of changing one or a few parameters. This makes it possible to relatively quickly and easily run some basic what-if scenarios. The program can also be used in a more extensive investigation, where perhaps 20 different schemes could be developed. Each scheme can be saved as a variant of the project so that the user has a record of the energy performance of each what-if scenario. ENERGY-10 also has an automatic ranking feature where several schemes or scenarios are ranked relative to the effect on the energy savings in a cost/benefit type of analysis.

One advantage of running what-if scenarios in a computer program that generates fairly reliable outputs is that the designer's intuition may be paired with the rational approach of the computer. The intuitive process is an excellent and essential tool in developing successful architectural designs, but sometimes the effect of changing a parameter may turn out to be counterintuitive.

An example of a counterintuitive outcome is explained in Chapter 8. The orientation of the Greenland Nature Institute was investigated. A rule of thumb for passive solar design is that the collector area, the south-facing glazing, should face due south or could perhaps be rotated away from due south by a maximum of 15 degrees. Although this rule of thumb might be valid within the latitude band of the 48 contiguous states in the United States, it is not necessarily valid for a high northern latitude.

The what-if scenario that was created for the Nature Institute rotated the building 90 degrees and moved most of the windows over on the south side (which now became the long side). The building as built has most of the windows oriented to the east and west (see Figure 6.2). As it turned out, rotating the building and moving the glazing to the south side did not have a significant effect on the amount of savings due to passive solar heating. This was a counterintuitive result. A possible explanation of this phenomenon can be found in the fact that the heating season is so much longer at high latitudes. Solar heat gains from the east- and west-facing windows are therefore useful for space heating for several months during the spring and fall shoulder seasons. In addition, with ambient temperatures below the comfort zone on a summer design day, a good ventilation scheme may negate the penalties commonly associated with excessive solar heat gain from south-facing windows.

An investigation of the lobby space at the Lewis Center at Oberlin College, by McDonough Architects, demonstrates another type of what-if scenario. Two large, double-height glass walls define the entrance lobby (see Figure 6.3). One of these glass walls faces south and the other faces east. In a study conducted by the author and performed by two graduate students at Arizona State University, a

Fig. 6.2 Greenland's Nature Institute. This shows the west façade at sunset on a clear April day.

what-if scenario was constructed where the east-facing glass wall was replaced by a well-insulated opaque exterior wall. An 8,760-hour thermal energy simulation was performed in eQuest, a front-end plug-in to the energy simulation program DOE2.

As expected, it was found that the east wall, as built, is a poor performer in terms of energy. When analyzed over an entire typical meteorological year, this wall contributes a net energy loss. The overall building performance would have improved if this wall had been constructed as a well-insulated opaque wall. This finding then generates follow-up questions. For example, how could the design

Fig. 6.3 Adam Joseph Lewis Center at Oberlin College. This shows south- and east-facing glass walls of the double-height atrium.

have been altered in order to maintain other qualities of the east-facing glass wall (views, inside-outside continuity, contact with nature) *and* improved on the energy efficiency?

SETTING UP A WHAT-IF SCENARIO IN ENERGY-10

In order to explain how ENERGY-10 may be used to set up a what-if scenario, we will use a fairly simple example. Other energy simulation programs (e.g., eQuest) have a more sophisticated building geometry interface, but ENERGY-10 has a lower threshold for first-time users of energy simulation programs.

In this example, we will investigate the effect of changing the glazing and shading parameters on the north- and south-facing exterior walls of a section of a typical office floor in a multistory building. The first step, therefore, will be to set up a model in ENERGY-10 of a slice of a typical floor sandwiched between other floors. The geometry of the section of the building is first described simply by entering width, length, and floor-to-floor height. The east and west walls of this three-dimensional shoebox can be determined as thermally neutral by entering an extremely low thermal conductivity represented by an R-value of 1,000. The same R-1,000 value may be entered for the ceiling and the floor, since we assume zero heat gain or heat loss to the spaces above and below the model space. Through these simple steps, we have now established a situation where heat flow is modeled for the north- and south-facing exterior walls only.

ENERGY-10 will automatically build two representations of this virtual massing model of the building. Default settings are used for thermostat set points, occupancy schedules, and the type of mechanical systems employed. ENERGY-10 will apply thermal mass to the interior for the low-energy case. Glazing properties and glass areas will also be entered by default.

The next task is to alter building 1, the reference case automatically built by ENERGY-10, in such a way that the various parameters are similar to that of the building we are investigating. ENERGY-10 will then run an 8,760-hour simulation for the building as built and compare the results to the low-energy version that ENERGY-10 built by default (building 2).

A copy of building 1 may now be created as a new building 2. This means that the user now has two similar buildings side by side. By changing glazing properties, glass areas, and shading types, the user can study the effect for each step by comparing the annual energy use of building 2 (altered) to building 1 (as built). This approach makes it possible to quickly compare a large number of alternative solutions by their annual energy use. The alternative that uses less energy on an annual basis is often the best solution, but other selection criteria may be established as well.

ENERGY-10 also can be set to make calculations in a *free-run mode*, in which the same alterations to the building design can be analyzed from a different perspective. In free-run mode, ENERGY-10 will shut off all mechanical systems so that the building uses no energy for heating, cooling, or ventilation. Instead of looking at the annual energy use output, the focus will now be on the internal air temperatures in the building as a function of the ambient conditions. The best alternative solution could now be the interior temperature swings. The goal in this approach would be to find the alternative that generates the most balanced building—the one that shows the smallest temperature swings in the interior.

LIMITATIONS AND VALIDITY

What-if scenarios as tested in building energy simulation programs are useful supplements to the intuitive sketching method in the same way that three-dimensional modeling programs provide useful feedback on massing and shading effects of multiple iterations to the project design. It is important to understand that building energy simulation models, like any computer tool, will only generate quality output if the input also meets high quality standards. In general, the output is less reliable for the more simplified models. This does not mean that simplified energy models used to generate what-if scenarios are invalid.

The benefit of performing what-if scenarios and analyzing their effect in building energy simulation programs lies in the comparison of alternative solutions. Although the actual numerical output may be less reliable, the relative differences in a series of iterations are valid as criteria for selecting which solution will create the most energy savings.

It is also important to keep in mind that the types of what-if scenarios described here should primarily be seen as decision-making tools, rather than as actual predictors of the annual energy use, indoor air temperatures, or other related parameters.

7

Summary of Part One

I t is always a good idea to set aside time to produce a detailed report from the findings of your investigation. The process of reporting is not only useful for the purposes of communicating with others or archiving your work, but quite often also helps clarify the results. Here follows a proposed table of contents for the report, including a list of deliverables that may be used as a checklist or guide to compiling the report. It is the hope that this proposal will be helpful, particularly in an educational context.

It has been suggested that the method of investigation described in the previous chapters may be tweaked into a design method—or an exploration that becomes an integral part of the design method. In this case, the report may take the form of a summary of the environmental impact of the various design schemes explored in schematic design.

STEP 15: REPORT CONTENT—DELIVERABLES

The table of contents for the report should follow the outline represented by steps 1 to 14. PDF (portable document format) files should be used consistently throughout the report. This makes it possible to read the report on any computer running the commonly used operating systems (Mac OS X, Windows, and others). PDF files print from most printers without any difficulty. If drawings or other graphic material are represented in PDF, the user may zoom in on details. This makes it easier to view large drawings on a standard computer monitor, as well as when the image is projected onto a screen during presentations to a larger audience.

1 Climate Data

The weather data file should be archived as an electronic data file in a commonly accepted file format, such as TMY or EPW. Summary reports, including design day data, can be exported and saved as PDF files. Documentation of horizon shading (skyline) should be included, if applicable.

2 Climate Analysis

The report from the climate data analysis, including the development of design strategies, should take the form of a written report accompanied by graphic output from the climate analysis program. Ideally, design strategies should be explained as conceptual diagrams (see Chapter 12 for examples).

3 Design Strategies

The report from the comparative analysis of heat flows, air temperatures, and solar radiation should take the same form as described for step 2.

4 Publications

A bibliographical database program, such as EndNote, should be used as an aid in the literature search. It is recommended that an abstract be produced for each item in the list of bibliographical references. An electronic copy of each item should be created as a PDF file (see Figure 7.1). There are two obvious deliverables from this step in the investigation. First, the bibliographical database file should be archived in a folder, including copies of the PDF files of all items. Second, an annotated bibliography (including the abstracts) should be printed to PDF.

5 Site Analysis

The report on the initial site analysis should include a site plan and property map at scale, a written explanation of findings from the site analysis, and a fact sheet including measurements, areas, and so on. Information regarding existing trees, roads, adjacent buildings, infrastructure, and zoning requirements should be included, if available. The report may take the form of a multipage PDF document.

6 Building Documentation

The building documentation should ideally take the form of a set of PDF files of each sheet in the construction documents set of drawings.

7 Interviews

The interviews should be recorded in digital video and then recorded onto a DVD after the first-cut editing is performed. The file from the editing program (Final Cut Express or similar program) should be archived on an external hard drive or a server volume.

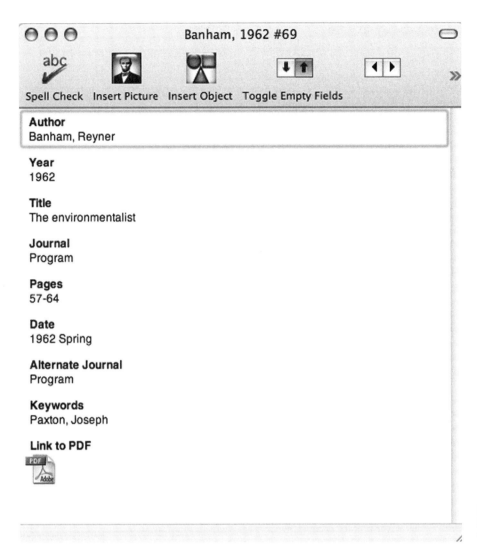

Fig. 7.1 Screenshot from EndNote, showing "Link to PDF" feature.

8 Transcripts

The edited transcript of the interviews should be exported to PDF and printed. The text editor file should be archived on an external hard drive or a server volume.

9 Claims

A summary of claims, including suggestions as to how to substantiate them, should take the form of a written report, formatted as described in step 5.

10 Preparing for the Site Visit

The plan for preparing for the site visit will also take the form of a written report, formatted as previously indicated.

11 Review Utility Records, On-Site Sources of Information

Utility records and other performance-related data should be tabulated in numerical format, and graphs should be created to illustrate the numerical data. Information gathered in step 11 should then be summarized in a written report, formatted as previously indicated.

12 Experimental Evaluation

The findings from the tests and the experimental evaluation should take the form of a scientific paper. The format required for submittal to a scientific journal or a conference may be useful as a format guide here.

13 Identify Scenarios

Conclusions from the process of identification of scenarios should be written up as an illustrated report along the lines described for step 5.

14 Run Simulations

Findings from running simulations on the various scenarios should be reported in a similar fashion to that described for step 5.

15 Report Content—Deliverables

As a general note, electronic copies of all digital files used in the investigation should be archived on an external hard drive (separate from the hard drive on the computers used). The reports from each of steps 1 to 14 should be compiled as one PDF file and printed.

Buildings

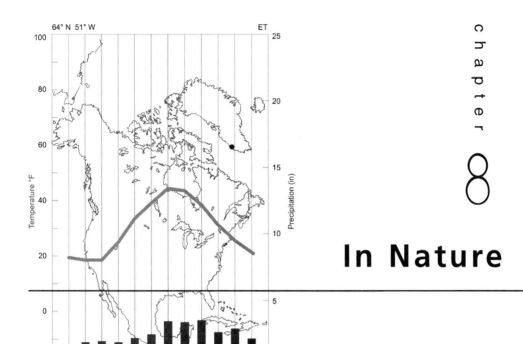

In Nature

Greenland Nature Institute by KHR Architects

Building Type: Office
Location: Nuuk, Greenland
Coordinates: 64°N, 51°W
Interviews: Ove Neumann, architect
    Klaus H. Nygaard, director
Site Visit: April 2005

Located just outside of the town of Nuuk, Greenland, at 64°N (see Figure 8.1), this modest office building houses offices and laboratories for the Greenland Nature Institute.

Sitting on a high point, it hugs the landscape and protects itself from the winds, much like the streamlined form of a seal (see Figure 8.2). The natural ventilation system is integrated with the architecture in a straightforward way, expressed by the hoods of the ventilators projecting out through the building skin. Tons of thermal mass, embedded in structural concrete walls, act as heat storage inside the building.

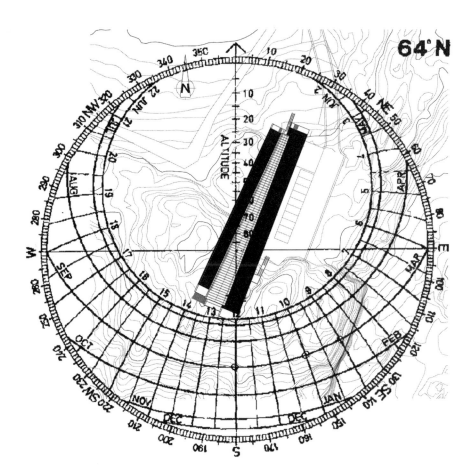

Fig. 8.1 Sun Path diagram for 64°N superimposed on the site plan.

Fig. 8.2 The Nature Institute as seen from the southwest with the Sermitsiaq Mountain as a scenic backdrop, on a clear April day.

Fig. 8.3 The "annex" (left) and the main building (right), viewed from the northeast on a clear April day.

BUILDING AND SITE

The building is the result of an architecture competition, to which several architecture firms were invited. The Danish architecture firm KHR AS won the competition. The majority of concepts introduced in the winning competition project made their way into the construction documents and eventually into the project as built.

The local home-rule government in Greenland—*hjemmestyret*—owns the 2,000-square-meter building, which contains offices, laboratories, and supporting facilities for the Nature Institute. The Nature Institute conducts research in the areas of fisheries, birds, sea mammals, and land animals.

The site is located at a high point in the landscape near the Nuuk airport, at the outskirts of new suburban settlements. With its dominant position, the site features great views to the south, west, and north. Although the temperature regime is mostly the same as the official temperatures for Nuuk, the winds at the site are commonly much stronger than average for this region on the west coast of Greenland.

A second building housing guest quarters and apartments was added in recent years (Lerum and Nygaard 2005). The two buildings now form an elongated outdoor space on the east side of the main building (see Figure 8.3). It is only the main building that is the object of analysis here.

LOCATION AND CLIMATE

The town of Nuuk is located at 64°N latitude on the west coast of Greenland. The coastal influence makes the temperatures less extreme as compared to inland locations, but it is still basically a cold climate with average temperatures below freezing for six or seven months in a typical meteorological year, as shown in Figure 8.4 (Siewertsen 2007).

A weather file in TMY file format was constructed with the software program Meteonorm. The outcome was calibrated against average monthly temperatures

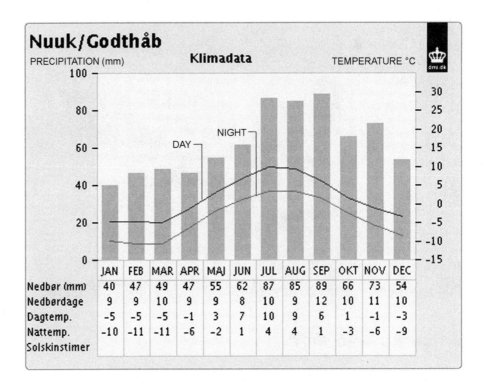

	JAN	FEB	MAR	APR	MAJ	JUN	JUL	AUG	SEP	OKT	NOV	DEC
Nedbør (mm)	40	47	49	47	55	62	87	85	89	66	73	54
Nedbørdage	9	9	10	9	9	8	10	9	12	10	11	10
Dagtemp.	-5	-5	-5	-1	3	7	10	9	6	1	-1	-3
Nattemp.	-10	-11	-11	-6	-2	1	4	4	1	-3	-6	-9
Solskinstimer												

Fig. 8.4 Average-day temperatures and solar radiation data. Monthly values are for a typical meteorological year.

obtained from the Danish Meteorological Institute. Weather data from the constructed TMY file were then processed using the software program Weather Maker (see Figure 8.5). While heating degree-days—at base temperature 65°F— amount to almost 13,000 for a typical meteorological year, there are no cooling degree-days for the same base temperature. Theoretically, there is a need for

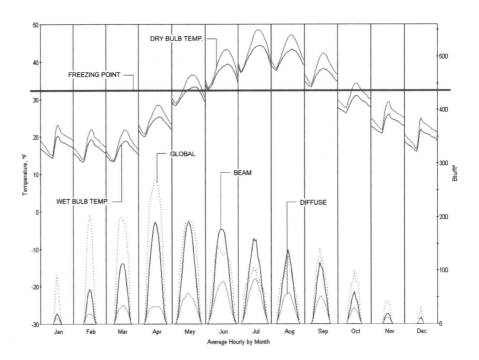

Fig. 8.5 Average-day temperatures and solar radiation data. Monthly values are for a typical meteorological year.

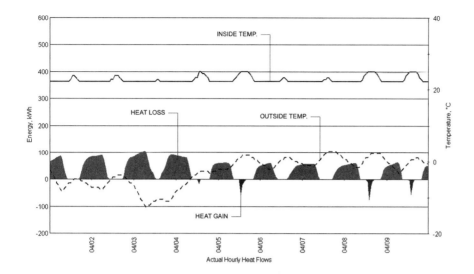

Fig. 8.6 Heat-flow diagram, ENERGY-10 reference case.

space heating all year. As we shall see later, this does not necessarily mean that a well-insulated building with a fair number of windows will not overheat. But it is still safe to conclude that heat loss through conduction—and through ventilation—is a major concern. The need for protection against the cold is enforced by the generally high wind exposure at the site.

A quick analysis using Weather Maker and ENERGY-10 shows how a well-insulated (ENERGY-10 low-E case) building designed for passive solar heating could overheat in mid-April when the ambient air-temperatures are around 0°C. The analysis was performed using the constructed TMY weather file for Nuuk and a model in ENERGY-10 that represents the Nature Institute building in a simplified fashion. It is worth noting that a conventional building will require a great deal of heating energy during the same period (ENERGY-10 reference case, shown in Figure 8.6). The easiest way to remove the excess heat from the low-E case building is by natural ventilation, since the ambient air temperature is low enough to provide cooling (see Figure 8.7). This explains why it is important to

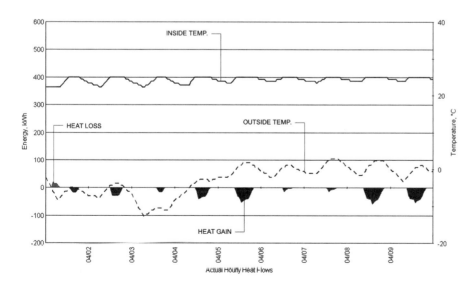

Fig. 8.7 Heat-flow diagram, ENERGY-10 low-E case.

combine a passive solar heating design strategy in cold-climate buildings with a design strategy for natural cooling.

What at first glance might seem like a climate where the only concern is to minimize the energy used for space heating could turn out to be more challenging in terms of design strategies for an energy-efficient and comfortable work environment.

PERFORMANCE BY DESIGN

In an interview in April 2005, Ove Neumann, the project architect at KHR, outlined the five major concepts that drove the design submitted to the architectural competition (Lerum and Neumann 2005):

1. Optimize energy-efficiency by introducing passive and active solar design principles.
2. Select sustainable materials.
3. Minimize water usage.
4. Use a comprehensive approach to indoor air quality.
5. Enter carefully into the sensitive arctic environment.

These five principles of sustainable design were carried forward into the successive phases of the project. One exception was the idea to use active solar technologies (solar collectors and/or photovoltaic panels), an idea that was dropped from the menu because it met stiff competition from artificially low costs of electricity from a recently completed hydroelectric power plant. The façades of the building are still proportioned and detailed in such a way that solar panels could be applied (on east and west façades) at a later stage.

DESIGN INTENTIONS TRANSCRIBED

The first major design move was to place the building as an elongated form along the prevailing wind directions. The building was aligned with the north–south axis and rotated 23 degrees to the east of north. The building form was then tapered both in plan and in section to resemble the streamlined, fluid dynamic shape of a seal, the symbolic sea mammal of the arctic (see Figures 8.8 and 8.14). The inside-out principle invented for the Pihl building (see Chapter 10) was then reintroduced in the design for the Nature Institute. Two 12-inch-thick concrete walls flank the central space (*panoptic room*), while the exterior walls are highly insulated, lightweight components. The panoptic room opens up to the landscape on the south side through a tall, 6-meter-wide slanting glass wall. The architects envisioned the low arctic sun penetrating the long panoptic room, allowing the concrete interior walls and floor to act as heat storage devices. Individual offices were placed on the east and west sides of the concrete walls defining the central space. Low horizontal window bands were introduced as a response to the overall low sun angles.

The three major construction materials introduced, in addition to glass, were the concrete walls and floors in the interior, the solid hardwood floors in the offices, and the Canadian cedar cladding on the exterior (see Figure 8.10). Extruded aluminum profiles were used in the window frames. Anodized alu-

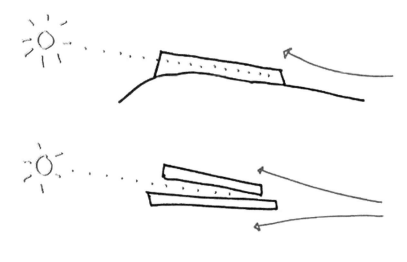

orientering mod sol og vind

Fig. 8.8 Conceptual drawings illustrate how the building was oriented relative to sun and wind, by KHR Architects.

minum does not require an initial application of paint and it eliminates the need for future paint jobs. These choices were made in order to minimize embedded energy from transportation of building components (concrete was made from local aggregates and on-site water) and to avoid toxic gases (by using untreated wood) and static electricity (by using waxed wood floors).

The emphasis on low water usage may seem odd at first. The reason for this design parameter is the fact that in a location where the average ambient temperatures are below freezing for six months, municipal water supply must be continually pumped and circulated in insulated above ground pipes to avoid damage from frost. Low-water fixtures were introduced to minimize the water usage in the building. There is no system installed for water purification and reclamation.

The comprehensive approach to indoor air quality defines the problem wider than the quality of the indoor air itself. Surfaces were not painted, so toxic gasses

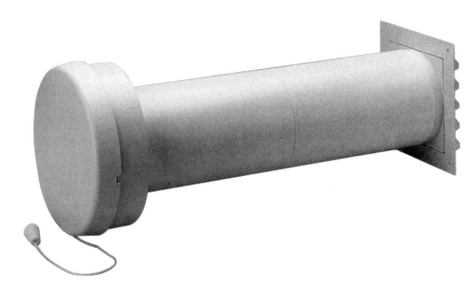

Fig. 8.9 The Fresh ventilator, by Therma-Stor, LLC.

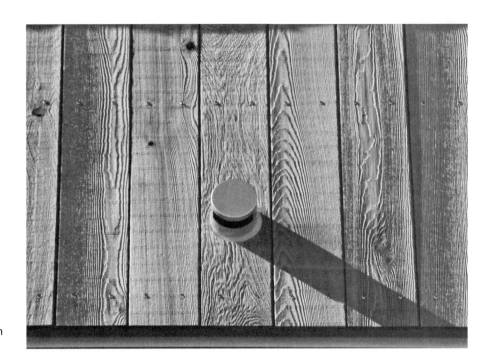

Fig. 8.10 Ventilator cap set in the Canadian cedar cladding.

were minimized or eliminated. The floors were polished concrete, concrete tiles, ceramic tiles, and unstained wood. From their previous involvement with building comfort research, the architects also noticed that most complaints were related to drafts. The architects' design responses were to use healthy natural materials, introduce a natural ventilation system with low airflow rates, design for good natural light, and use well-insulated exterior walls combined with high-

Fig. 8.11 Sunlight creates a shading effect on the artwork on the west-facing high-mass concrete wall in the lunchroom.

mass interior walls, which resulted in a draft-free interior with a mean radiant temperature that would be stabilized well inside the comfort zone.

The transformation of the last of the major design parameters into built form was a compact building with a relatively small footprint that was carefully set down among boulders and other high points in the rocky landscape of the site (see Figure 8.26).

CLAIMS

The architects have made few claims that are explicitly and specifically expressed. But embedded in the design intentions and their transformation into architectural form lay generalized claims that deserve closer examination.

One claim that stands out is that the streamlined shape of the building is an appropriate response to the high wind exposure at the site. Although the metaphor of the seal may be a productive one in generating design impulses, the seal can constantly adjust its direction of movement to respond to the prevailing ocean currents or the prevailing winds when surfaced. The building does not move, and, as we all know, wind is unpredictable. The prevailing wind direction is not only from the north, but also quite often from the south. Northern to northeastern winds occur predominantly in the winter season, while the summer winds come from the south (see Figure 8.12). The wind is elusive; it does not stay on a steady course. With constant average wind speeds exceeding 12 meters

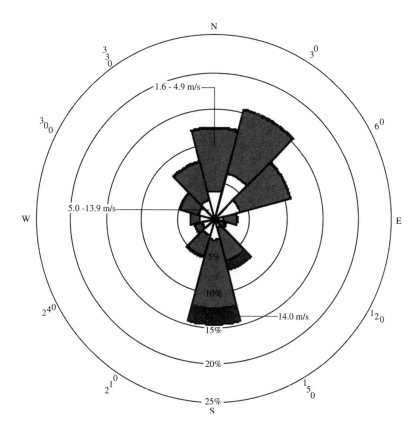

Fig. 8.12 Wind rose for Nuuk, Greenland.

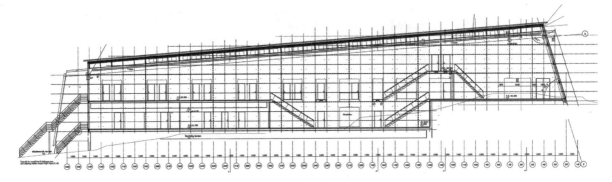

Fig. 8.13 Longitudinal section cut through the central circulation space, looking east.

per second or more over sustained periods of time, the wind will frequently create shifting negative and positive pressure on the roof and the sides of the building. This has resulted in windows being torn off the building and air being sucked out where it was supposed to be drawn in. The streamlined form does not prevent the building from needing to be totally closed up in windy weather, which, in turn, results in a complete shutdown of the natural ventilation system.

There is also an embedded claim concerning the stabilizing effect of the high-mass concrete walls and exposed floors on the indoor air and mean radiant temperatures. Recorded surface and air temperatures, measurements that were backed up by positive statements from the users during the interviews, verify this claim. The large south-facing glass wall is an exception here. Electric radiant tube heaters are mounted on the interior side of the aluminum mullions of the glass wall in order to prevent low glass temperatures from bringing down the mean radiant temperature in the winter. Together with the electric radiant floor heating, the tube heaters take the edge off any cold draft radiating from the glass.

Fig. 8.14 Sculpture of a seal near the Nature Institute's main entrance.

During the first day of the site visit in April 2005, both the floor heating and the tube heaters were on full blast. The lunchroom was quite hot at that time, with the sun shining in through the glass. When this was pointed out to the building maintenance person, he changed the thermostat setting and the tube heaters went cold.

The idea that the solar gains through the large south-facing glass wall will be distributed throughout the entire central space from the south to the north end and stored in the thermal mass cannot be substantiated. There is a firewall that separates the spacious lunchroom at the south end of the panoptic room from the rest of the central space that runs the entire length of the building (see Figure 8.13). The lunchroom then becomes a greenhouse or conservatory, where the heat builds up even on an April day when outdoor temperatures are around freezing. The northern end of the building is generally much colder than the southern end. At times during the winter months it is not possible to achieve indoor temperatures in the offices above 17°C.

The claim that the building is designed for low water consumption seems to be reasonable, but it was not tested or investigated, since no water meter is installed.

Fig. 8.15 View of the panoptic room, looking south.

The concept of a comprehensive approach to indoor air quality is definitely working. Although there were complaints about the quality of the work conditions in the first two years post occupancy, a later questionnaire circulated among all users turned back mostly positive responses to the indoor air quality and work environment. The opinion of three office workers, including the director, represents an exception to the general user satisfaction.

Their offices are located on the upper floor, facing west. When the doors to the central space are closed—as required by fire code—these offices experience zero airflow from the wall vents to the central space. When the doors are open—illegally—there is an air exchange with the upper strata of the lunchroom, where the air temperatures are generally very high. These offices therefore tend to overheat during normal working hours. Figure 8.15 shows the configuration of the central circulation space with doors to the individual offices on both sides. The library and three offices are located at the second-floor level on both sides of the bridge.

PERFORMANCE AS BUILT

Measuring and data-recording devices were set up in the lunchroom to monitor the surface temperatures at the inside of the glass, the floor surface temperature, and the room temperature near the south-facing glass wall. The resulting data (see Figure 8.16) show that the glass surface temperature did not fall much below the comfort zone, even when the tube radiators were off and the outdoor air temperature fell below 0°C. A possible explanation could be that there is an irradiative exchange between the cool glass and the warm floor, an exchange that is reinforced by the sloping vertical angle of the glass wall.

A wind meter had been installed on the roof of the building from the very start. This device would prevent the clerestory windows from opening during strong winds (see Figure 8.17). When weather conditions were fair, the windows would open automatically to allow for the air inside the central space to escape

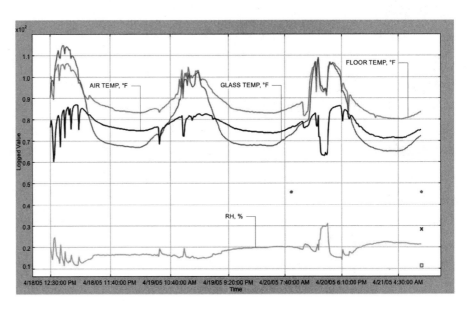

Fig. 8.16 Dry bulb temperature, relative humidity, and radiant temperatures in the lunchroom over a three-day period in April 2005.

by means of natural ventilation. As the wind wore the ball bearings down, however, the wind meter malfunctioned and was not repaired or replaced. The windows are now operated manually, which means that they are generally closed during nighttime hours and opened only during fair weather when there seems to be a demand for more fresh air inside.

Three smoke tests were conducted in order to determine how the natural ventilation system worked (Figure 8.18). First, a smoke candle was ignited in one of the west-facing offices that open up to the lunchroom on the main floor. The wall vent in the office was opened and the windows were closed. The clerestory windows at the top of the lunchroom space were opened. An air exchange through the open office door was clearly visible. Cooler air escaped from the office through the lower half of the door opening, while warmer air from the lunchroom seemed to be returning into the office. There was a clearly visible path of air and smoke moving from the office, across the lunchroom floor, and into the kitchen on the opposite side. There is a mechanically vented hood in the kitchen, which caused a negative pressure to suck the air across the floor. The smoke eventually filled the lunchroom space and escaped through the clerestory windows (and the kitchen hood). Smoke also entered the tall meeting room next to the kitchen. Since there is no place for air to escape from the upper portion of this space, smoke was trapped here for several hours (see Figure 8.19).

The second smoke test involved an office on the main floor, on the west side of the tall central space and north of the firewall (see Figure 8.20). This time a flow of cold air could be felt falling down from the open clerestory windows. These windows near the roof did not just let the hot air out, but also introduced fresh, cold air into the central space. Since the air temperature in the office now was higher than the air in the central space, the air exchange through the open door followed a pattern different from what we saw in test number one. Air from the office now escaped through the upper half of the door opening, while colder air

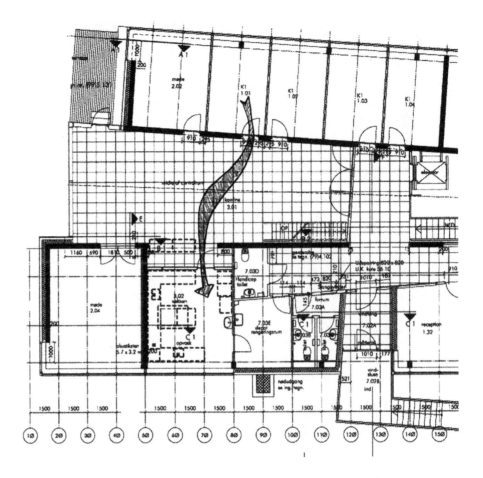

Fig. 8.18 Plan diagram shows direction of airflow from an office through the lunchroom, driven by negative air pressure created by the extraction fan in the kitchen.

Fig. 8.19 Smoke remained near the ceiling of the meeting room several hours after the smoke test.

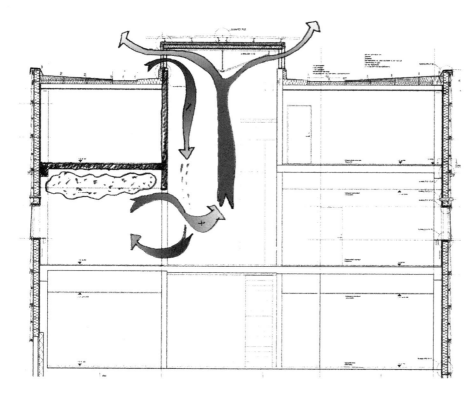

Fig. 8.20 Airflow diagram showing findings from the second smoke test. There is evidence of air exchange (not only air extraction) between the office and the central circulation space and also between the central space and the outdoor air.

from the central space seemed to be replenishing the office through the lower part of the opening.

Finally, a third smoke test was performed from the director's office at the top floor of the building—facing west. This office has one window near the corner facing south and a rather long row of windows facing west. Two smoke candles were ignited inside the office. The two wall vents were kept open. The windows were closed at the start of the test but were later opened. The patterns of smoke movement were more complex this time (see Figure 8.21). The office is connected to a small corridor, which again is connected to both the north and the south portions of the central space through fire doors. The two fire doors were kept open during the test. It became evident that the small corridor acted as an air duct between the panoptic room to the north and the lunchroom to the south. The direction of the airflow in this short corridor was first south to north, then north to south. The direction seems to be determined by the pressure difference between the two parts of the panoptic room, which again is determined by the number of clerestory windows open in each zone and the wind direction outside the building. There was an air exchange between the office and the short corridor. When the direction of the airflow was from south (lunchroom) to north (panoptic room), hot air entered the director's office. The smoke was very slow in moving out of the director's office, so the windows were opened. There was practically no wind outside. Air could now flow in through the windows and push the smoke out into the lunchroom through the short corridor.

None of the smoke tests provided convincing evidence of the actual capacity of the wall vents to supply fresh air to the offices. A parallel test was set up during the third smoke test to investigate this puzzle. A temperature sensor was placed inside one of the wall vents approximately a third of the length in from the inte-

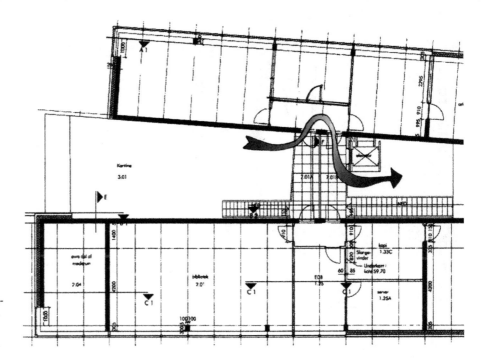

Fig. 8.21 Airflow diagram shows how the air moved from the lunchroom (warm) to the north end of the circulation space (colder), bypassing the fire wall via open doors.

rior wall toward the outside end of the vent. A second sensor recorded the inside surface temperature of the glass. The sensors were connected to a HOBO data logger that also recorded the room air temperature near the vent. The theory was that if a significant flow of air entered the space through the vent—at ambient temperatures 0°C—the temperature inside the vent would be clearly below the indoor air temperature.

The results show that these two temperatures were quite similar, which leads to the conclusion that the vent did not work as intended (see Figure 8.22). There are

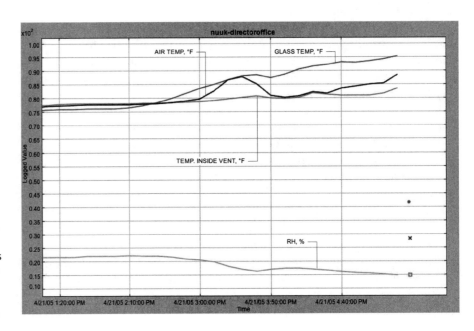

Fig. 8.22 Air temperatures, glass surface temperatures, and relative humidity in the director's office, including air temperatures measured inside a vent on the west-facing exterior wall.

several possible explanations for this. One is that the spongelike air filter inside the vent could potentially represent a significant pressure drop. A more likely explanation is that the inside mechanics of the Fresh 80 and Fresh 100 type vents include a thermostat-activated damper that is designed to shut down the airflow to a minimum when the outdoor temperatures approaches 0°C. This is an energy-saving feature of the product that is designed for a normal situation in a conventional residential building in a cold climate. The thinking behind it seems to be that when outdoor temperatures fall below a certain level, say 5°C (40°F), the stack effect in the natural ventilation system increases as the need for heat removal decreases. In this situation, lower airflow means less energy used to heat the incoming air. The situation observed at the Nature Institute on a clear day in April, however, was quite different. Although the outdoor temperatures fell below freezing, there was still a need to remove heat (and supply fresh air) to the director's office.

Records of the monthly energy use were made available for four years of operation since 2001. The records show that the building checks in at a total specific energy use of 152 to 198 kWh/m² per year for the years 2001 to 2004. This measure of performance is quite impressive when compared to a 2007 energy standard of 140 kWh/m² per year for energy-efficient office buildings in Norway (Forskrift 2007). The annual heating energy use for 2001 to 2004, by month, is compared to the monthly heating degree-day data in a typical meteorological year (see Figure 8.23). The energy use graphs for these four years are quite consistent. The energy graphs show a greater difference from winter (January) to summer (July) than the HDD graph, which indicate that the building does make use of solar radiation for space heating in the summer.

The energy use for space heating, including fans for the mechanical portion of the ventilation system and motors for the heat recovery system (mechanical ventilation only), represents the largest portion of the total energy use. Energy use for lights and plug loads is quite low. There is reason to conclude that the natural ventilation system makes a significant contribution to the energy efficiency of the building. Simply because it functions quite poorly when it comes to flushing fresh air through the offices, the resulting low levels of outside air mean that

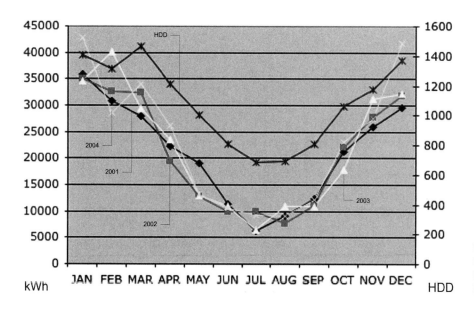

Fig. 8.23 Annual energy use by month, from utility data made available by the building owner.

less energy is used to heat that air. A study by the author (Lerum 1996) shows that limiting the outside airflow rate is the primary energy-efficiency measure in office buildings at high latitudes.

SIMULATIONS

While Weather Maker was used in conjunction with ENERGY-10 for the weather data analysis, ENERGY-10 alone was used to run hour-by-hour energy performance analyses of three variants of the building (see Figure 8.24). These three variants would all retain the same basic geometry as a simplified, shoebox model of the actual building. ENERGY-10 automatically built the two first variants: the reference case and the low-E case. A third case was then built on the low-E case, but with close to actual window areas allocated to the four building elevations.

The simulation results show that the auto build low-E case in ENERGY-10 would use a total of 155 kWh/m² per year. This was a dramatic reduction from the reference case, which would use 350 kWh/m² per year. This improvement in energy efficiency was mostly associated with a big cut in the energy required for space heating, but was also an improvement in the utilization of daylight as an energy-saving measure. This enormous improvement was made possible by improved insulation values, better window, fewer windows, a different allocation of windows among the four façades (fewer north-facing windows), and several other energy-efficiency strategies as defined by the authors of the ENERGY-10 program.

Fig. 8.24 Diagram of actual hourly heat flows, as simulated in ENERGY-10.

The shoebox variant of the Nature Institute with actual window areas and orientations would use 162 kWh/m²-Y. It is interesting to note that this is near the actual energy use as recorded over a four-year period. The increase in total

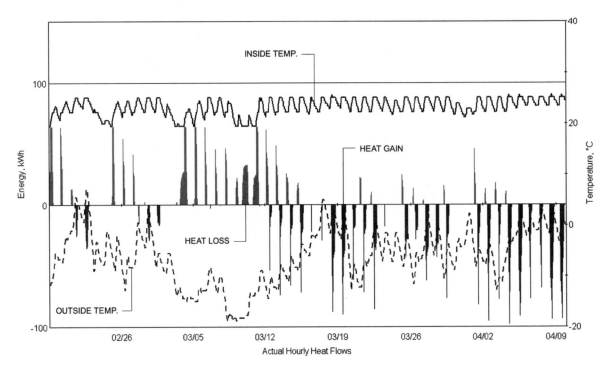

Fig. 8.25 The Nature Institute at sunset on a clear April day.

annual energy use can be traced back to a doubling of the net space heating energy, from 6.3 to 13.1 kWh/m² per year. These numbers do not include fan energy, plug loads, and other miscellaneous loads commonly associated with ventilation. A closer look at the hourly heat flow graphs in ENERGY-10 discloses another important difference between the low-E case and the Nature Institute case. When there is a need for space heating, the Nature Institute case requires more energy per hour. Similarly, when there is a need to remove heat from the space (by the use of outside air), the Nature Institute case requires larger amounts of heat removal. In other words, the Nature Institute case, with the double amount of total gross window areas, is more prone to overheating when the rooms are exposed to sunlight and is also more prone to lose heat through the same larger window areas for the remaining hours when there is no heat gain from solar radiation (see Figure 8.25). These findings bring into question the claim that the window sizing and orientation were carefully calculated.

WHAT IF?

One might think that an elongated building such as the Nature Institute should be oriented along the east–west axis for maximum use of passive solar heating. A second simulation scheme was therefore set up in order to test this hypothesis. Again, the low-E case built automatically in ENERGY-10 was used to compare with the previous variants. The results show that while rotating the building seems to have little or no effect on the total annual energy use (160 versus 162 kWh/m² per year), the building that is aligned with the long sides along the east–west axis would probably have less problems with asymmetrical overheating and glare, as seen in the existing building. But a rotated building would also require a totally different internal spatial organization, since most of the windows would be facing south.

Fig. 8.26 The Nature Institute, west-facing façade.

This is a very significant finding. Although the rule of thumb for passive solar buildings is to let the long sides face south, this scheme is not the only one that can work in the arctic—at high latitudes. Here a certain amount of east- and west-facing glass may prove beneficial in harvesting solar heat during periods of the year when there is still a need for energy to bring the interior of a building into the comfort zone (see Figure 8.26).

The low-E case variant of the first simulation run proved that the energy performance could be improved by reducing the total window area to about 50 percent of what is the case in the existing building. This finding suggests that the window scheme for the east- and west-facing offices could have been arranged differently. If there were a narrow, horizontal band of windows placed like clerestory windows near the ceiling, and if these windows were combined with smaller view windows at eye level when seated, overheating could have been reduced and glare avoided. Such a scheme is similar in its general approach to the window placement and sizing at the earlier Pihl & Søn building by the same architects (see Chapter 10).

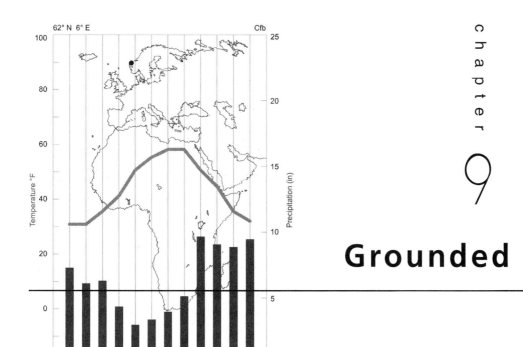

Grounded

Ivar Aasen Centre for Language and Culture by Sverre Fehn

Building Type: Museum, Interpretive Center
Location: Ørsta, Norway
Coordinates: 62°N, 6°E
Interview: Oddvar Hegge, mechanical engineer
Site Visits: July 2000; July 2005

Celebrating the work and life of Ivar Aasen, who developed the New Norwegian written language *Nynorsk*, the Aasen Centre is located at the Aasen family farm on a south-facing slope near Ørsta, Norway (see Figures 9.1 and 9.2). The building is elongated east–west with large south-facing windows, heavy construction (exposed concrete) to absorb the heat, clerestory windows to distribute light, and the north side dug deep into the ground, protected by a thick blanket of grass-covered soil.

Fig. 9.1 View of the Aasen Centre from the green roof.

Fig. 9.2 View of the Aasen Centre from the southwest.

BUILDING AND SITE

The Aasen Centre is situated next to the farmhouse where Ivar Aasen was born. The steep hillside presented itself with a site condition where the architectural response was to dig the building into the ground. This created a building with one dominating façade towards the valley below. The structural system incorporated white concrete cast in place using formwork built with rough sawn wood planks. Diagonally placed leaning walls act as structural slabs between floor and ceiling. (Fehn 2001b)

On the site plan printed in the most prominent publications of the project (Fehn 2001b; Statsbygg 2001), the building is oriented with its longitudinal axis along a horizontal line. This could lead to the conclusion that the long façade toward the valley was facing due south. A closer investigation shows, however, that the building is rotated 35 degrees off the east–west axis (see Figure 9.3). The shadows on the official site plan are an approximate reflection of the sun angles on summer solstice at 5 P.M., although the shadows seem to be foreshortened. The building is described in *Byggekunst:*

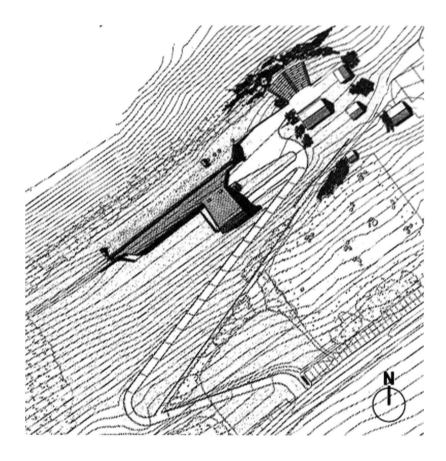

Fig. 9.3 Official site plan. The Aasen Centre located immediately west of the Aasen farm.

The main layout is as follows: the areas facing the valley were reserved for Ivar Aasen's life and research, divided into rooms by a row of inclined wall plates. The first room presents mementoes from his life, set against the view out to the Valley and the mountains. The next room contains his main heritage, the Nynorsk grammar, the dictionary, and the language. The Kristiania Room shows the interior of his two rooms in Theatergaten in Oslo, his desk, book collection, and other objects. The slanting walls give an impression of his attic chamber. The next section presents his travels throughout Norway, and the sequence ends with a small library of central Nynorsk authors. The fight of the formal dialect for its existence runs as a thread throughout the exhibition (see Figures 9.4 and 9.5).

The spatial sequence along the retaining wall to the back opens with a room of sound and signs, where work by the composer Arne Norheim, "the birth of language," uses a computer to produce harmonies made up of the smallest constituent parts of language: the phonemes. The computer reacts to the presence of people in the space, which determines the final composition of sounds. The murals by the artist professor Ole Lislerud are based on signs from different systems of writing.

The library stretches over two stories and connects the lower research and administration level with the museum above. The auditorium follows the natural topography and has access from two levels. The reception and the restaurant bring the vault to an end and face an amphitheater above the original Aasen homestead.

The structure is made in white in-situ concrete using timber shuttering. The imprint of the standard boards of the shuttering transfers the

Fig. 9.4 Signs on a concrete wall in the main exhibition area.

memory of the paneling of traditional timber architecture, and the materials infuse the architecture with a timeless way of building. The face of the building toward the valley is the large wall of the auditorium where Ivar Aasen's signature is written in steel across the concrete (see Figure 9.6; Fehn 2001b).

BUILDING SPECIFICATIONS

- Green roof: 200 mm concrete cast in place, vapor barrier. 200–300 mm high-density rock wool insulation, membrane, drainage sheet, ~ 200 mm topsoil and turf.
- Flat roof: 200 mm concrete cast in place, vapor barrier, 200–300 mm extruded polystyrene foam insulation, two-layer roofing.
- Retaining wall: 300 mm concrete cast in place, drainage sheet, 100 mm extruded polystyrene foam insulation.
- Main floor: 200 mm concrete cast in place, 50 mm rock wool, built-up floor cavity, 22 mm plywood, 25 mm sound-absorbing board, 22 mm wood fiber board, 20 mm solid oak flooring.
- Lower floor: compacted gravel, 40 mm concrete poured in place, vapor barrier, 100 mm extruded polystyrene insulation, 80 mm reinforced concrete slab, 3 mm rubber flooring.

Source: Construction documents provided by Oddvar Hegge (Lerum and Hegge 2006).

LOCATION AND CLIMATE

The climate on the west coast of Norway is not as harsh as one would think, judging from the high latitude. Since the Gulf Stream brings warm water up along the Norwegian coast, the weather is generally milder than what you might find at similar locations at these high latitudes. Norway is situated in a belt of westerly winds, which brings continuing supplies of maritime-tempered air masses from the west. This influences to a high degree the climate of the coastal regions (see Figure 9.7).

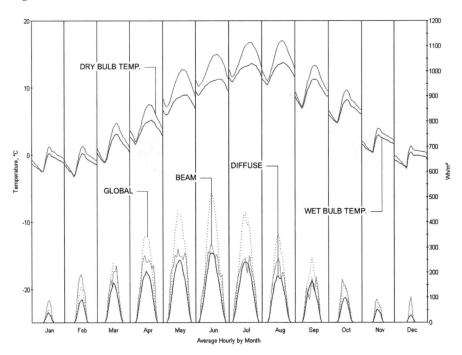

Fig. 9.7 Average-day temperatures and solar radiation, by month.

The west coast of Norway is a maritime macroclimate without any dry periods and without strong variations in temperatures. The annual normal temperature amplitude ranges from 15°C to 14°C as you go up the coast. The annual average temperature is obviously falling as you travel north, from 7.6°C at Lindesnes to 2.5°C at Helnes at 74°N latitude (Wolleng 1979).

In order to fully appreciate and understand the distinctive characteristics of the climate at the location, it is necessary to have access to hour-by-hour data. A weather file in TMY file format was constructed with the software program Meteonorm™ 5.1. The outcome was calibrated against average monthly temperatures obtained from Terje Wolleng's book *Climate Data for Norway* (Wolleng 1979). Weather data from the constructed TMY file were then processed using the software program Weather Maker, giving the results shown in Table 9.1.

Although heating degree-days—at base temperature 18.3°C—amount to 4,356 for a typical meteorological year, there are only 13 cooling degree-days for the same base temperature.

These numbers strongly indicate that the building is located in a heating-dominated climate. A well-insulated, correctly oriented building, however, may still need cooling for parts of the day, even during late winter and early spring. Figure 9.8 shows the results of a quick ENERGY-10 simulation for one week in February. Although heating is required from the early morning until early afternoon, there is also a need for moving heat out of the building during the afternoon and early evening on sunny days.

Figure 9.9 is produced from Weather Maker. It shows a two-week period in January where the temperatures outside are below freezing for most of time, but then rise to almost 10°C on January 20. Although there may be occasional sunny

Table 9.1 Summary of climate data in a typical meteorological year, from Weather Maker.

	Average Dry Bulb Temperature, °C	Average Wet Bulb Temperature, °C	Average Daily Horizontal Solar Radiation, Wh/m²	Heating Degree Days, Base 18.3 °C	Cooling Degree Days, Base 18.3 °C
JAN	-0.6	-1.1	198	578	0
FEB	-0.8	-1.3	714	528	0
MAR	1.9	1.1	1585	511	0
APR	5.0	3.7	3081	405	0
MAY	10.3	7.8	4360	259	0
JUN	12.9	10.4	5018	173	1
JUL	14.5	12.5	4353	135	6
AUG	14.3	12.4	2979	140	6
SEP	10.5	9.4	1824	243	0
OCT	7.2	6.5	854	344	0
NOV	2.3	1.7	290	475	0
DEC	0.0	-0.6	117	566	0

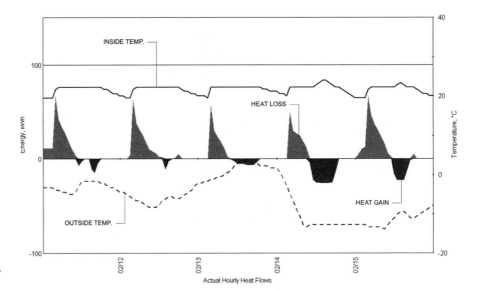

Fig. 9.8 Actual hourly heat flows in February, as simulated in ENERGY-10.

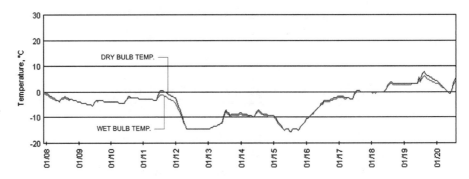

Fig. 9.9 Ambient temperatures during the second week of January in a typical meteorological year, from Weather Maker.

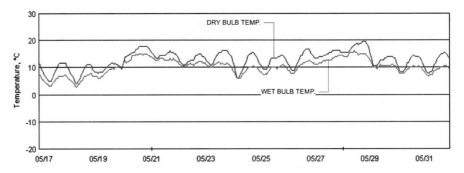

Fig. 9.10 Ambient temperatures toward the end of May in a typical meteorological year, from Weather Maker.

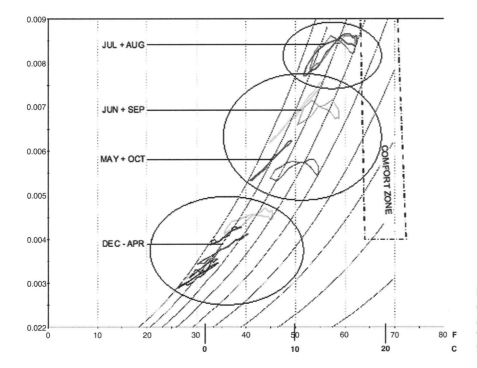

Fig. 9.11 Psychrometric chart of average day ambient temperature fluctuations, by month, from Weather Maker.

days where heat must be removed from the building, heating is needed most of the time during winter.

Figure 9.10 shows a week toward the end of May. In a typical meteorological year, the outdoor temperature now averages 10°C and reaches 20°C occasionally during the day. Nighttime temperatures are 10°C or lower. Knowing what we have seen from the ENERGY-10 analysis, the building may now need to release heat from the interior on any sunny day. The moderate outdoor temperatures, particularly at night, clearly show the possibility of using night vent cooling as a passive, low-energy strategy for space conditioning.

Outdoor temperature fluctuations during a typical day for each month are plotted on the psychrometric chart shown as Figure 9.11. July and August stand out as summer months with relative high humidity, but with ambient temperatures that are still well below the comfort zone for most of the time. May, June, September, and October are shoulder-season months, when passive heating and cooling strategies can be used to create a comfortable environment with minimal use of energy for space conditioning. The winter season basically lasts from December through April, with temperatures below 7°C most of the time.

DESIGN PHILOSOPHY

The architect, Sverre Fehn, was not available for an interview for this book. It therefore became necessary to rely on secondary sources, such magazine articles, in order to arrive at an understanding of the building as seen through the eyes of the designer.

Sverre Fehn is often seen as an architect whose approach to issues of sustainability, nature, and ecological design is more philosophical and poetic than sci-

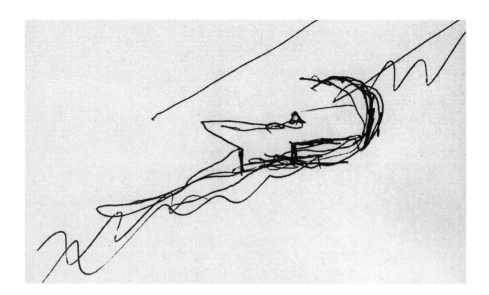

Fig. 9.12 Drawing by Sverre Fehn.

entifically calculated (see Figure 9.12). As an invited lecturer at a workshop on ecological design in Denmark in 1994, Fehn started out by making it clear that he is not an architect who specializes in ecological design, but simply an architect. That said, he continued with presenting a number of design criteria for ecological architecture. He spoke about the field of tension between the low technology of the past and the high technology of today. He spoke about the tension between history and nature. Sverre Fehn addressed his audience by describing how in his work he seeks the confrontation between the two technologies, and that he often feels that the two are passing by each other. By passing, but not touching, each other, the two technologies show mutual respect (see Figure 9.13). He spoke about the relationship to the earth and to the inner history of the burial grounds,

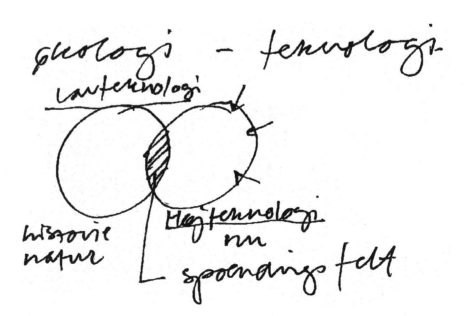

Fig. 9.13 Drawing by Lone Wiggers.

the poetry of the buried, and how constructed objects are placed in nature. Fehn then went on to show his built ecological project, the well-known eco-house at Norrköping (Wiggers 1994).

Looking back on his travels to Morocco as a young man, Sverre Fehn spoke about tattoos as he referred to the French author Michel Tournier and his book about the three wise men. This book is actually titled *The Four Wise Men* in the English translation (Tournier 1982). He explained how tattoos may be seen as incisions into the skin, which is the envelope of the human body. If you compare architecture to the human body, you see how the skin defines the space of your own body (see Figure 9.14). When you make a cut into the skin and prevent the wound from growing, you can cause "buildings" to grow on the surface of the skin with fire, knives, needles, and color: yellows and reds. The signs inscribed into the flesh develop a third dimension. The painting becomes a relief, a sculpture. A piece of art has been imprinted into a physical landscape.

Sverre Fehn's drawing of Pegasus—the winged horse—is imprinted on a wall-mounted marble tile at the Aasen Centre, as seen in Figure 9.15. For Fehn, the image of Pegasus represents another sign of the concept of making incisions into the earth in order to provoke a reaction: "Everywhere the winged horse struck hoof to earth, an inspiring spring burst forth" (Wikipedia 2007).

Fehn then explained how the Vikings sailed the oceans in their wooden ships, and how the ships were brought up on land and incisions were made into the landscape for the ships to be buried in the earth. In the afterlife, the Vikings continued to sail their ships on a journey into the land of death, illustrated in Figure 9.16 (Wiggers 1994).

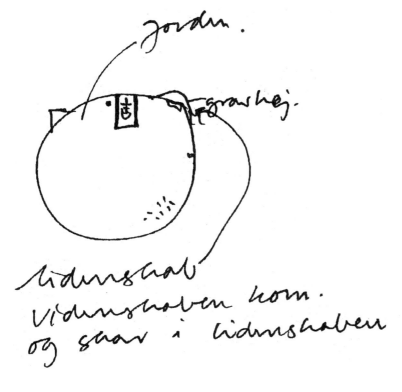

Fig. 9.14 Drawing by Lone Wiggers: "As science arrived, incisions were made into the passion."

Fig. 9.15 Pegasus: Drawing by Sverre Fehn on a wall-mounted marble tile at the Aasen Centre. "Everywhere the winged horse struck hoof to earth, an inspiring spring burst forth."

"In the project of the Museum for the big battleship at Stockholm, I placed the object under the surface of the landscape to dramatize the story of the lost ship at the bottom of the sea at the harbor. In the Museum for the death culture of the Viking a whole section of the building was moved into the field to express the 'life' of death under the earth" (Fehn 1999a).

In the *Byggekunst* article, Fehn described his approach to the Aasen Centre:

The idea behind the project was to bring together a museum presenting the story of Ivar Aasen's life with the cultural center for "Nynorsk," the Norwegian formal dialect which Aasen constructed. The chosen site, a dramatically steep hillside, adjoins Ivar Aasen's birthplace and presents a unique architectonic challenge. The building had to be dug into the sloping ground, which gave it a dominating façade facing the valley. The meeting of the

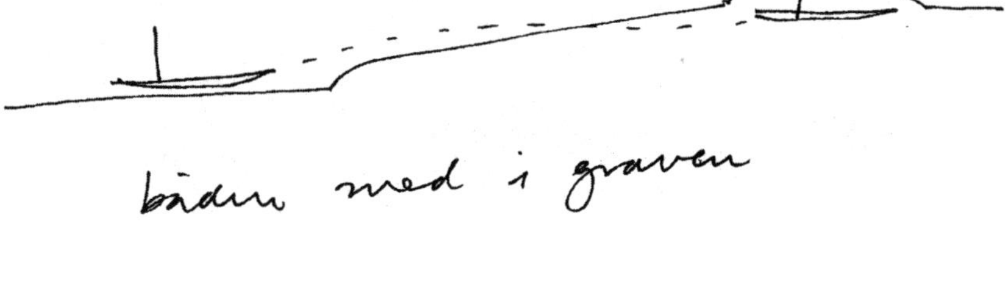

Fig. 9.16 "The boat is brought along into the grave (the burial mound)." Drawing by Lone Wiggers.

båden med i graven

user's program and the architectonic construction became a strong point of tension, and we were given the time to go through the exciting process of bringing this program together with the approach to the site. (Fehn 2001b)

INTENTIONS TRANSCRIBED

Mountains, snow, landscape—it has a great meaning to me. You have this great surrounding nature that you must conform to—build into the topographical landscape. It is the space of nature that provides the language and creates architecture. It is the great counterpoint. Nature and culture must find a dialogue. If you simply submit to nature, you risk a resulting state of lethargy. (Møller and Fehn 1997)

I see materials as letters we use to write our poetic thoughts. Detailing is the story of the meeting point between materials. We work with letters, an alphabet, we write a story. The story and its structure are inseparable. The poetic idea needs the support of structures to exist. We should have a story to tell [see Figure 9.18]. (Fehn 1999b)

If the narration we here call architecture does not possess a structure, it remains meaningless. Architecture is also irrational, but an irrational idea must be based on a rational structure. In the Gothic cathedrals, stone is used with extreme economy; a structure cannot be more elegant. (Møller and Fehn 1997)

The construction is the nerve of the building. I continually build models in paper during the design process in order to find the roots of the construction. . . . I have all my life tried to run away from the Nordic tradition. But I realize that it is difficult to turn away from yourself. (Fehn 1999a)

Concrete has two lives, one coming before and the other after hardening. The strength that emerges from the hardening process is a mystery and happens in an instant. Iron is intrinsic to this form of construction in which the mass of the concrete rides the strength of the metal. The relationship between concrete and steel is dependent, since each material alone lacks sufficient strength. With the advent of glue the tree's tectonic size is totally transformed and wood itself becomes a substance. Its color remains naturally determined, but its dimension becomes artificial and unlimited—mystery no longer resides.

Fig. 9.17 Drawings by Sverre Fehn.

  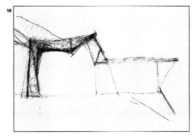

Fig. 9.18 The exhibition area on the main floor. View toward the southwest.

> With time certain architects will accept age as evidence of a tiredness, which has a beauty of its own, allowing raw material a dimension of life and wisdom. (Fehn 1993)

ENERGY PERFORMANCE

Oddvar Hegge was the mechanical engineer on the project. In the interview, he gave the following responses (marked "OH").

OH: Fehn always reminded me that he did not want the mechanical systems to be seen in his buildings; he simply wanted the systems to work!

The architect has made no explicitly or specifically expressed claims about the energy performance of the building. The following sections review the various aspects of the building and how well they perform as built.

Outside Air Requirement

OH: There is now in Norway a requirement that 100 percent outside air is used for ventilation. In this situation, since a large portion of the annual energy use is associated with pre-heating fresh air supply, ways to improve energy-efficiency are: to reduce the air flow rates to a minimum needed to maintain indoor air quality (IAQ), and to recover the heat from the exhaust air stream. System controls allow for a reduction in the airflow rate to two-thirds. Rotating heat recovery units with efficiencies of 60 to 70 percent were installed.

Displacement Ventilation

Displacement ventilation is used in the café and reception area (see Figure 9.19). The air supply is through a grill made out of wood and designed by the architect to integrate with the building structure. Sverre Fehn used this approach in other buildings, such as the Aukrust Centre in Alvdal, Norway. The exhaust air from this area returns through the kitchen and bathrooms, and also through wall vents on the north wall. He decided not to use displacement ventilation in the exhibition areas on the main floor, since wall-mounted air supply grills might have reduced the general flexibility of these spaces.

Forced Air Mixing

A mixing principle is used for air distribution in the tall spaces along the north side of the exhibition area (see Figures 9.20 and 9.21). There are similar air-

Fig. 9.19 Displacement ventilation supply air grill in the café.

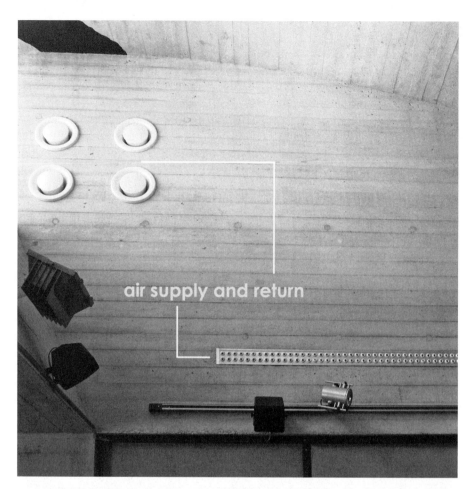

Fig. 9.20 Forced-air supply grill and return vents near the ceiling on the first floor.

air supply and return

Fig. 9.21 Forced-air supply grill near the ceiling on the first floor.

supply grills at the junctures of the inclining concrete walls that form the *open books*.

Heating and Cooling

A direct expansion type chiller with a 130 kW compressor and six-fan condenser was installed (see Figure 9.22). This system provides chilled water at 7°C to 12°C, an average of 10°C. Cooling radiators (chilled beams) were installed in the ceilings near the south-facing windows in the exhibition area. In order to avoid condensation problems, chilled water at minimum 16°C is supplied to the chilled beams, shown in Figure 9.23.

The cooling system is also used for humidity control. If the outside air is too humid, the air is subcooled and then reheated. The opposite phenomenon is seen in the winter, when a water spray is used to increase the humidity of the dry outside air that is introduced to the building interior. Both these procedures increase the annual energy use significantly.

Heating is generally supplied through the ventilation air, with additional electric resistant heaters mounted on the floor near the windows in the exhibition areas.

Systems Integration

In Sverre Fehn's many museum buildings, such as the Aukrust Centre in Alvdal, mechanical systems are integrated with the structure in a truly elegant way (Fehn 2001a). At the Aasen Centre, the main conduits for air supply and return are concealed under the built-up floor at the main exhibition level. Circular vents mounted directly in the concrete ceiling provide air supply to and return from the rooms on the lower floor.

Fig. 9.22 Condenser unit on the roof near the southwest end of the building.

Fig. 9.23 Ceiling-mounted "chilled beams" and fin-tube type radiant heater on the floor next to the southeast-facing window wall.

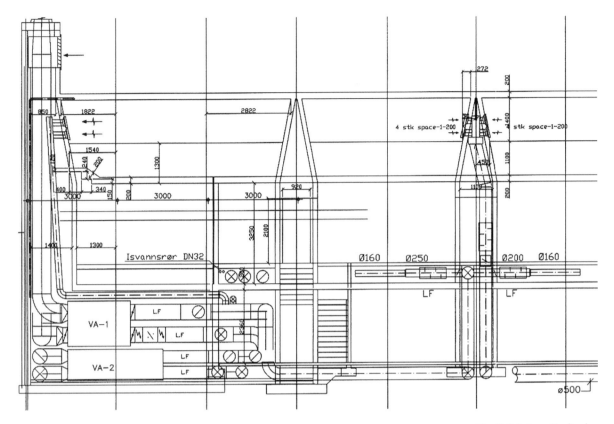

The secondary air supply and return ducts in the main exhibition spaces above are concealed within the vertical structural elements made of cast-in-place concrete (see Figure 9.24). Air supplied by the displacement ventilation system is introduced through carefully designed grills in the walls made with wooden slats.

This approach eliminates the need for any suspended ceilings and leaves the beautifully cast concrete walls and ceilings with their abundant supply of thermal mass fully exposed to the interior.

The capacity of the heating and cooling system, however, seems to not fully meet the peak demands of the winter and summer design days. Radiant heaters are mounted on the floor next to the large floor-to ceiling windows in the exhibition area. In these rooms, there are also chilled beams (cooling radiators) mounted in the ceiling. Seen against the background of Sverre Fehn's elegant mechanical systems integration, these heating and cooling elements are obvious add-ons that were not intended by the architect.

Annual Energy Use

Figure 9.25 is reproduced from the utility company Tussa's Web site (Tussa 2007). The graph shows electric energy use for a typical day of each month. Data for 2004 and 2005 are based on historical energy use. The bars for 2006 show projected energy use based on historical data for previous years.

With an annual energy use of more than 500,000 kWh for the whole (all-electric) building, the annual specific energy use amounts to approximately

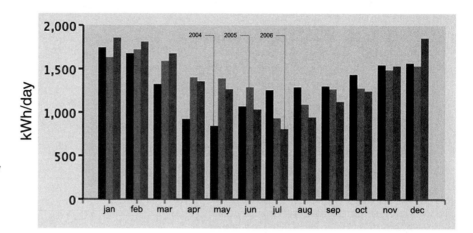

Fig. 9.25 Annual energy use, by average day per month, for 2004 (actual), 2005 (actual), and 2006 (projected).

330 kWh per square meter per year. This is a higher number than we would expect from the location and the design of the building, which is basically tuned to allow for passive heating and cooling strategies to be utilized. As compared to the average annual specific energy use for museum buildings owned by the Norwegian government, the specific energy use for the Aasen Centre is more than double the national average. As seen in Figure 9.26, the annual average specific

År	Totalt forbruk		Areal	Graddager	Spesifikt forbruk	
	Avlest	50% g.d.korr.		(veid middel)	Avlest	50% g.d.korr.
	MWh	MWh	m2 * 1000		kWh/m2	kWh/m2
1999	4130	4336	30	3808	137,1	143,9
2000	4894	5331	34	3554	143,2	156,0
2001	5320	5405	34	4058	155,6	158,0
2002	5088	5327	34	3828	149,2	156,2
2003	4995	5247	34	3804	146,9	154,3
2004	5006	5293	37	3757	135,3	143,1
				Normalår		
Snitt	4906	5156	34	4188	144,5	151,9
1	2	3	4	5	6	7

Fig. 9.26 Annual energy use in museum buildings owned by the Norwegian government. Column heads translate as (1) year; (2) total energy use (measured); (3) total energy use (50% degree-day correction); (4) total floor area; (5) degree-days; (6) specific energy use (measured); and (7) specific energy use (50% degree-day correction).

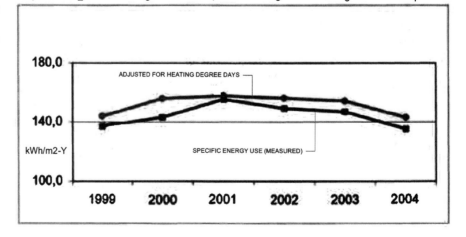

energy use for state-owned museum buildings in Norway (2004) was less than 150 kWh per square meter per year (Statsbygg 2005).

During the interview with mechanical engineer Oddvar Hegge, and in e-mail exchanges with facilities manager Knut-Johann Jørgensen, a possible twofold explanation for the relatively high energy use emerged: The building does not fully utilize solar radiation for space heating because the blinds always come down when the sun hits the building. This shading strategy is also used for the clerestory windows, where the low winter sun would not necessarily cause any damage to the exhibited artifacts. Also, the potential for night vent cooling is not utilized during the periods of the year when heat needs to be removed from the building and mechanical cooling is required. The most obvious explanation for the failure to utilize the potential for low-energy strategies that are inherent in Fehn's design is that the building owner (Statsbygg) set very strict limits for temperature and humidity ranges. These design requirements supposedly limited the use of low-energy space-conditioning strategies.

Interior Surface Temperatures

In order to investigate the claim that temperatures and relative humidity are kept within narrow ranges of amplitude, surface temperatures were measured at the inside of the building on a sunny summer day in 2005. The resulting surface temperature measurements were recorded on sectional diagrams of the building. The placement of the sections is indicated in the diagrammatic plan included in Figure 9.27.

The recordings show that there were significant temperature differences of up to 16°C between the ceilings downstairs and the curved ceiling above the café upstairs. In general, the building was warmer upstairs than downstairs and warmer at the east end than at the west end of the main floor. The museum personnel also noted that the building felt stuffy as they arrived at work early on a sunny summer day.

These measurements, although taken during a snapshot in time, clearly show that the temperature ranges are much larger than the limits included with the design requirements (see Figures 9.28 to 9.31). Since the building obviously

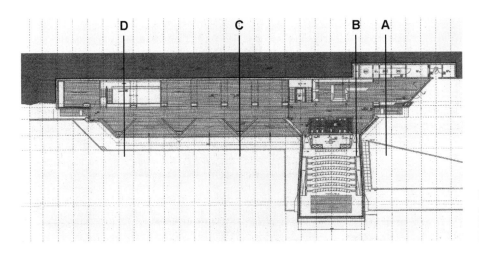

Fig. 9.27 Plan of first (main) floor. Section lines A–D refer to Figures 9.28–9.31.

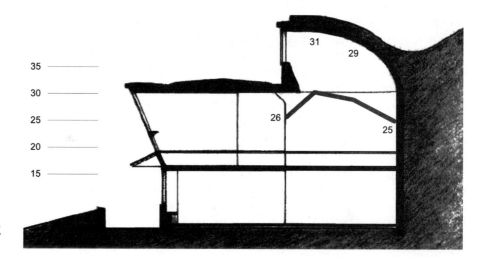

Fig. 9.28 Surface temperatures on July 27, 2006, at section A.

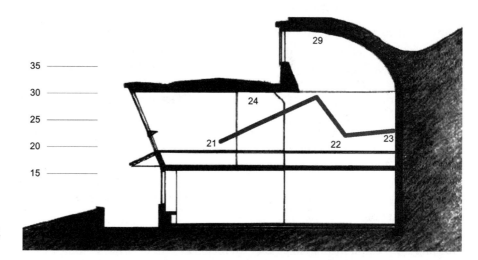

Fig. 9.29 Surface temperatures on July 27, 2006, at section B.

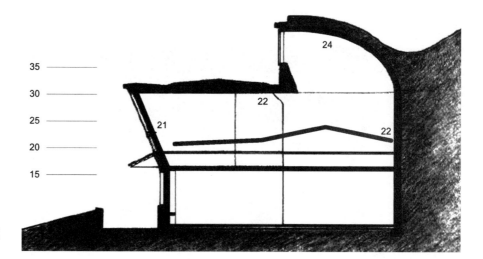

Fig. 9.30 Surface temperatures on July 27, 2006, at section C.

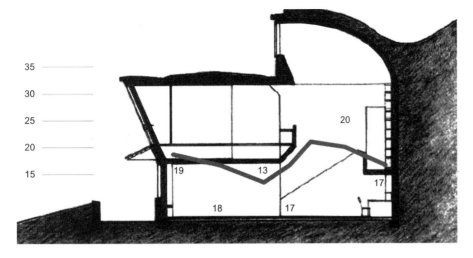

35
30
25
20
15

20

19   13

18   17   17

Fig. 9.31 Surface temperatures on July 27, 2006, at section D.

operates without severe damage to the exhibited artifacts within these wide temperature ranges, the design requirements might be revisited. A natural ventilation system with high-mass night vent cooling could easily be implemented through a low-cost redesign, which could include operable clerestory windows and fresh air intake through the built-up floor.

The East Window

A large window wall at the end of the café faces east, as shown in Figure 9.32. Heat gain from solar radiation through the glass on a sunny summer day may explain, in part, the indoor air temperature asymmetry that was recorded with the

Fig. 9.32 The east-facing glass wall in the café.

Table 9.2 Solar gain in W/m² through an east-facing window on June 15.	
Time	**W/m²**
04:00	231
05:00	508
06:00	662
07:00	723
08:00	697
09:00	599
10:00	437
11:00	227

infrared thermometer. An analysis of the solar radiation incident on the glass was performed for a clear day in mid-June. Solar radiation data were obtained from Terje Wolleng's climate data book (Wolleng 1979, p. 96).

Solar radiation data at the actual location—through single-pane glass for an east-oriented window on June 15—are listed in Table 9.2.

The average hourly solar radiation transmitted through a single-pane glass for the hours of 6 to 9 A.M. is 670 W/m². If one roughly assumes that two-thirds of the solar radiation is transmitted through double-pane low-E glass, and if we assume a net glass area of 25 m², then the hourly solar gain amounts to $670 \times 0.67 \times 25 = 11,223$ W. In other words, during the first half of a summer day, the heat from the glass wall in the café compares to an 11 kW radiant heater. This internal heat gain comes in addition to heat generated by a row of 300-watt uplights and an array of spotlights of 35 to 50 watts each. During the site visit on July 27, 2005, all electric light fixtures were switched on.

Internal Heat Gain

Figure 9.33 shows one of the many 300-watt uplights used to light up the curved exposed concrete ceilings in the exhibition areas. Figure 9.34 (taken in 2000 before the exterior blinds were installed) shows how daylight would provide sufficient light levels and enrich the perception of the interior spaces.

Shading

While the floor-to-ceiling windows on the main exhibition level, and the clerestory windows, are shaded by movable blinds, as shown in Figures 9.35 and 9.36, the lower-level offices are protected by a fixed overhang. This overhang is constructed with large slate tiles mounted on a structure made from laminated wood.

An analysis of the shading provided by the lower-floor overhang was performed using a section of the building. Figure 9.37 shows the section of the lower-floor overhang with profile angles at noon for winter solstice, spring

Fig. 9.33 The 300-watt wall-mounted uplights.

Fig. 9.34 View of the library from the lower floor, toward the northeast.

Fig. 9.35 Southeast-facing glass wall shaded by movable blinds (upper floor) and a fixed overhang (lower floor).

equinox, and summer solstice superimposed. It is evident from the diagram that the overhang was designed to allow the low winter sun to heat the spaces inside while the higher summer sun angles are cut off from reaching the glass. Due to the rotation of the glazed façade 35 degrees east of due south, the noon profile angle on winter solstice, December 21, is zero. There will be several weeks around winter solstice when there is no significant solar heat gain.

The tilt angle of the large windows on the main floor was generated by the geometry of the inclined concrete walls. The tilt may eliminate problems with visual comfort from the inside of the building, such as glare and reflections. This

Fig. 9.36 Detail of fixed overhang and movable blinds.

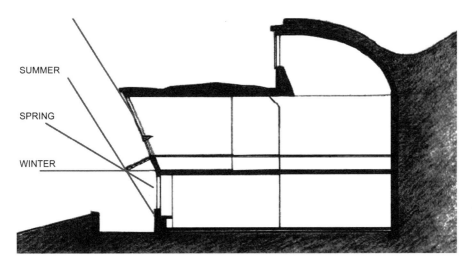

Fig. 9.37 Profile angles (sun altitude angle measured in a plane perpendicular to the glazed wall) at winter solstice, equinox, and summer solstice.

particular configuration of the main façade may also help reduce the solar gain around summer solstice, but lower sun angles during most of the summer daytime hours may cause overheating. Without a fixed overhang on the upper floor, movable blinds became a necessity for sun control.

WHAT IF?

Passive Solar Heating

In Figure 9.38, the spring equinox sun angle is superimposed on a typical section of the building. For almost six months out of the year, the sun's rays will light up the curved ceiling without reaching the back wall of the exhibition areas. The clerestory windows do not represent any discomfort from glare, since they, with rare exceptions, are out of the view of the visitors. If light control during the winter months were needed as a result of high luminosity inside the building, perforated blinds could be installed on the inside of the windows. This

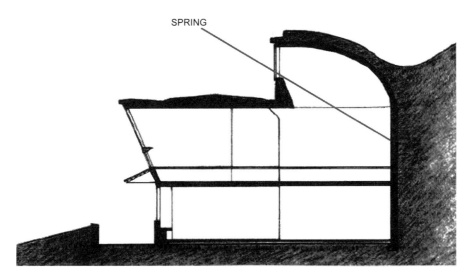

Fig. 9.38 Profile angle at noon on March 21 and September 21.

arrangement would maintain control of interior light levels while admitting heat from solar radiation as needed.

Night-Vent Cooling

The potential for low-energy cooling from high-mass night ventilation was investigated through computer simulations. A simplified model of the building was generated in ENERGY-10, and the necessary parameters were set up to run a few night ventilation hour-by-hour calculations. Simulating night-vent cooling is somewhat complicated and not straightforward in ENERGY-10. Basically, the procedure assumes the following:

- There is a high nighttime airflow rate generated from outside air entering the building.
- There are large areas of thermal mass exposed to the interior.
- The building is opened up for airflow at night and closed during the following day.
- The windows are protected from solar radiation and daylight controls are applied.

Figure 9.39 shows temperature variations during a warm week around August 21, when the noon sun angles start to dip below 50 degrees above the horizon. Ambient temperatures reach above 25°C for three days during the beginning of this period.

Night-ventilation cooling was simulated in ENERGY-10, with no mechanical cooling applied. Figure 9.39 shows how the indoor temperature drops at night, but still within several degrees of the minimum outside air temperature. The daytime maximum indoor temperatures are below ambient for the two first days and then just a degree or two above ambient for the third day. As the ambient air temperature drops below the comfort zone for the last three days, the indoor temperature, due to the high thermal mass, remains within a comfortable range.

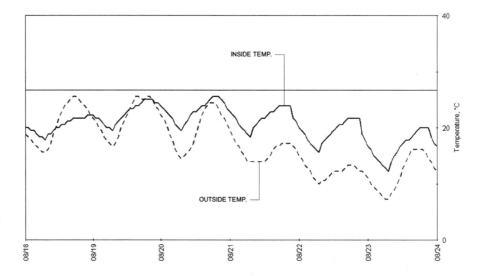

Fig. 9.39 Ambient and indoor air-temperature fluctuations with high-mass night-vent cooling during a warm summer week, as simulated in ENERGY-10.

SUMMARY OF FINDINGS

This highly acclaimed building by the architect Sverre Fehn exhibits several major characteristics of a high-performance, low-energy design: The building is designed to admit daylight across the entire width of the section. The sun is controlled by a fixed overhang at the lower level and by movable exterior blinds on the remaining south-facing windows. Abundant amounts of thermal mass are exposed to the interior in the form of cast-in-place concrete walls and ceilings. An east–west directional incision was made in the sloping landscape and the building was set deep into the hillside, protected by a well-insulated green roof. This approach to program and site generated an elongated building where most of the glass is facing south.

When the annual energy performance of this all-electric building is somewhat disappointing at a specific annual energy use of above 300 kWh/m^2 per year, one immediately starts looking for clues and answers from the building itself. As it turns out, the obvious potential for application of low-energy strategies is clearly underutilized. Although requirements for interior light levels and for air temperature and humidity control in a museum represent a design challenge, this challenge could have generated exciting solutions for high-efficiency space conditioning. It is tempting to conclude that the architect may have been underserved or ill-served by the mechanical systems specialists on the design team.

Perhaps clues at a deeper level of understanding can be found in the words of the architect himself:

> You ask why I became an architect?
>
> There were no artists in my family. My father was a lawyer and my mother mixed poison—I mean, she was a pharmacist. I was born in Kongsberg and at the age of four moved to Tønsberg. They said I was "good" at drawing. But I have never revealed to anyone before, the real reason that I became an architect. I was a precocious, only child and always in the company of my parents. I listened to the conversations they had with their friends. One of their close friends was an engineer and taught at the technical college in Trondheim. My parents were very interested in hearing about the conditions there, about the engineering education, and the field of engineering in general, and finally my father asked: "What about the architects at that school?" The engineer answered: "Architects, they never study, they just run around with large hats and enjoy themselves." It was then I decided to become an architect. (Møller and Fehn 1997)

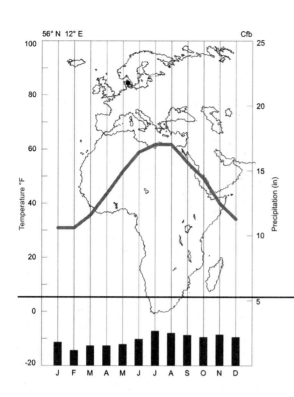

Light Breezes

Pihl & Søn Headquarters by KHR Architects

Building Type:	Office
Location:	Lyngby, Denmark
Coordinates:	55°N, 12°E
Interviews:	Jan Søndergaard, architect
	Sergio Fox, engineer
Site Visits:	April 2005; February 2006

Situated in a suburb of Copenhagen, Denmark, the office building for the construction company Pihl & Søn became its signature: a built example of the firm's excellence in modern construction rooted in crafts and tradition. With its elegant design and modern expression of tectonics, a main feature of the building is the integration of natural ventilation and daylight design (see Figure 10.1). The fully automated lighting system responds to daylight levels and to occupancy.

Fig. 10.1 Central atrium space showcases the daylight design.

BUILDING AND SITE

The building is situated in a suburban setting in the town of Kongens Lyngby northwest of Copenhagen. The L-shaped building is aligned with the street grid, which is rotated almost 45 degrees relative to due north, as shown in Figure 10.2.

The site plan in Figure 10.2 is from the journal *Casabella*. The north arrow on the drawing shows that the orientation of the building was off by 19 degrees. This is yet another example of the inaccuracy of information presented in architecture journals. This inaccuracy seems to be prevalent as it pertains to the orientation of site plans—or lack thereof.

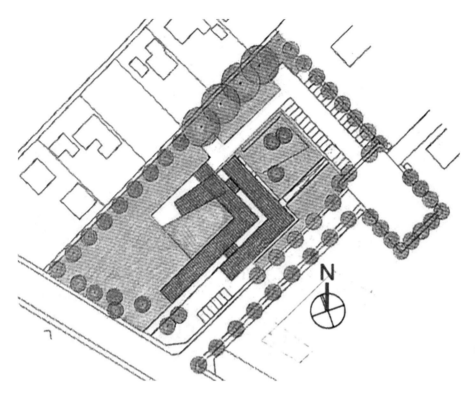

Fig. 10.2 Site plan.

Openings in the elegantly detailed brick façade are either large glazed curtain walls or moderately sized windows. For the most part, the smaller windows correspond to individual offices while the exterior glass walls correspond to common areas such as the large, tall atrium or the south-facing corridor (see Figures 10.3 and 10.4). However, a number of private offices are located behind floor-to-ceiling glass walls.

Fig. 10.3 Main entry plaza.

Fig. 10.4 Typical office window arrangement.

The rotation of the building away from due north means that there are expansive glass areas facing southeast, southwest, and northwest (see Figure 10.5). There are no architectural shading devices on the building. The large glass walls therefore represent a potential liability in terms of solar heat gain in the summer and heat loss due to convection in the winter.

Fig. 10.5 Exterior glass walls facing southwest and northwest.

LOCATION AND CLIMATE

The area in and around Copenhagen does not have such a severe climate as one might expect at 54°N. Summer temperatures reach an average high of around 20°C for three to four months, while the winter temperatures fluctuate around 0°C, as shown in Figure 10.6.

A weather file was created using the computer program Meteonorm. The weather file was converted to the TMY format and imported into Weather Maker.

The design-day dry bulb temperature for winter is near –12°C, and the summer design-day dry bulb temperature is just above 27°C. At the base temperature of 18°C, there are 3,900 heating degree-days and only 21 cooling degree-days. As we shall see later, this picture of a heating-dominated climate will change as we're looking at a high-performance, low-energy office building. The need for heating energy may be reduced significantly by design, but heating will still dominate over the need for energy to cool the building.

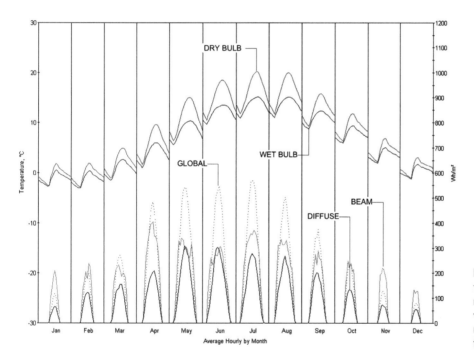

Fig. 10.6 Average-day temperature and solar radiation data. Monthly values for a typical meteorological year, from Weather Maker.

Table 10.1 Summary of climate data for Copenhagen in a typical meteorological year, from Weather Maker.

	Average Dry Bulb Temperature, °C	Average Wet Bulb Temperature, °C	Average Daily Horizontal Solar Radiation, Wh/m²	Heating Degree Days, Base 18.3 °C	Cooling Degree Days, Base 18.3 °C
JAN	-0.4	-1.2	516	579	0
FEB	-0.4	-1.4	1128	524	0
MAR	2.1	0.8	2011	506	0
APR	6.0	3.9	3831	380	0
MAY	11.2	8.5	5030	235	0
JUN	15.1	12.1	5142	115	1
JUL	16.4	13.5	5334	81	10
AUG	16.3	13.5	4239	85	10
SEP	12.8	10.9	2659	172	0
OCT	9.2	7.7	1428	286	0
NOV	4.6	3.6	657	408	0
DEC	1.2	0.4	354	534	0

WINTER

Temperatures for a week in mid-January stay below freezing for most of the time. During the seven-day period (in a typical meteorological year) analyzed as shown in Figure 10.7, temperatures reach above freezing for only a few hours.

The solar radiation graph in Figure 10.8 for the same week shows that every second or third day is a sunny day, with beam radiation values reaching 700 watts per square meter.

The energy simulation program ENERGY-10 was used to analyze a simplified shoebox representation of the building as if it were located in Copenhagen. Figure 10.9, the heat flow graph produced from ENERGY-10 for the same period, shows that heating is required most of the time in order to compensate for heat loss through convection. Cooling is needed for only a few hours. With outside air temperatures below freezing, cooling is easily provided by natural ventilation.

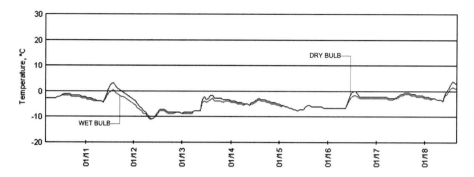

Fig. 10.7 Winter dry bulb and wet bulb temperatures, from Weather Maker.

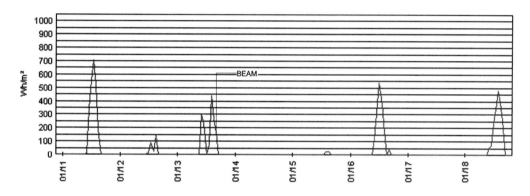

Fig. 10.8 Winter direct beam solar radiation, from Weather Maker.

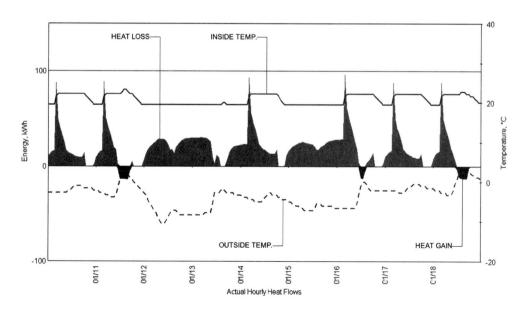

Fig. 10.9 Winter actual hourly heat-flow data, from ENERGY-10.

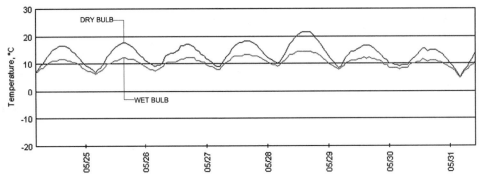

Fig. 10.10 Dry bulb and wet bulb temperatures for a week in May, from Weather Maker.

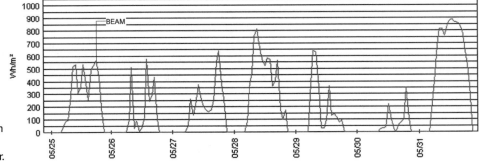

Fig. 10.11 Direct beam solar radiation for a week in May, from Weather Maker.

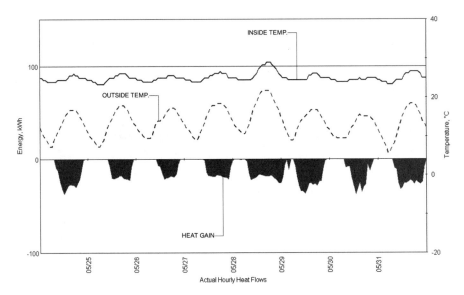

Fig. 10.12 Actual hourly heat-flow data, as simulated in ENERGY-10.

SPRING

During a week toward the end of May, outside air temperatures fluctuate between 10°C and 20°C (see Figure 10.10). The outside maximum temperature reaches above 20°C only one day.

The solar radiation graph in Figure 10.11 for the same period shows that most days are sunny or partly cloudy. The heat flow graph from ENERGY-10 in Figure 10.12 shows that cooling is required at daytime every day. Since the daytime temperatures now reach 20°C, natural ventilation may not be sufficient as a low-energy cooling strategy. Nighttime temperatures, however, frequently go below 10°C. Night ventilation cooling with high thermal mass may therefore be the cooling strategy of choice during the spring and early summer season.

SUMMER

Figure 10.13 for a week in mid-August illustrates temperature fluctuations on the warmest days in a typical meteorological year (TMY). Daytime high temperatures now reach above 25°C, but most nights are still cold enough to provide sufficient cooling of a high-mass building interior. Since some nights are quite warm, a substantial amount of thermal mass is needed to carry the building through a couple of extraordinarily warm days.

The solar radiation graph in Figure 10.14 for the same period shows that beam radiation now reaches nearly 1,000 watts per square meter. It is therefore essential to protect the windows that are exposed to the sun by correct orientation and sufficient shading. The heat flow graph from ENERGY-10 in Figure 10.15 shows that some form of cooling (heat removal) is now needed 24 hours a day.

This comparative analysis of climate data and energy performance data as analyzed in Weather Maker and simulated in ENERGY-10 shows that energy is still needed to heat a typical office building even if this office building was designed with a low-energy performance standard in mind. This quick analysis also shows that with good design, correct window orientation and sizing, and appropriate selection of materials, an office building at this location may be kept comfortable year-round without any conventional mechanical cooling.

Fig. 10.13 Summer dry bulb and wet bulb temperatures, from Weather Maker.

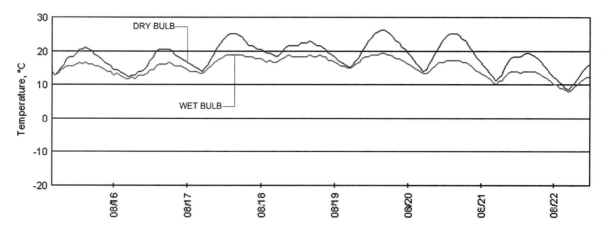

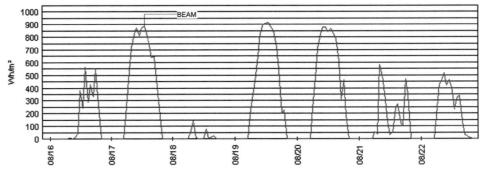

Fig. 10.14 Summer direct beam solar radiation data, from Weather Maker.

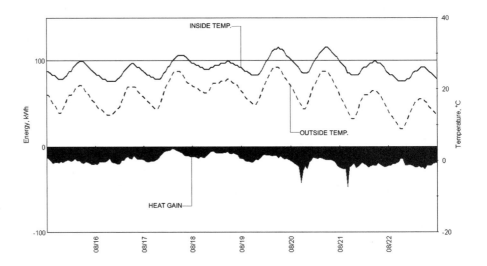

Fig. 10.15 Actual heat-flow data for a summer week, as simulated in ENERGY-10.

JAN SØNDERGAARD INTERVIEW

What follows is the response of Jan Søndergaard (JS), shown in Figure 10.16, to prepared interview questions (Lerum and Søndergaard 2005).

JS: I have difficulties separating and isolating the many aspects of architecture. As a starting point in the design process, I prefer to search for what relates to the place, to tradition, and to culture. But it is also about renewing tradition, and it's about bringing in elements from our profession. I find issues of tectonics to be very motivating—the tectonics that's included in the concept of architecture.

Then there are other elements that make things happen, such as the way buildings are produced and manufactured most efficiently with today's technology. And then above all there is the ecological question, which includes the large discussion about sustainability. I believe that all these questions can be answered, but they cannot be answered one at a time.

It's actually about applying thinking about architectural design as common sense—and that is incredibly exciting. I see architecture as something holistic

Fig. 10.16 Jan Søndergaard at the northwest
entrance.

where one problem and its solution generate another problem and other solutions all the time. As we apply this way of thinking, we can now introduce sustainability into the equation. Sustainability is a piece of the puzzle, and you cannot start creating architecture only from hypotheses or statements about sustainability. Our approach is to introduce sustainability in the context of a larger holistic process of design.

What is driving me as an architect is a methodological approach to the profession. I do not want to discard architecture as art, because architecture is art. But it's not sufficient to look at architecture exclusively as art. A methodological approach to the profession brings about an acknowledgment that our profession is a complex one where many parts interact all the time. We need to be able to keep all this information, all these components in play all the time. One concept will be introduced and it will then engage another concept and motivate new ways of thinking about re-creating and renewal. So all the elements have got to be in play all the time. That is my methodological way of working as an architect: to always work in different layers from various hypotheses and try to reach comprehensiveness.

This comprehensive approach is also applicable to the team of engineers that is involved in a building design. On the Pihl & Søn design team, Sergio Fox emerged as the person who could encompass all the disciplines of engineering. He was also in command of structural issues. We were looking at saving 60 percent on the energy budget, so we had to find ways where we could go behind the technology and create things that were inexpensive and could achieve many goals at the same time. There is a tendency to specialize in today's design environment. Specialization is necessary in order to be able to go deep into the analysis and resolution of complex, specialized tasks, but Fox was the man who pulled it all together, who brought about a comprehensive understanding of the many aspects of building.

Brick

JS: In the beginning there was a discussion about brick: To what extent could we accept and respond to a requirement of using red brick? There was a zoning requirement to use red brick as the predominant façade material, and at this point we [KHR] had never used red brick in our designs and we could not imagine using it. I thought about it for a long time and came to an agreement with myself that it was a quite strange and nonproductive approach if we started out thinking that we could not use a specific material without really understanding why. And then I realized that we often dislike new red brick buildings because they have not had a chance to mature over time. A brick building will normally require 50 years of aging before the exterior has taken on the patina that brings out the inherent beauty of fired clay. And as you start thinking about it, the city of Copenhagen is all red brick. So I was rethinking the concept and asked myself: How can we produce a brick building that has the beauty of old brick? And this question led to another question: How could one produce brick in such a way that beauty, materiality, and sense of quality would emerge?

Reinventing the Old Way of Brick Making

JS: We convinced a brick manufacturer to open an old, cone-shaped kiln, and from there we produced brick in the old coal-fired way it was done traditionally. Bricks that are placed near the perimeter of a circular kiln become overheated to such an extent that the iron in the clay is burned into the brick surface. By using brick that was fired in this way, we were able to create a building that looks like it's been weathering for many years [see Figure 10.17]. This approach was questioned, but you need to understand that the brick produced this way did not cost more than brick produced using modern firing techniques. The circular kiln process requires more work in handling of each individual brick, but in the end the manufacturer was very pleased with the result. It was a success story also from the manufacturer's point of view.

Fig. 10.17 Brick veneer with exposed steel detailing.

Creative Resistance

JS: In our work there is always the desire to avoid starting out with preconceptions and hypotheses that have been unchanged for a long time. If it becomes a habit to make decisions the way it's always been done, you cannot create anything new. It is when you're challenged with new requests or unusual and unexpected input from outside that the situation demands of you to start thinking from scratch. It's when you meet resistance as an architect that *reality is inspiring creative thought*. When things do not turn the way we expect and we encounter resistance to our ideas, that's when there is an opportunity to develop something new. Increased attention to problems of natural resource extraction and renewed awareness of ecology and sustainability can be seen as a resistance to business as usual. This resistance may be seen as a pointer to a need to solve new problems with new tools. It is this resistance that drives the need to re-create.

Honesty

JS: We decided to use brick on the exterior of the building in such a way that the brick was not used as a material to form load-bearing walls, but was instead used as a weather-protective skin. This approach created a lot of discussion about honesty. The discussion started with questions about honesty in architecture: Are we expressing honesty when we use brick as veneer on the exterior of the building? This was one question that then led to another discussion—and that was about whether it was right to take away from the brick its ability to form a load-bearing construction. This discussion came at a time when exposed prefabricated concrete elements were used frequently in the exterior of buildings.

During this time it was a common approach to assemble prefabricated concrete elements, but I disliked that approach much because this system focused on a different agenda in its system approach. I did not like much the way architecture was expressing the process of prefabrication and repetition. Raw concrete as a façade material also tends to take on a dreary, depressing look on rainy days.

Inside Out

JS: As this process of thinking and discussion evolved, it came as a liberation to me when we decided to turn things inside out. We decided to place exposed, reinforced concrete as thermal mass facing the interior of the building. We were using cast-in-place concrete, and by doing so we were able to bring out the beauty of the concrete to be enjoyed by the users inside the building. So what turned the whole thing around was the realization that exterior brick now could make sense because we used it for its sensuality as a material that faces the city and as a material that makes for a perfect protective screen facing the natural environment [see Figure 10.18].

This new approach allowed us to explore other ways to approach the idea of honesty in architecture. We decided to express the fact that the brick now was used as a nonstructural material. When brick used in this way had to span large window openings, we exposed some elements of the steel beams behind. When you look at the brick façade of the new building you can see markings in steel that indicate where we have used steel beams behind the brick. In this way the building is telling the story in an honest way about how it was built.

As natural ventilation was introduced to the design scheme, we were able to apply building physics as we took into consideration the effect of thermal mass in the concrete walls that were exposed to the building interior. The idea was to bring out the beauty of the concrete cast in place, combined with the functionality of the thermal storage capacity of concrete to aid in the performance of the natural ventilation system.

Air Carried by Light

JS: In addition to the hypothesis about natural ventilation and thermal mass, there was a second and more poetic hypothesis. This concept was about combining natural ventilation with bringing daylight into the offices. At Pihl & Søn we arrived at a solution where narrow bands of clerestory windows are located next to the exposed concrete ceilings. These clerestory windows are also used to bring fresh into the building. Through this approach to combining daylight utilization with natural ventilation, we arrived at the concept of light carrying air from the outside environment to the inside of the building [see Figure 10.19].

Natural Cooling

JS: We did not introduce heat recovery from the exhaust air in a conventional way. The large atrium, however, is mechanically conditioned, and there are air-extraction dampers next to the main entry doors where the air is brought back into the mechanical room below. As the exhaust air passes by the incoming supply air, heat is exchanged. We're also using the water in the reflecting pool outside the atrium for summer cooling. A circulation pump keeps the water in the pond moving through a small water treatment plant. The primary function of the pond is to reflect light into the building in the afternoon, but by circulating water we can also take advantage of the evaporative cooling effect at the surface of the pool [see Figure 10.20].

"There is certainly a passive evaporative cooling effect, an 'oasis' effect, with the building itself shading the pool and evaporation creating a cooler micro-climate in the immediate vicinity of the U-shaped courtyard. We have never tried to measure it, but Konya gives figures of 3 to 5 degrees under ambient in his book." (Sergio Fox, e-mail communication, September 18, 2006).

Fig. 10.18 Structural high-mass concrete wall with exterior insulation and brick veneer.

Fig. 10.19 Window arrangement in a typical office.

Heat Recovery

JS: There is no heat recovery from the part of the building that is naturally ventilated. We were discussing this many times, and we reached to the conclusion that it would not be cost effective. An office building like this require heat to be removed from the interior for most of the time in a typical year, so for eight months or so the heat recovery system would not make any sense at all. Heat recovery ended up being a small item that did not make it into application among the many strategies that we were considering. Even in the winter, a heat recovery system from natural ventilation plays a minor role. As we improve on energy efficiency and introduce improved energy conservation features such as

Fig. 10.20 Floor air supply grill in the atrium. Reflecting pool outside.

tightly controlled, on-demand ventilation rates and advanced glass properties, there is less need for heating the building, and therefore heat recovery becomes less important.

SERGIO FOX INTERVIEW

What follows is the response of Sergio Fox (SF) to prepared interview questions (Lerum and Fox 2006).

Light

SF: The professionals, but perhaps even more importantly, the users, they like the lighting. It's about how you experience the quality of light and how you measure the quantity of light. While there may be many different views on the quality of light, it is generally seen as very pleasant. We know from measurements that the light levels are good. You get a fairly good 2 percent daylight factor. So quantitatively it's good and qualitatively it's good. Other architects who came in to evaluate the light, and also the users, were pleased with the way the light works throughout the building. In a survey the users were asked a lot of questions on the indoor parameters. They said that they liked the lighting.

Intelligent Users

SF: We wanted to design an intelligent building and ended up realizing that we were dealing with intelligent users. Let the users decide, don't give them the Big Brother idea that here we got an intelligent system and you don't have to think about it. If it's an intelligent system, what are the people? No, intelligent people and a system that serves them—not the other way around. That was an important lesson. It also worked with the solar shading. When the sun started to shine in, the blinds would come down automatically. But again, some people didn't want the solar shading down. Sometimes they like to see sunlight enter the room. You could say that quantitatively it was very bad, but if subjectively they wanted just to feel that it was them that decided, they would move the blinds back up. So again, a human interface: They wanted to decide, they didn't want the system to decide for them.

We've learned a lot, and it has been a good learning process. It's very good to come back after 12 years and learn that the same principles are still being used. It was one of the weaknesses of the original system that we thought we had an intelligent control system. It was, if you like, too intelligent. It decided that the sun was shining on this; therefore we want to close down the blinds. That irritated some people.

Natural Ventilation

SF: During the design process, we were under a lot of pressure to put in a full mechanical ventilation system. The mechanical engineers made their calculations and told us that the temperatures inside the building would reach into the mid-thirties. They presented the analysis, but Jan was very much against this. He would have to put in suspended ceilings, which would have lowered the overall floor-to-ceiling height and increased the cost. So that's why we actually started this idea of a hybrid ventilation system. We introduced the automatically controlled operable skylights and operable windows. But the question was: What if it's very warm and there's no wind, will it work? So we placed extra ventilators on the roof. We call them *horizontal chimneys* or *jet engines* [see Figure 10.21]. This invention allowed the users to press a button and draw air through the whole house at a rate of three air changes per hour. So that became what you might call *hybrid ventilation*. It was this natural ventilation system with a safety belt. The jet engines are mostly used at night, but it was nice for the director to be able to say we have this facility. So the basic system is just two sets of windows in each office: one automatic at the top and with a motor connected to the whole control system, and a plain manual window—and then the skylights at the top, which also open automatically, but with a manual override. It is a natural ventilation system with a "just in case" mechanical exhaust.

Mechanical Ventilation

SF: There's a mechanical heat exchange system in the floor of the central atrium space. We looked at what might become a problem, draft from the two entrance areas, and exchanged the heat with the fresh air and then supplied some air back in through floor vents along the tall glass façades on the northwest side. In this way we were able to provide comfort and introduce a bit of background ventilation as well. There is no chiller or other form of refrigeration. Fresh air is preheated and supplied to the atrium at 0.5 air changes per hour.

Comfort

SF: The primary function of the mechanical system was actually to avoid drafts. People don't close their doors, so it's a very open house and consequently, there could be significant temperature gradient stratification in a tall space. We did a smoke test in the main foyer and found that there was three or four thousand cubic meters an hour of air exchange internally from the heat rising in the main foyer, generating high velocities, almost up to 0.6 to 0.7 meters per second. This is why I work now with the principle of local climate zones, so people always have the ability to control their own temperatures and air movement. User requirements are increasing, and naturally so. For personal productivity, and for the productivity of the company as well, it's important to provide this psychological advantage.

There is also a time component to thermal comfort. We looked at thermal stress on the artwork inside the Winter Palace in St. Petersburg. It is widely accepted that artworks need very tightly controlled conditions in terms of air temperature and relative humidity. The argument sounds initially as if it is logical, but if you look at material technology, the actual artwork can easily adjust to changing conditions if the change happens slowly. It's the rate of change that's important. It's not a question of whether the air temperature is kept constant at 24°C plus or minus 0.5. It's a question of whether the change is from 24° to 24.5° over 10 minutes, which produces more stress to a painting than if the air temperature changes from 24° to 26° over a period of two days. It's the rate of change. This is true also for human thermal comfort.

Fig. 10.21 Roof-mounted extraction fans (*jet engines*) located next to the skylights above the atrium.

Logos versus Pathos

SF: I think it's been an extremely interesting voyage with the Pihl & Søn building. Despite the pressure to use a traditional mechanical system, we managed to make a building that is interesting and simple and one that functions. They said it was necessary to install a full air-conditioning system with a guaranteed minimum of two air changes per hour, heat recovery, and all the bells and whistles. But somehow the logic didn't seem necessary. You can use a complex CFD analysis tool to simulate air movement in small offices connected to a tall atrium space, but what were the people doing? They open windows when it gets warm, so we get a strong breeze effect. If you were able to include that phenomenon in the calculations, the results would probably be very different. The consultants decided to play it safe: What if only a few windows were open? Then you could get up to 34°C inside the building. That sounds frightening to a client. But somehow, I had a gut feeling that told me that the 34°C scenario was not going to happen. It's been an interesting experiment. Jan's idea with the light, he had no real way of actually deciding what the light quality would be, he had an idea that it would be good. And I had an idea that the air movement would be good. We had to trust our instincts very much. It was the logos against the pathos, if you like.

It was predicted that we could get very heavy carbon dioxide concentrations due to lack of air movement, but basic science had taught me there is a phenomenon called *diffusion*. Even if there is no air movement, you're going to get diffusion of gases. Dalton's law teaches us that diffusion will prevent local CO_2 concentrations to build up. But even the most sophisticated simulations did not factor in diffusion. I could talk to an engineer about diffusion and he'd say, well maybe you'll get lucky. Today we can see from the measurements that the CO_2 levels are normal. We get 400 ppm up to 800 ppm, numbers that are within the acceptable limits. The users all say that the air quality is surprisingly good, despite the fact that we're working with very low air changes.

Annual Energy Use

SF: Since the central heating system designed for the first building phase was dimensioned for a later extension, we had this problem with an enormously large gas boiler trying to cover a very small load. The boiler was actually coming in and out a lot, especially in the summer when we are just covering the hot-water load. After the first year of operation, they found that more gas was used in the summer than in the winter. That doesn't make a lot of sense, but when you're operating a 350 kW gas boiler just to heat a little bit of hot water and you add a 3 kW circulation pump, you're using a lot of energy to heat a small amount of water. Since the large circulation pump runs continuously all year round, the electric consumption associated with providing domestic hot water in the summer, when space heating is not needed, is quite extensive. It would be very logical to have solar panels and an electrical backup here.

AS BUILT

Daylight Design

A Danish Building Research Institute (SBI) publication on "Architecture, Energy, and Daylight" reports on an analysis of measured data from the Pihl & Søn headquarters building (Christoffersen, Petersen, et al. 2001). Figure 10.22 summarizes daylight factors found in four typical offices.

A minimum daylight factor of 2 percent at the workplace is adopted as a daylight design guideline for energy-efficient buildings in Denmark. In general, the report concludes that this minimum daylight factor is exceeded at 3 meters distance from the exterior window wall in all offices included in the test. Glare was not reported as an issue, except for the lunchroom (canteen), where the fully glazed end wall creates severe discomfort from glare for seated persons facing that same wall (see Figure 10.23). This comfort issue can easily be resolved by changing the orientation of the tables in such a manner that people are seated facing the sidewalls.

In the southeast-facing office on the first floor (lower-left office in the diagram), the daylight factor varied from 9.5 percent near the window to 0.6 percent at the back wall. The daylight factor at a distance of 3 meters from the window was 2 percent. The report concludes that since most of the work stations are located by the window or at a maximum of 3 meters from the window, there is no need for supplementing daylight with artificial light except for a few hours out of the total work hours in a year.

In the southeast-facing office on the second floor (upper-left office in the diagram), the daylight factor varied from 10 percent near the window to 2 percent at the back wall, almost 5 meters from the window. This significant improvement relative to the office below is due to two factors: There is less horizon shading from next-door buildings, and the clerestory window is three times higher at the second floor (southeast side only) as compared to the clerestory windows in the ground floor and first floor offices.

The effect of each of these two factors is further explained by including the northeast-facing office on the second floor (upper-middle office in the diagram) in the comparison. The clerestory windows in this office are identical to the

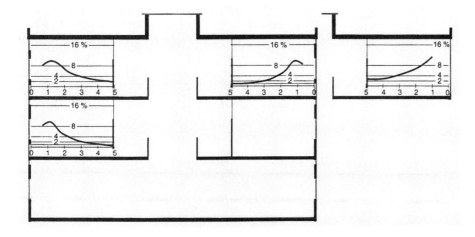

Fig. 10.22 Daylight levels in the offices, from By&Byg 013 results.

Fig. 10.23 View of the lunchroom with wall-washing skylights (left), clerestory windows (right), and high performance light fixtures integrated into the ceiling.

southeast-facing office on the first floor. The daylight factor at the back wall of the northeast-facing second floor office was found to be 1 percent. It is therefore fairly safe to conclude that the decreased horizon shading accounts for an increase from 0.6 percent to 1 percent (at the back wall), while an increase in the height of the clerestory window from 0.2 meters to 0.6 meters led to a doubling of the daylight factor at the darkest part of the room.

There is a full floor-to-ceiling glass wall in some of the offices on the second floor (upper-right office in the diagram). Radiators in front of the window wall cause a minor decrease in the daylight entering the room. Although the daylight factor at the back of the room now increases to 3 percent, there is still a significant asymmetry in the daylight levels across the section, from the window wall to the back wall.

The analysis of the measured data from these four typical offices shows that the window arrangement, including a band of operable and motorized clerestory windows combined with a band of operable view windows in each office, creates favorable daylight conditions for most working hours in a typical year. An increase in the height of the clerestory windows would lead to improved daylight levels toward the back of the room.

Lighting Energy Power Level

General electrical lighting for each typical office is provided by one specially designed light fixture hung from the ceiling. This light fixture is equipped with 2×38 W PL fluorescent tubes screened by a low-luminance grill. The light level at a typical workstation is 350 lux, decreasing to 100 lux toward the back wall. The combined installed power level associated with general and task lighting is 8 W/m², which is less than half the design guideline (15–20 W/m²) for cellular office layouts in Denmark.

Natural Ventilation

The findings presented here are derived from an interview with Sergio Fox at the Pihl building on February 23, 2006, followed by a conversation in Kongens Lyngby the same day. Although based more on systematic speculation than on actual measurements on the day of the site visit, the analysis presented here is based on years of experience and reflection and should therefore be regarded as valid.

These are flow patterns that may be understood as modes of operation of the hybrid ventilation system. In an environment where wind is absent or insignificant, airflow is commonly driven by thermal differentials, which, in turn, cause variations in air pressure.

VENTILATION: OUTSIDE AIR SUPPLY

In normal ventilation mode, the system will open the clerestory windows in the offices as well as the clerestory windows on both sides of the skylights in the atrium (see Figure 10.24). It is assumed that the upper region of the atrium is warmer than the air inside the office. The pressure difference between the upper region of the atrium and the office will pull hot air out of the atrium and pull outside air into the office (see Figure 10.25). In a typical office, the user may override the system and reduce the airflow by closing the motorized clerestory windows. There is also an override on the operable clerestory windows on both sides of the atrium.

When outside air temperatures rise above the indoor air temperature on a summer day, extract fans connected to the skylights will start. There is a 26°C set point that governs the operation of the extract fans. The extract fans—also called jet engines—are placed horizontally on the roof. Jan Søndergaard refers to these devices as *horizontal chimneys*. According to Sergio Fox, the fans rarely operate during daytime hours, simply because the indoor air temperatures are within the comfort zone even on warm summer days.

The jet engines are frequently used on summer nights during warm periods. This allows the system to cool the internal thermal mass of the building during nighttime hours and let the mass absorb internal heat during the following day.

Ventilation: Offices Only

The Pihl & Søn headquarters building is an *open office* environment. In general, all office doors are open all day. If doors are closed, however, the natural flow of air through the office from the outside to the atrium is shut off (see Figure 10.26). It is still possible to ventilate the office, simply by opening the lower window. If the clerestory window in the office and the lower window are open simultaneously—and the heating is on—outside air will enter the room through the lower window and leave the room through the window near the ceiling.

Fig. 10.24 Detail of operable clerestory windows with exposed steel detail indicating structural steel beams behind the brick.

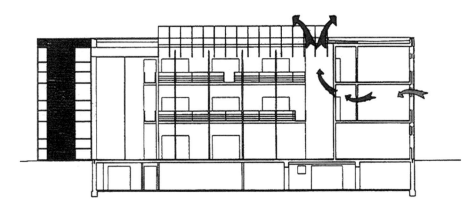

Fig. 10.25 Airflow diagram; "normal" mode.

Ventilation: Internal Air Exchange

With the office doors open to the atrium and the office windows closed, there will still be an air exchange between offices and the large central space (see Figure 10.27). As long as the central space is ventilated, this mode will provide sufficient ventilation for the offices. CO_2 and other pollutants will be removed from the offices both by airflow to and from the atrium and also by diffusion.

Assuming that the office is slightly cooler than the atrium, air will flow out of the office through the door at floor level and in to the office through the upper half of the door opening, as illustrated in Figure 10.27. Figure 10.28 shows how this convective loop will be reversed if the office heater is on and the office air temperature is higher than the atrium.

Turbulence in the West Wing

The floor-to-ceiling glass walls in the corridors of the west wing face southeast. These corridors are not conditioned by any heating or cooling system. When the first-floor offices were unoccupied during winter days, the lower corridor was quite cold because the motion sensor–controlled radiators were turned off. This caused a convective loop to occur, as illustrated in Figure 10.29. Air would flow in and out of the corridors through fire doors that were left open. Warm air from the atrium entered the upper corridor, cooled off and fell down the stairwell, and returned into the atrium near the floor. According to Sergio Fox, smoke tests and measurements indicate that the airflow induced by the convective loop was 3,000 to 4,000 m³ per hour, with velocities up to 0.7 meters per second.

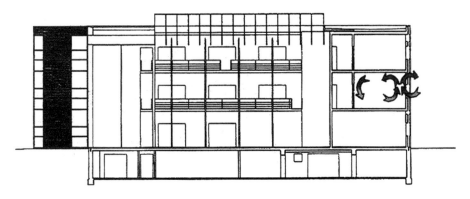

Fig. 10.26 Airflow diagram; office doors closed.

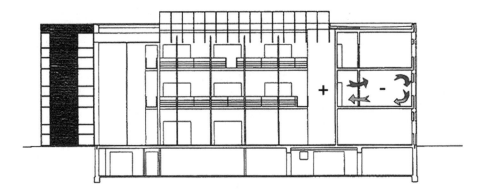

Fig. 10.27 Airflow diagram; open doors, closed windows.

Dilution or Diffusion?

A Danish Building Research Institute (SBI) report on natural ventilation at the Pihl & Søn headquarters building identifies the governing principle behind natural ventilation as dilution: "During winter the ventilation concept for achieving acceptable indoor air quality is based on the *dilution* principle" (Bergsøe 2001).

Dilution, as the term pertains to ventilation in buildings, involves reducing the concentration of pollutants in the air. Concentration is the measure of how much of a given substance is mixed with another substance.

> The *dilution* equation, also known as the Basic Room Purge Equation, is used in industrial hygiene. It determines the time required to reduce a known vapor concentration existing in a closed space to a lower vapor concentration. The equation can only be applied when the purged volume of vapor or gas is replaced with "clean" air or gas. For example, the equation can be used to calculate the time required at a certain ventilation rate to reduce a high carbon monoxide concentration in a room." (Wikipedia 2006)

Figures 10.30 and 10.31, reproduced from the SBI report, illustrate measured values of indoor temperature, CO_2 concentration, and fresh air-supply flow rate in two almost identical offices. During a period of five workdays starting on Monday, December 1, 1997, the CO_2-concentration level peaked around 700 to 750 parts per million (ppm), which is within an acceptable range. The difference in CO_2-concentration levels in the two rooms is almost insignificant. The fresh airflow rates, however, do not show a similar conformity. Although the air exchange

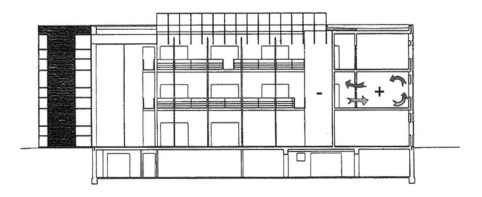

Fig. 10.28 Airflow diagram (winter); open doors, closed windows.

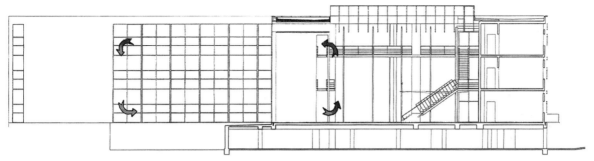

Fig. 10.29 Airflow diagram; convective loop with air exchange between atrium and unconditioned office corridors with southeast-facing glass wall.

rate in room 3 frequently peaks between 5 and 10 liters per second per m^2 of floor area (which translates to an hourly air exchange rate of 4 to 8 ACH), the corresponding air-supply flow rate for room 5 peaks between 1 and 2 liters per second (0.8 to 2.5 ACH). This phenomenon cannot be explained by referring to the dilution principle alone. (The report does not identify the phenomenon specifically and therefore does not provide any explanation.)

During a telephone conversation with Sergio Fox on October 22, 2006, the author questioned the air supply numbers in Figures 10.30 and 10.31. There might be factor 10 error in the Y-axis scale here. It is not likely that the CO_2 concentration would reach 750 ppm if the air exchange rate were above 8 ACH (room 3, Tuesday, December 2, 1997). The factor 10 error may be caused by incorrect use of units. If the air exchange rate were measured per person, not per square meter of floor area, the airflow rate would be approximately one-tenth of what can be read out of the figures.

As explained earlier in this chapter, indoor air quality may be maintained even with all the windows closed, as long as the adjacent two-story lobby space is mechanically ventilated. CO_2-concentration levels in an office with no fresh air supply from the outside, but with an open door to the adjacent space, could still be kept below the 800 ppm commonly accepted limit for good indoor air quality. This phenomenon is better explained by *diffusion* than by dilution.

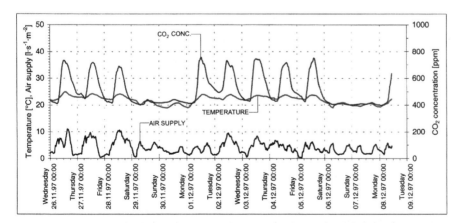

Results of measurements in office 3 during almost two weeks. The temperature [°C], taken 1.1 m above the floor, has been recorded every 30 minutes. The CO_2 concentration [ppm] and the air supply [l·s⁻¹·m⁻²] have been recorded approximately every 10 minutes. The curves have been smoothed in order to emphasize the overall trends.

Fig. 10.30 Measured temperature, airflow, and CO_2 concentration data, from Danish Building Research Institute Report: NatVent Work Package 2 (Bergsøe).

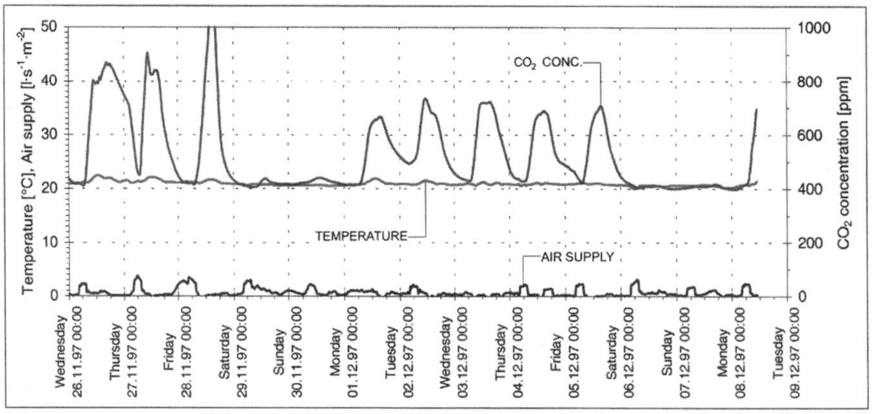

Fig. 10.31 Measured temperature, airflow, and CO_2 concentration data, from Danish Building Research Institute Report: NatVent Work Package 2 (Bergsøe).

Encyclopaedia Britannica defines diffusion as a "process resulting from random motion of molecules by which there is a net flow of matter from a region of high concentration to a region of low concentration. A familiar example is the perfume of a flower that quickly permeates the still air of a room" (Encyclopaedia Britannica 2006). A gas distributes itself over a room by diffusion. While steady-state bimolecular diffusion is governed by Fick's first law, steady-state thermal diffusion is governed by Fourier's law.

Annual Energy Use

The building owner provided annual energy-use data for 2003, 2004, and 2005, by monthly distribution of gas and electricity use. Energy-use data for the years 2003 and 2004 are consistent, but the 2005 data are less reliable. The irregularities in the 2005 data are due to the fact that Pihl & Søn built and moved into phase 3 of its corporate headquarters that year. Figure 10.32 shows monthly energy use for 2003.

The total energy use for the years 2003 and 2004 average 760,000 kWh, which translates to a specific energy use of 170 kWh/m^2-Y. The split between gas and electricity use for 2003 and 2004 was about 50/50.

At 170 kWh/m^2 per year, the overall energy efficiency of the building is quite good, particularly if seen in light of the fact that it was not primarily designed for extremely low energy use. Although the first phase of the Pihl & Søn headquarters was built in 1994, the new (2006) Danish building regulations specify 95 kWh/m^2 per year as a target for total annual energy use. A typical Danish office building still uses 300 to 400 kWh/m^2 per year.

Although the monthly use of electric energy is fairly constant over the entire year, the monthly gas usage data reflect the increasing need for space heating as the midwinter months approach. This is a bit puzzling. It is commonly assumed that a modern, well-designed, and well-built office building will hardly use any energy for space heating. One would think that such a building could be heated entirely by body heat from occupants, heat from equipment use, heat from lights, and heat from passive solar design features. In reality, this assumption is a myth generated by the lack of calibration of building energy simulation results against the actual energy consumption. While solar gains may balance heat losses during an average heating season, a typical January month in Denmark

Energy Use 2003

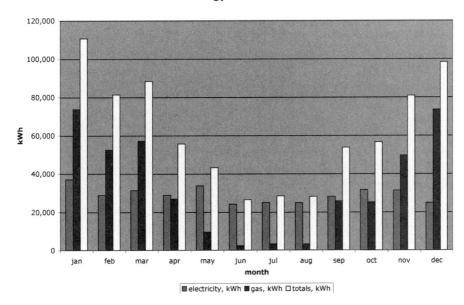

Fig. 10.32 Monthly distribution of natural gas and electricity use in 2003.

has only 26 hours of sunshine. The average outside air temperature in Copenhagen is –0.4°C for both January and February and the winter design-day temperature is –12°C.

With limited availability of performance data as it pertains to temperatures, airflow rates, and distribution of gas usage between domestic hot water and space heating, one can still discuss possible explanations for the variations in monthly gas usage. The following explanations were generated using a method of educated guessing.

1. It is safe to conclude that the natural ventilation system saves energy in the summer since there is no energy use for chillers or other mechanical cooling devices. With ventilation rates in the 0.8 to 8 ACH rage, however, this system may not be as energy-efficient in the winter. The energy used to heat the incoming fresh air may turn out to be higher than what is strictly necessary in order to maintain indoor air quality. Energy use for fresh air supply to office buildings in cold climates plays a significant role in the total annual energy budget (Lerum 1996).
2. The level of energy use for space heating is also influenced by the fact that there is no heat recovery from exhaust air, which may turn into a significant factor if the air exchange rates are consistently above the minimum requirement for indoor air quality.
3. The large expanses of glass walls facing southeast, northeast, and northwest represent a significant amount of heat loss by conduction and convection during the coldest winter months. The role of the glass areas in the overall summary of annual energy use may be investigated in greater detail using an hour-by-hour energy simulation computer program.

WHAT IF?

In a highly acclaimed office building that also enjoys a high degree of user satisfaction, two areas of inquiry stand out in terms of possible what-if scenarios to be investigated:

1. Large glazed walls face southeast, southwest, and northwest (see Figures 10.3 and 10.33).
2. One large boiler is used to provide both space heating and domestic hot water.

Glazed Exterior Walls

There are no external shading devices on the large glazed portions of the exterior walls (see Figure 10.34). The size and the orientation of these glass walls may be a liability in terms of excessive heat loss in the winter, combined with unwanted solar heat gain during the eight months when energy for space heating is not required.

Elevation drawings are required in order to perform a more detailed investigation of this issue. Alternatively, an analysis of solar heat gain factors may be satisfactory here.

Decentralized Water Heaters

A gas-fired boiler delivers hot water to the space-heating system as well as hot water for the lavatories. If a 350-kilowatt boiler and a 3-kilowatt circulation pump

Fig. 10.33 Reflecting pool next to glass walls facing southwest and northwest.

Fig. 10.34 Director's office with floor-to-ceiling exterior glass walls.

are kept running for 8 to 10 months when space heating is not required, there may be a large energy-saving potential in providing decentralized electric or gas-fired water heaters. Decentralized water heaters would allow the boiler to be shut down for at least two-thirds of the year.

SUMMARY OF FINDINGS

One lesson that we could take away from the analysis of the annual energy use data relates to natural (or hybrid) ventilation systems in office buildings in moderately cold climates. While mechanical devices (such as the jet engines at Pihl & Søn) may be required to maintain sufficient airflow rates on hot summer days, automatically controlled and mechanically operated dampers may be required to avoid excessively high airflow rates on cold winter days and nights. In other words—and as often stated—natural ventilation systems in cold climates tend to provide high air-change rates when you do not need air for cooling (winter) and lower air-change rates when you need it the most (summer).

The headquarters building for the Pihl & Søn contractors, located in Lyngby just northwest of Copenhagen, is still a high-quality design that is also a high-performance office building. The building design by acclaimed architects KHR combines outstanding architectural quality with a high degree of user satisfaction and low overall energy use. By eliminating the need for ductwork and other mechanical systems most commonly hidden above suspended ceilings, the designer allows fresh air to be brought into the workspaces "carried by light," as poetically expressed by the architect Jan Søndergaard. The natural ventilation system takes advantage of the thermal mass provided by concrete walls exposed to the building interior, which in turn was a result of a rethinking of the way brick has traditionally been used in buildings. The passive heating and cooling system, assisted by a mechanical background ventilation of the atrium and by roof-mounted exhaust fans, not only reduces the costs associated with energy use for space heating and space cooling but also shifted the allocation of funds in the construction budget from mechanical systems to elements that enhance the architectural quality of the design.

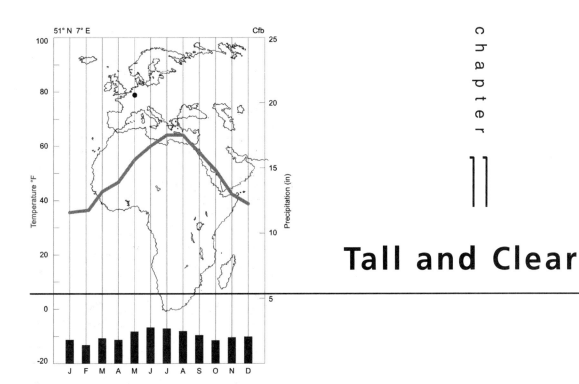

51° N 7° E   Cfb

Tall and Clear

Building Type:	Office
Location:	Bonn, Germany
Coordinates:	51°N, 7°E
Interviews:	Gordon R. Beckman and Steven S. Cook, architects
	Stefanie Reuss and Monika Lauster, climate engineers
Site Visit:	November 2005

With the building of the Post Tower, a new chapter has been opened in the history of the Deutsche Post World Net. As we made a successful transition from a national enterprise to a global service corporation, we wanted our headquarters to be a symbol of transformation and a platform for communicating new ideas and developments. Our plan was to show what takes place inside the building and to demonstrate the openness with which this international logistics corporation, Deutsche Post World Net, does business. So we envisioned a building of maximum transparency and flexibility. The design similarly represents the company's inherent dynamism and modernity. (Blaser 2004)

Situated on the banks of the Rhine River in Bonn, Germany, the Post Tower stands tall as a symbol of the "office of the future." The new headquarters building for the Deutsche Post World Net, shown in Figure 11.1, was designed by Murphy/Jahn for maximum transparency and climate engineered by Transsolar for energy-efficiency according to ecological principles. A tightly knit design team headed by architect Helmut Jahn, climate engineer Matthias Schuler, and structural engineer Werner Sobek arrived at a building design that stands out as a highly integrated and sophisticated example of the new European tall office building.

> The Post Tower makes a statement for a new way of building. Its components are minimal, integrated with engineering and thus serve architectural, structural and mechanical purposes at once. Its aesthetic and appearance derives from the coordinated whole of these systems and components. The goal is that perfection can only be achieved if nothing can be taken away. Transparency, ecology and user comfort are the resulting benefits. (Blaser 2004)

BUILDING AND SITE

The building is situated in a suburban setting on the banks of the river Rhine in Bonn, Germany. The tower, with its elliptical footprint, is rotated 21 degrees relative to due north. The two main curved façades are oriented SSE and WNW (see Figure 11.2).

The building makes use of sources of "free" energy available at the site. Cool water is pumped up from the ground and circulated through the building. This arrangement eliminates the need for compressor-driven mechanical cooling. After the cool water has passed through the building, it is now at a higher temperature, depending on the actual instantaneous cooling load. The water is released

Fig. 11.2 Aerial view of the site, from Google Earth.

to a basin and then through a small artificial creek back into the Rhine. The purpose of the retention pond is to bring the temperature back to that of ambient surface water before it is returned to the river.

Hot water is delivered to the Post Tower from publicly owned cogeneration power plants via a district heating system. This makes it possible to heat the building from low-grade energy using waste heat generated from cooling the electricity production process.

BUILDING SPECIFICATIONS

- Glass façade 162.40 m
- Roof level 151.55 m
- Offices 3.55 m
- Ground floor 10.00–15.00 m
- Sky gardens 32.00 m
- 1 lobby level
- 1 level conference rooms
- 4 sky gardens
- 37 levels offices
- 1 level executive conference area (penthouse)
- 1 level mechanical (20th floor)
- 5 levels parking, mechanical, storage (UG)
- Circumference 179 m
- Gross floor area typical office floor: 1,534 m^2
- Gross floor area typical level sky gardens: 1,930 m^2
- Gross floor area above ground: 65,323 m^2

(Blaser 2004)

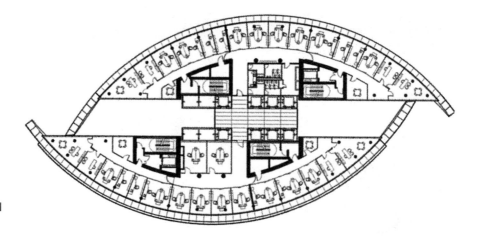

Fig. 11.3 Plan of typical floor in Post Tower.

Fig. 11.4 Cross-bracing at the ground floor elevator lobby.

Fig. 11.5 The shingled south façade and the glazed end walls of the sky gardens.

As shown in Figure 11.3, the form of a typical office floor plan is generated by half shells that are separated by nine-story sky gardens. A two-story space and a penthouse with a screened roof terrace define the executive areas at the top of the building. Two groups of glass elevators, separated by glass floors, serve all floors. It is essentially two buildings that act together as one structure by means of large diagonal cross-bracing, as shown in Figure 11.4.

Skin

The building envelope is dominated by a fully glazed double-skin façade that enables natural ventilation and protects the interior from noise, rain, and wind (see Figure 11.5). Perforated Venetian blinds are placed between the two glass shells of the façade, for sun protection and glare control. Fresh air is preconditioned as it passes through the double-skin façade. The displacement ventilation principle is used for air distribution. Heating and cooling is primarily provided by a radiant system embedded in the coffered exposed concrete slabs.

LOCATION AND CLIMATE

An hourly weather file for Bonn was created in TMY file format using Meteonorm. This weather file was compared to an EnergyPlus weather file for Köln. The comparative analysis of the two files proved that the synthetic file for Bonn is valid. Both the Bonn file and the Köln file depict a typical meteorological year based on 30 years of local climate data. The climate consultant Transsolar had used a weather file for 1995, based on one year of climate data acquired at

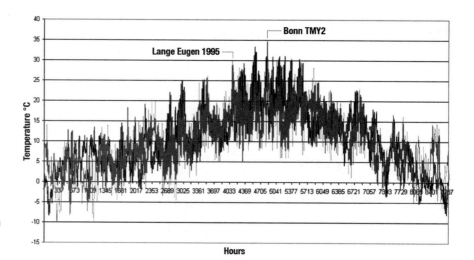

Fig. 11.6 Hourly ambient air-temperature data from two weather files superimposed.

the Lange Eugen building near the Post Tower site (Reuss 2006). Graphs of hourly temperature data from the Bonn file and the Lange Eugen 1995 file were scaled and superimposed, as seen in Figure 11.6.

As expected, the two weather files do not exhibit a direct match when compared hour by hour, but the overall fit is fairly good, with seasonal extreme highs and lows at the same levels. The summer extreme daytime ambient temperature reaches 35°C and the winter extreme nighttime ambient temperature reaches –10°C. The winter design-day temperature for Bonn is –10.6°C (99%) and the summer design dry bulb temperature is 30°C with a coincident design wet bulb temperature of 23.3°C.

One difference between the two files is seen in the summer nighttime lows. The 1995 Lange Eugen file shows summer night lows frequently reaching 10°C, while the Bonn TMY file shows summer nighttime lows at or above 15°C. This difference in summer nighttime lows may not be very significant, since it is widely accepted that nighttime cooling of thermal mass works whenever the ambient dry bulb temperature reaches a minimum of 18°C (65°F).

At a base temperature of 18.3°C, there are 3,250 heating degree-days and only 75 cooling degree-days, which at first glance could lead to a conclusion that the building will mainly need heating and very little cooling. As we have seen earlier (Chapters 8 and 10), this picture of a heating-dominated climate will change as we look at a high-performance, low-energy office building. The need for heating energy may be reduced significantly, and the chances for the building to overheat may be avoided by an intelligent envelope design.

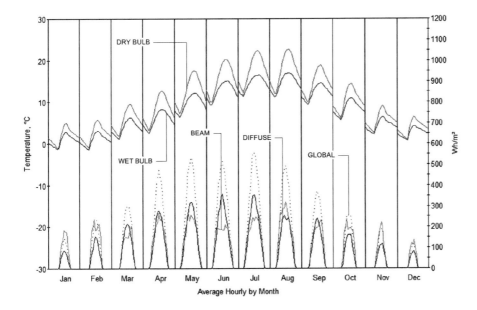

Fig. 11.7 Average-day temperature and solar radiation data, monthly values in a typical meterological year, from Weather Maker

WINTER

Temperatures for a week in mid-January stay below freezing for most of the time. During the nine-day period (in a typical meteorological year) analyzed here, ambient daytime high temperatures barely reach above freezing on every third day (see Figure 11.8).

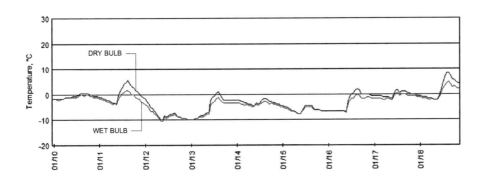

Fig. 11.8 Winter dry bulb and wet bulb temperatures, from Weather Maker.

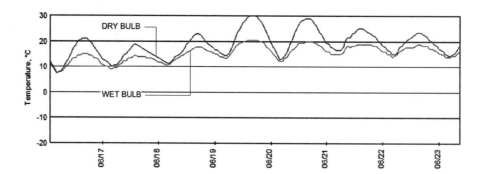

Fig. 11.9 Dry bulb and wet bulb temperatures for a week in mid-June, from Weather Maker.

SHOULDER SEASONS

Daytime temperatures typically reach 25°C during the early summer and early fall shoulder seasons. With nighttime low temperatures frequently reaching 10°C, the climate lends itself to passive strategies for thermal comfort, such as high-mass night vent cooling. Even in mid-June, when daytime temperatures reach into the upper 20s (°C), nighttime cooling of the thermal mass may work well since the nighttime lows typically are in the 10°C to 15°C range, as shown in Figure 11.9.

SUMMER

Figure 11.10 for a five-day period during the third week of July illustrates temperature fluctuations on the warmest days in a typical meteorological year (TMY). Daytime high temperatures may now reach above 30°C, combined with some warm nights when the minimum dry bulb ambient temperature does not reach below 20°C. Mechanical cooling will be needed for extreme summer conditions like these.

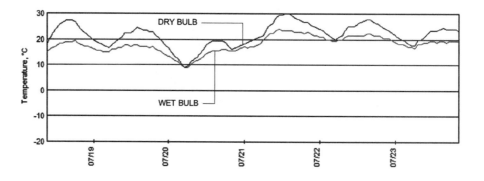

Fig. 11.10 Ambient dry bulb and wet bulb temperatures during a warm summer five-day period in a typical meteorological year, from Weather Maker.

Architecture: Interview with Gordon R. Beckman (GB) and Steven S. Cook (SC) at the offices of Murphy/Jahn, Chicago, September 19, 2005 (Lerum, Beckman, et al. 2005).

Climate engineering: Interview with Stefanie Reuss (SR) and Monika Lauster (ML) at the Post Tower site in Bonn, Germany, November 18, 2005 (Lerum, Reuss, et al. 2005).

Design Philosophy

GB: We always look at buildings as technological pieces which can help us to control the environment. We talk about Mies's buildings across the way. And then we talk about our buildings as just an advancement of that with today's available technologies—for human comfort and for living. A typical floor elevator lobby has glass floors that let daylight through the building in order to minimize the use of power for lights. [Figure 11.11 shows] the technological aspects of the building and also the character of the building, which is really derived from putting together the parts in the best way.

Team

SR: We got involved in the project through the competition for the Deutsche Post (DP). From the very start, there was a very close teamwork among the architects at Murphy/Jahn, the climate engineers at Transsolar, and the structural engineer Sobek. The team had already been established prior to the DP competition. It was a very good teamwork between the three parties. I think this

Fig. 11.11 View of a typical floor elevator lobby, with X-bracing and glass floors connecting the two halves of the tower.

is a team that was established when they first started working on the Bangkok International Airport. The Deutsche Post and before that the Bayer Leverkusen project started to create a team that was working very well.

Now we [Jahn, Schuler, Sobek] have done several projects together, so we know a bit about how they are thinking—and they know what's important from the energy point of view—so there is a very good understanding for what's important for the other parties in the team. That helps a lot. You have to be open to the problems and the work of the other team members. You can't say, "I am the structural engineer and we need this column here and this column there"—you have to be open minded and see the whole building as an integrated design.

Political Context

GB: After the Wall came down in Berlin, the city of Bonn wanted to make sure that something could happen there. While they were having large government ministries move to Berlin, they thought that they needed to find a way to induce certain of those ministries to remain in Bonn. One of the ideas was to have the postal ministry, which was a very large ministry in Germany, move their headquarters into a new building. The corporate strategy behind it was to go public. They did not want to be a ministry anymore. They wanted a new building that created a corporate image. From the standpoint of the owner, that was very significant. From the standpoint of the city, the city wanted to create a demonstration project that actually had an energy consumption that had to be 25 percent below the already stringent European energy code.

Building Code

GB: The buildings we do in Germany are all based on building code requirements that in effect maximize the span to about 8 meters. You always find an office and a corridor, and it goes back to the International Congress of Architects in the thirties, but that is still today what we work with there: a strong requirement for daylight for every individual, a strong requirement for natural ventilation, and requirements both for cellular offices and open offices.

SC: You can't do back-office space in Germany in the traditional American manner. Every and each workspace has to be within a few meters of a window.

Concepts

GB: [Figure 11.12] shows that even at the very early stages of the project we were already thinking about these concerns, especially in a project like this where it is basically mandated that you design for energy efficiency. This concept is looking at not only the views of the Rhine River, but also the average wind patterns in this location. The building is oriented not only towards the views, but also to take into consideration the prevailing winds.

Transparency

GB: You should remember that by the time this building was going up, a big influence on this building was that the Post was going public, it was becoming a pub-

Fig. 11.12 Wind and views. Concept sketch by Helmut Jahn.

licly held company. There was this desire to be seen and to be known that you're on top of your game, not just another ministry that moves letters around.

SC: The Deutsche Post was expanding into something bigger than simply being a letter carrier. They were in the process of becoming a corporate, global transport company, which was a conglomerate of many new companies. They were purchasing companies, and they are still purchasing companies. So they see themselves as a global player, not simply as the postal system in Germany. They wanted the German public to see that this ministry was reborn with this new transparent character and they wanted their employees to know that they were on display, that they were part of a bigger world, that they were being watched, that this was part of the new open culture, and that they were not just going to be able to sit in their offices and not be seen and not be monitored. They wanted the new organization to be a real open company.

GB: The whole issue of bringing natural light into the building was a very significant item for the owner in terms of creating a quality work space. The issue of transparency then actually enables the people who work there to see each other, to know who is there. The building they came from was a building of long corridors, with individually closed-off offices, where you could go to your office in the morning, walk in, sit down and do your work, and you would have absolutely no idea if anyone else was working in the building. You would not see anybody. And they found out from their corporate image and from the corporate culture they wanted to create that it was completely the wrong design approach.

So part of it was to create this transparency where you can meet with your division in the sky gardens, you can go there for events, you can stand in your building and you can look through and you can see all the different offices. Beyond that, the idea of creating a building that is flooded with natural light was also a key design feature that we wanted to create.

SC: You can look up three floors from the sky gardens and see that people are working. You can see everybody working and experience all the activity. It is extremely open, it is an extremely transparent work environment. [See Figure 11.13.]

GB: It's always a challenge to design a 100 percent glass building, even in climates like Germany, because glass does not insulate as well as insulated panels and you've got to take care of the solar gains. But it can be done. We just have to know what we are doing.

SR: I think that there are some parts of the building where I would say that it would be OK if they would be insulated, and that is from the window sill height to the floor. But if the client tells us that he wants 100 percent transparency, then there is always the advantage that you are sitting in this tower and there is a very nice view to the outside—it is a different feeling if you can look outside with a view angle that is unobstructed all the way down to the floor. For a high-rise building I understand the view of the architect that it gives a different kind of feeling to the space. You need at least 30 to 40 percent of glass in the façade just for optimal use of daylight. From the energy point of view, a perfect façade would be 2 meters insulated opaque wall from the floor up, and then a band of clerestory windows for daylight, but then you could not have a look outside. That is just the optimum from the energy point of view, not the overall optimum.

Fig. 11.13 View of south-facing shingled glass façade.

Thermal Conductivity of the Double-Skin Façade

SR: The U-value of the inner, double-pane glass wall is 1.1. This has been tested and certified by the manufacturer. They have to certify all the components—the glass, the gas, and the coatings. Taking into consideration the double façade as well, the U-value goes down to 1.0 or 0.9, depending on how much you open the flaps. We have got temperature sensors in the double façade, so if it gets colder than 15°C, we keep the flaps closed if possible, depending on the wind pressure. With the flaps fully closed, you get an U-value of about 0.9. It is, however, not the primary control strategy to keep the U-value low. Primarily you want to keep the wind pressure within certain parameters by controlling the flaps.

Energy Concepts

SC: I think one of the most successful things in this building is the cooling system. They don't pay anything for cooling. They created groundwater wells that essentially are fed by the Rhine River and use those as their cooling base. And the slabs of the building are all exposed in the offices—we ran pipes through those—exposed to the ceiling, and when you are in the space and when the slabs are cooled down, it is extremely comfortable. It is one of the most comfortable offices I have even been in. And you get your individual controls with the fan coil unit. They run cool water additionally through the fan coil units so the base cooling is created by the slabs and if it is not sufficient, you can modify that as needed.

So you have a slow system, which is the system in the concrete, and the quick response system in the fan coil units. The exhaust air actually goes through the corridors—there are enough slots and openings in the wall system of the offices—the glass wall system—that the exhaust air is drawn out through those openings in the wall system and then at the ends of the corridor it gets blown into the atria where it tempers the air. [See Figure 11.14.]

GB: As we get into the outer edges of the shingled façade, that's where the air is coming in. Through the operable windows at each end of the atrium is where the air is exhausted to the outside of the building.

SC: The atria are also used for cross-ventilation. During the right time of the year when you have really wonderful fresh air, especially in the transitional fall and spring seasons, they can completely flush the building by opening these things and just let this good air come through.

GB: The beauty of this kind of system is that there are no vertical shafts that go up through the building. All the ventilation and all the comfort is taken care of on a floor-by-floor basis through the façade. So you save an enormous amount of real estate not having to have those systems.

SC: We sized the joints around the glass up at the top in order to accommodate the return airflow through the office corridor system. So the air is going out into this corridor, and then it is pulled down the corridor and then it is vented via a fan unit and blown into the atrium.

Double-Skin Façade

GB: The south side is shingled to take into account the solar loads and the north side is flat. On a hot summer day, air will move up inside the cavity of the double-

Fig. 11.14 View of transparent and translucent interior glazed walls, as seen from the corridor on a typical floor.

skin façade. A vertical airflow on the outside of the blinds allows the heat to be vented out at the top of each nine-story segment. The atria have large operable windows at both sides, and it's all motorized. [See Figure 11.15.]

GB: Here you see the difference on the south side where it extends one meter thirty five—or one meter fifty, and then here on the north side the distance is one meter.

SC: When you do these expensive façades, what you have to study carefully in your computer fluid dynamics is the size of the various components. The idea on the south side was that the air rose and would draw in colder outside air as it went out. It would also draw in cooler air at the bottom so that when we have sun coming in on the south side these would be closed—and we create a chimney starting to bring air upwards. In that way it assists in drawing in cooler air in this inner zone here. So that you would not have the superheated air actually up against the building. It was stood off—it was pressed out further. There is also a firebreak for each nine-story segment. A firebreak floor was designed with an F90 steel construction.

Here we've got just wind needles. They are thin stainless steel stand-offs, and the whole façade is hung every nine floors—the hanger structure comes out here and basically with these stainless steel extruded mullions the whole nine floors of exterior skin is hung. [See Figure 11.16.]

GB: By using the little wind needles you take care of the resistance this way—these are inserted at every single module point. Those become very small as well.

SC: The key to doing this façade was actually splitting the forces into their most direct components and then really only having horizontal forces in the needles and really only having vertical forces in the hanger rods. Once you do that, not doing more than one thing, you can make them very small in profile.

GB: The needles are only about 30 millimeters in diameter. The operable glass

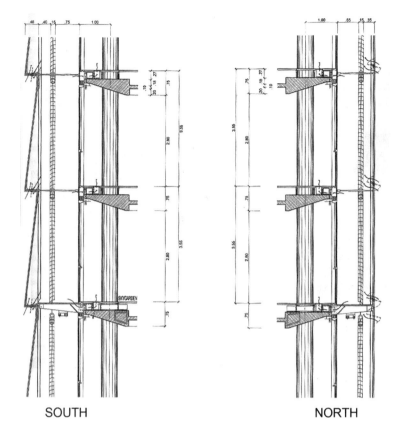

SOUTH   NORTH

Fig. 11.15 Section through the double-skin façade.

dampers are really nothing more than response technology applied in a more sophisticated way to control the airflow. The system also deals with the different pressures on the windward side and leeward side of the building.

SC: In a building like this, there is a higher demand in computer programming to program the systems to perform all the functions—the standard ventilation and then all those other things.

GB: The building management system on a building this size usually has two or three thousand connection points. This thing has about 20,000 points. There are 4,000 individual motors that operate the various components.

Blinds

GB: The blinds act as basic cooling devices that provide shading, since you're essentially placing a filter in front of the inner layer of the double-skin façade.

SC: The key is to keep the solar gain off—you tolerate some additional heat in the outer cavity, but the solar gains are basically kept completely on the outside of the blinds.

GB: We were looking at two different shading options for perforated blinds, one with small holes and one with bigger holes. That affects the view out because even when you are keeping most of the solar gains out by keeping these things closed, you still have an openness to the outside. The finer perforations generally give you a greater sense of transparency.

Fig. 11.16 View of the wind needles and the motorized louvers (flaps).

Airflow Rate

SR: The airflow rate is variable concerning what the person wants. When you enter your room, you insert your key card and the fans come on and it gives you as much fresh air as you need for one person. If you want more air, then you can vary the fan speed. But after a certain time—10 minutes or so—the fan speed will go down to a level where it transports as much air as one person needs by code.

Raised Floor

SC: To do this kind of system you need a raised floor. It is one of the key features—you have to have a raised floor. The fan coil units are placed in the floor along the perimeter of the façade [see Figure 11.17]. We were able to size

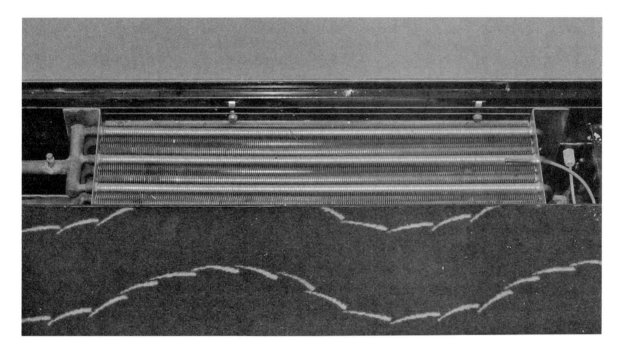

that unit so that it could fit within the thickness of the raised floor. The raised floor houses all the electrical, all the heating, and the pipes for the sprinkler heads below. If you are using the visible concrete slab—there is no hung ceiling—and all the lighting for the office below is routed through, and all the electrical for the floor above.

GB: The holes coordination was a nightmare.

SC: You've got to draw plans with all the floor systems, you can't just draw a floor plan, you've got to draw a whole lot of detail sections that show how pieces come together.

Smoke Tests

GB: These are tests that actually show the airflow, how it pools at the bottom of the office. It was actually a ventilation study to see where is the air going—the air that's coming out of that fan coil, how is it distributed throughout the office. Smoke is used to show the movement of air visually. Cool air comes across the floor and come up slowly as it heats up so that you get essentially a displacement system. [See Figure 11.18.]

SC: If it went up along the exterior wall and then out into the corridor, then you would have a problem.

Daylight Design

GB: There are light sensors so when the daylight is bright enough, the lights automatically go off along the edges. In the United States where we have 40-foot depths, it's a whole different game. The systems that we are talking about here are very well adapted in this kind of a building where you are naturally ventilating just a small area and where you are naturally illuminating just a small area.

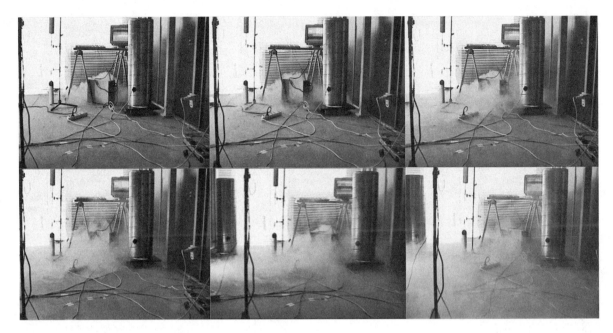

Fig. 11.18 Smoke was used to test the performance of the displacement ventilation system inside a typical office with the fan coil unit engaged.

User Interface

SR: When the person leaves the room, the lights will shut down, the window will close (if open), the person should say, "I'm leaving," but if he does not do that, then at 6 in the evening the light turns lower. If you are still in your room after 6 P.M., than you have to manually switch on more light. The blinds are controlled automatically, but if the user wants to override, he can do so. After two hours the blind controls go back to automatic. If you open the window, the fan coil unit shuts down. I think that it is very common that people are happier if they can influence their environment. That was one of the goals we had when we started. While designing a high-rise building, we still wanted the users to be able to open the windows, because we know that is so important. Even if you can get enough fresh air from the mechanical system—or even if you can change the fan speed for your personal ventilation rate—to open a window is just different. I think that contributes to the very high level of comfort that the users experience in the Post Tower. [See Figure 11.19.]

SR: It can get very hot inside the double façade of the Post Tower, but people still open the windows and they turn off the air cooling. And they know it. The fan will stop and they get warm air coming into the room through the open window. That's something I really like.

ML: It has something to do with the personal comfort situation that people establish for themselves. Sometimes when you have a hot day outside your body adapts to the warm weather, and if you walk into an air-conditioned space you will feel cold. Even 26°C may feel too cold sometimes if it is very hot outside. Here, when it is hot people are happy about it. This summer we had one week cold, one week hot, one week cold. During the hot weeks, people enjoyed it. So if you are in an office building, you like the warm air coming in. I am dressed for the warm weather, so I open the window. It is not good to always have the same temperature in the room.

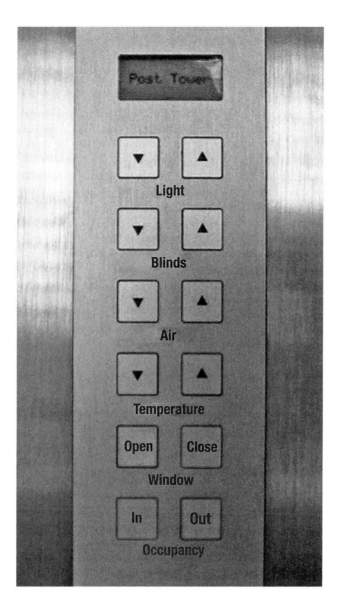

Fig. 11.19 Control unit installed near the door in a typical office enables the user to influence air temperature, light level, operable window, blinds, and airflow.

Operable Windows

ML: The client responded to a demand for operable windows requested by the postal workers trade union. The German building code requires that each worker have access to daylight and a view through a window, but there is no explicit requirement for the window to be operable. The client decided to side with the trade union and specified that operable windows were included in the Post Tower design. As climate engineers we supported that decision. In the beginning there was a discussion with the architect, but then there was Transsolar, and there was the client, and the trade unions. Our approach was that if we were going to use operable windows in a high-rise building, we wanted to make sure that they would work without compromising the thermal comfort inside the building.

Fire Safety

The tower is segmented into nine-story segments in order to control the heat gain that builds up—and for fire safety reasons.

SC: You can kind of see [in Figure 11.20] the nine-story segments. At the very top we have a two-story high segment where the executive offices are located. The stairs are all intercommunicating stairs so that you don't have to take the elevator if you are only going up one or two floors. These are fire exits in the building that have glass surfaces, so at the levels where we have the sky gardens, we have F90 glazing. Then when you get above the sky gardens, you have 30-minute glazing. The owner actually invested quite a lot of money in creating the interior

Fig. 11.20 The Post Tower. View from the east.

transparency of the stairs. [See Figure 11.21.] We also have a microdroplet system in the atria—basically a fog system. It is not a standard sprinkler system—it creates a dense fog which eliminates the ability for a fire to continue to grow.

Light, Air, and Energy

SR: Daylight design contributes tremendously to the energy efficiency of the whole building. In the Post Tower, they basically need electric lights only when it is dark outside. And since we do not have a centralized forced air system, they have a very low pressure drop. If you had a central air system in a building like this, you would have all the vertical ducts—and since these vertical shafts take up so much space, they try to make them smaller, which in turn would increase the pressure drop. So I think that on that issue we achieved a lot. But in the end if they install refrigera-

Fig. 11.21 View of the emergency stairs; with fire-rated glass wall facing the sky garden.

Fig. 11.22 View of a typical duplex office as seen from the corridor, with coffered exposed concrete ceilings.

tors for cold drinks with only three insulated walls and a glass door; these refrigerators could use a lot of energy. So there are elements that we do not control. We do all that we can do, but there is a limited range where we can operate.

Energy-Use Data

VL: Does that system also have the ability to store historic data on the performance of the building?

GB: About a year ago this building had been operating for a year or so and we all sat around and asked, "Can't somebody just go there and have the Post do a case study to find out how it really is performing—after the fact?" At that time nobody wanted to spend the money to do that little study. We keep pushing here for the real results where we get to know what is the real outcome. I am not sure that anybody knows yet.

With a couple of more things on the BMS we should be able to sit in our office a year later and see how this building is actually performing. I think that is kind of the next step. This was a client that really wanted to push the limits in terms of what could be done and it cost real money and it takes a real effort.

Elevators

GB: The Post Tower is one of the first buildings to use destination dispatch on the elevator controls, which means that you get essentially a better performance in terms of the elevator service, reducing the number of elevators, and reducing the size of the equipment.

SC: If you are working there, you have a pass card and you swipe it in front and it knows where your office is and it will tell you which elevator to take. Or if you are a guest, you can type in your destination and it will tell you which elevator to take. The elevators are clustered together and depart from a common elevator core. [See Figure 11.23.]

Fig. 11.23 View of the glazed elevators.

GB: If there are 20 people coming in the door, all the ones that want to go to floor 5 to 8 are told to get on cab A and all the ones who want to go to floor 8 to 20 are told to go to another cab.

SC: It is an example of how computer technology can be applied to make building systems more energy efficient.

SR: If you come in and tell the system that you want to go to level 24, then the system calculates and tells you to wait for lift G, for example. So you go to G and the door opens and it takes you directly to your floor. But after you have entered the elevator car, you cannot change your mind and tell the elevator to stop at level 18 instead. Since the elevator cars are fully glazed, and the sky garden floors are fully glazed as well, you are standing in the lift and the floors rush by. People had to get used to it. I think it's great.

VL: How much energy do the elevators use?

ML: The manufacturer (Schindler) claims that energy is regenerated when the lifts use their brakes. That's how the hybrid cars work. This is the claim, but we are not sure how energy efficient these elevators are, as installed. We would love to be able to measure the energy used by the elevators, but we do not have that capability yet. We think that the elevators use a lot of energy.

SR: We had a discussion about what is the total energy needed to operate the elevators. There were numbers between 10 and 20 percent of the total energy use. When these numbers are taken into account, it obviously influences the total energy efficiency of a high-rise building.

Embedded Energy and Sustainability

VL: There is also the embedded energy that goes into the building. In a low-rise building, you can use other types of construction (than reinforced concrete) that have lower embedded energy. In the Post Tower there is a large amount of concrete and steel and glass, all of which have a high embedded-energy content—especially the glass. As compared to the energy required to operate a building over 20 to 25 years, the energy that goes into constructing a low-rise building is still relative small. So normally the embedded-energy issue is not a big deal, but that equation could change for a high rise.

SR: That might be true, but then you have to make sure that the building is used for a long time, because it took so much energy to build it. There is one (speculative) office building in Frankfurt. They built it, but it was so uncomfortable that they could not rent it out. So they had to demolish it. It was never used. That type of operation is definitely not sustainable. So good design is required in order to promote sustainability.

Cost

VL: In his book on the Post Tower, Werner Blaser states that there were so many cost savings from the integrated design that the total cost would come out approximately equal to a standard office building.

GB: This is not an inexpensive building.

SC: The Post Tower is also a corporate headquarters and the cost for this building was comparable to similar corporate headquarters that had been built during the same time period. You should not compare the Post Tower to a regular office building, that's not an appropriate comparison. If you compare it to other high-end corporate headquarter buildings that were done in Germany at the same time, we were actually cheaper. It was an experiment to design a high-rise that had that level of energy savings. It was a level of experimentation that you seldom find in the United States.

AS BUILT

Heating and Cooling

Energy for heating and cooling is distributed throughout the building by a four-pipe system using water as the energy bearer. The primary heating and cooling device is a slow-acting radiant system consisting of water pipes embedded in high-mass concrete slabs with exposed ceilings. Ventilation air is preheated and precooled by fan coil units in each office. The fan coils are installed in the raised floor along the exterior walls.

Since the building is situated on the banks of the Rhine, the groundwater is influenced by the river. The groundwater temperature is fairly constant at 12°C to14°C during the entire cooling season. As the chilled water circulates to the fan coils, it has reached 16°C.

It is important to understand that there is a symbiosis between the use of groundwater for cooling and the radiant system that is used as the primary means of removing heat from the interior. A conventional forced-air-conditioning system would require greater airflow rates, duct work to accommodate recirculating air, and lower supply air temperatures. This would, in turn, require a lower chilled water temperature, which can only be supplied from a

Total Energy Consumption

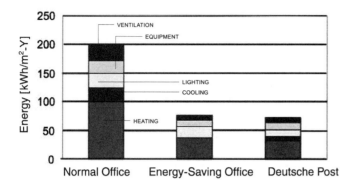

Fig. 11.24 Predicted energy use.

chiller. The radiant system embedded in the concrete ceilings is therefore an integral and crucial component of the low-energy cooling concept.

Annual Energy Use

As a result of the collaboration of building envelope, building structure and a building environmental system, the energy demand of this building is predicted to be less than 100 kWh/m² per year for heating, ventilation, cooling and artificial lighting (Blaser 2004).

Based on energy simulations using the local weather data for 1995, the design team had predicted an annual specific energy use of less than 100 kWh/m² per year for heating, cooling, ventilation, and artificial lighting (Blaser 2004). A graph of expected energy savings produced during the design phase (Figure 11.24) shows a specific annual energy use of 70 kWh/m² per year, as compared to 200 kWh/m² per year for a normal office building with air conditioning. Note that the numbers in this graph include energy use for equipment.

Transsolar has published a graph showing the actual (estimated) annual specific energy use. The numbers (Figure 11.25) are based on measured energy use for 2003, but it is also important to note that there is no breakdown in the mea-

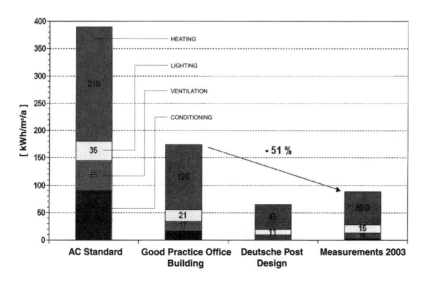

Fig. 11.25 Energy use as estimated by Transsolar, based on measured data for total energy use 2003.

sured data into heating, lights, cooling, ventilation, plug loads, and other end-use categories. It is also important to note that energy use for equipment is not included in the numbers presented in Figure 11.25.

The annual specific energy use for heating, ventilation, cooling, and artificial lighting for the building as monitored by Transsolar in 2003 is still below 100 kWh/m² per year, and is less than 50 percent of the predicted annual energy use for a good-practice office building with air conditioning. But the numbers presented in Figure 11.25 have not been substantiated by published actual energy use data. Energy use for vertical transportation (elevators), computers, printers, coffeemakers, and refrigerators is not included. It is assumed that energy use for circulation pumps, fans in the floor units, motors for operable windows, and motorized dampers in the double-skin façade is included.

SR: For the cooling we only included the electricity needed for pumps. And for the heating, the amount of hot water from the district heating system is measured. So the heating is direct and the cooling is indirect. Cooling provided by the groundwater is basically free cooling.

Fig. 11.26 Motorized dampers (louvers, flaps) at the south-facing shingled glass wall.

It is unclear whether energy use for control systems, exterior lights, and façade lighting (art project) is included. There may also be a percentage of the total energy use that is unaccounted for. The building owner, as well as the architect and climate engineers, have been reluctant to provide documentation of the total specific annual energy use, by monthly distribution (as of January 2007).

Controlling Air Pressure Created by Wind

The air pressure in the cavity in the double-skin façade is controlled by motorized dampers or flaps (see Figure 11.26). In a typical office, the airflow rate will be influenced by the pressure differences between the façade cavity and the office. It also depends on the pressure difference between the office and the corridor, and the pressure difference between the corridor and the sky garden.

The glass wall between the office and the corridor is designed with leakages in order to provide for a cross-flow of air exiting the office. Vents built into the raised floor facilitate cross-flow from the floor of the corridor to the wall of the sky gardens (see Figure 11.27). The nine-story-tall sky gardens run through the entire length of the building, intersected only by the elevator lobby bridges on each floor. This arrangement makes it possible for air to pass through the sky gardens from the high-pressure side to the low-pressure side.

Ventilation

The supply of fresh air necessary for maintaining indoor air quality is provided by a hybrid (mechanical/natural) displacement ventilation system. The fan coil units allow for a controlled supply of air from the outside through the double-skin façade. The air is extracted from the offices through the corridors and then through the sky gardens. There are no vertical or horizontal air-

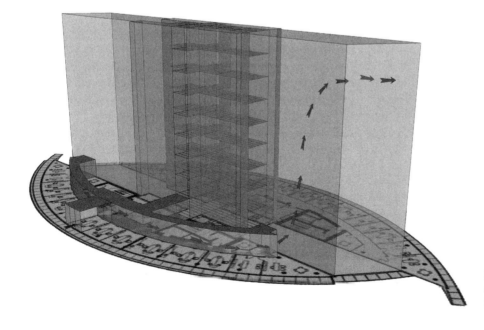

Fig. 11.27 Three-dimensional view of typical airflow path.

distribution ducts in the ventilation system. During normal weather conditions with little or no wind, the exhaust side is entirely powered by negative pressure created by a stack effect in the sky gardens. Operable windows near the ceiling and near the floor of the sky gardens, and at both ends of the building, are controlled to take advantage of negative wind pressure to pull the exhaust air out of the building (see Figure 11.28). Controls of the operable windows in the sky gardens work in tandem with the controls for the glass dampers in the double-skin façade.

SR: Usually in the winter, the façades in the sky gardens are basically closed. Air from the offices moves into the sky gardens, and only the upper flaps on the negative wind pressure side of the sky gardens are open.

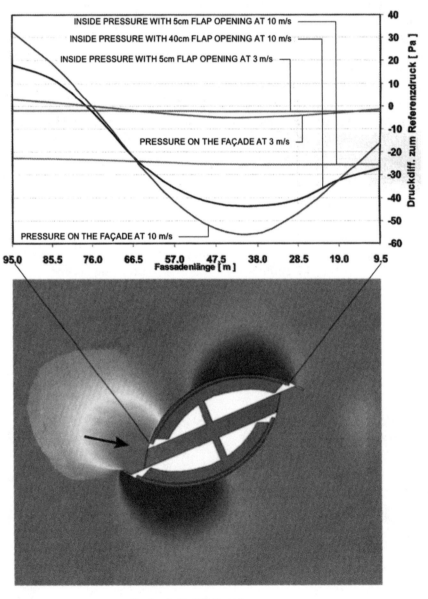

Druckverlauf bei Windanströmung

Fig. 11.28 Analysis of predicted air pressure along the façade as a result of variable wind speed and glass damper openings.

Fig. 11.29 View of the south-facing façade with blinds in the cavity of double skin.

Blinds

The perforated blinds installed in the cavity of the double-skin façade operate in three modes: (1) pulled up with no obstruction of sun, light, and view; (2) lowered and in horizontal position; and (3) lowered and in vertical (closed) position. The perforation makes it possible to obtain a high degree of sun control while maintaining daylight transmittance and views (see Figure 11.30).

The effect of the perforation of the blind was tested in the afternoon on a clear day in November 2005. Figure 11.30 shows how a view of the landscape is main-

Fig. 11.30 View of the perforated blinds from within a typical office, with louvers in the open position (left) and the closed position (right).

tained even with the blinds in closed position. The blinds are automatically controlled by the building energy management system, but users may override the control system. The system will then kick in and return the blinds to optimal position after two hours.

Condensation

SR: Even for the ventilation units, where the inlet water temperature (in cooling mode) is 16°C, there is no condensation. If you would get condensation, there is a small basin (or pan) where the condensed water is collected, but it is assumed that the water will dry up. There is no drain provided. And they do not have a problem with it.

This claim was tested by analyzing the climate conditions on a design day. The design-day data were extracted from the TMY weather file using Weather Maker.

According to Ress, on a summer design day, the design dry bulb temperature is 30°C with a design wet bulb temperature of 23.3°C (TMY file for Bonn). The

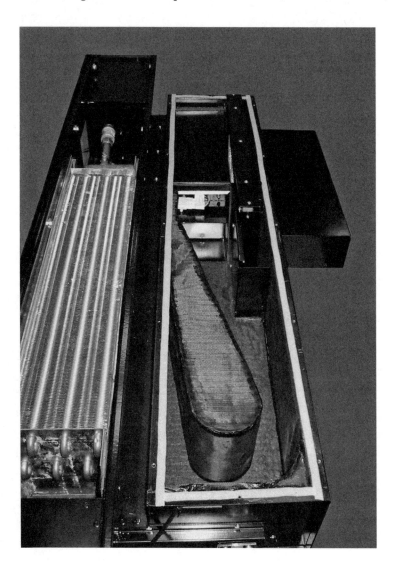

Fig. 11.31 The fan coil unit, as designed and built especially for the Post Tower.

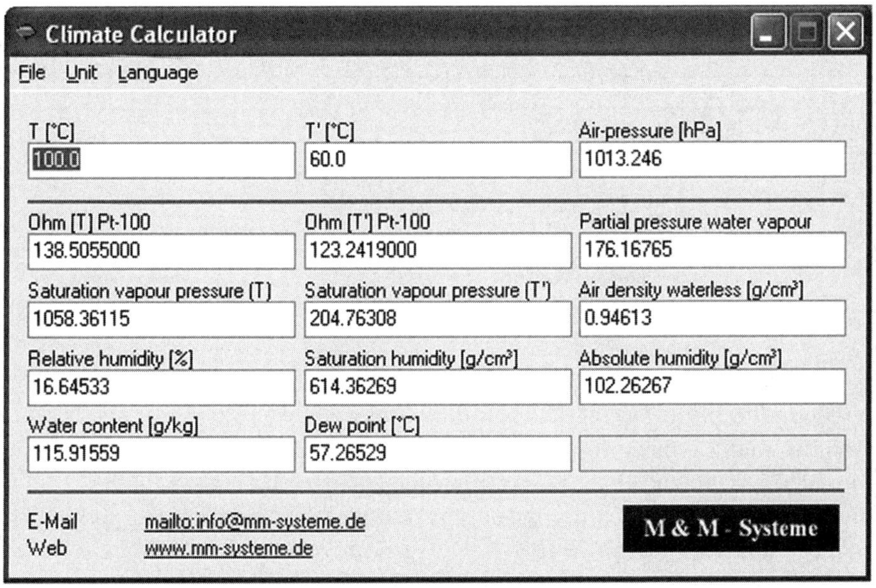

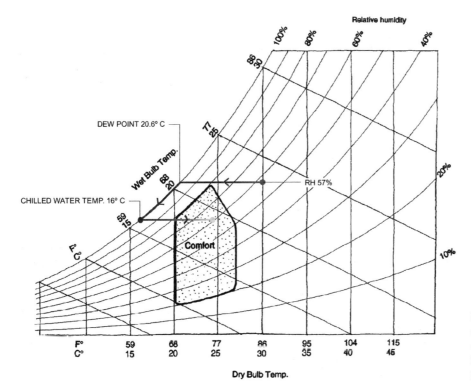

Fig. 11.32 Screenshot of Climate Calculator™, from M&M Systeme.

inlet chilled water temperature at the cooling coil inside a fan coil unit is 16°C. The computer tool Climate Calculator™ was used to find relative humidity, humidity content, and dew point temperature (see Figure 11.32).

With a dry bulb temperature of 30°C and relative humidity at 56.6 percent, the dew point temperature at summer design-day conditions is 20.6°C. As air supplied from the outside passes over the cooling coil, condensation will occur in theory, as illustrated on a psychrometric chart (see Figure 11.33).

Fig. 11.33 Summer design-day condensation on the cooling coil, as illustrated on the psychrometric chart.

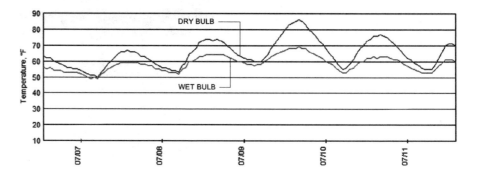

Fig. 11.34 Ambient dry bulb and wet bulb temperatures during the second week of July in a typical meteorological year, from Weather Maker.

Using the Climate Calculator, the saturation humidity at a dew point of 20.6°C was found to be 18.1 g/m³. The saturation humidity at 16°C is 13.8 g/m³. If one assumes that a typical duplex office has a floor area of 25 m² and a volume of roughly 75 m³, the hourly airflow rate would be 75 m³/hour with an air exchange rate of 1 ACH. During a design-day peak hour, the accumulated condensing water would be (75 × (18.1−13.8) = 322.5 g/hour, or 0.3225 liters/hour. It follows from this analysis that 11 ounces of water would accumulate in the fan coil drip pan during a peak design-day hour.

In a typical meteorological year, July 9 is very close to a summer design day, as illustrated in Figure 11.34. A closer look at the hour-by-hour temperature fluctuations on this particular day shows that the time window when condensation may occur inside the fan coil unit is limited to a few hours in the early afternoon when climate conditions could be characterized as extreme. The dew-point temperature drops below the chilled-water inlet temperature rather quickly to 14.7°C in the early evening, to 12.2°C around midnight, and reaches a minimum of 10.6°C in the early morning hours the next day. This analysis supports the claim that accumulation of condensation water in the drip pan of a fan coil unit could happen only on a few days out of a typical meteorological year, and only on a few hours out of those days. Condensation water in the fan coil unit, if any, would dry up within a 24-hour cycle.

Figure 11.35, provided by Transsolar, shows that the ceiling temperature inside a typical south-facing office on a hot day is fairly constant at about 22°C, while the room air temperature reaches a maximum of 25°C. It is therefore safe to conclude that there is no risk of condensation on the exposed high-mass concrete ceilings inside the building.

Daylight Design

The electric light fixtures in the offices work with the coffered ceilings. Most of the light is directed toward the ceiling and then reflected back into the room. The power level used by the electric light fixtures varies with the level of daylight in each workspace.

Small sensors in the ceiling measure the actual lux level. Buttons on the control console by the door allow room occupants to determine their personal lux level. By default, the light level set point is 300 lux, but it can be increased up to 500 lux. The system automatically adds as much electric light to the available daylight as needed to get to the set lux level at any time of day.

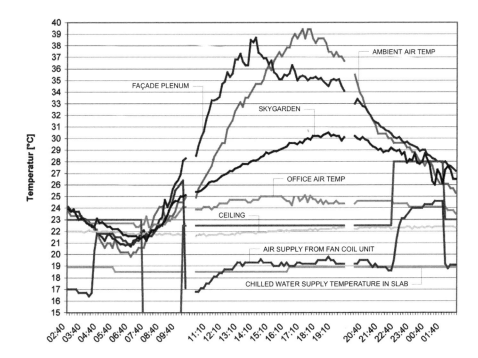

Fig. 11.35 Temperatures in a south-facing office on August 6, 2003.

USER SATISFACTION

A survey of user satisfaction at the Post Tower was conducted by the University of Koblez-Landau. A 55-person team headed by Dr. Rotraut Walden carried out the research project. Dr. Walden is among the most respected experts in the field of architectural psychology in Germany. A method of empirical social research was used to find answers to the 254 questions included in the questionnaire (KA 2004, p. 17).

Workplace performance and well-being were the main criteria that guided the questions included in the survey, since these criteria are seen as significant in designing a work environment for the "Post of the Future." Cooperation and communication are other criteria that the Deutsche Post sees as important to promote a better workplace. Transparency has been emphasized by Deutsche Post as a vehicle in the process of transforming the German Postal system into a modern, self-governing corporation.

Although the team characterizes the office layout and the general configuration of the technologically advanced Post Tower as outstanding, it was found that less emphasis had been placed on the need for the employees to influence their personal workspace. A need for more privacy and freedom to personalize the individual workstations was expressed (University of Koblenz-Landau press release 2004). A newspaper article based on an interview with Dr. Walden points out the lack of green plants and wood in the personal work space as an area of potential improvement (KA 2004, p. 17).

A final report by Dr. Walden is completed, but will not be published until July 2007 (Reuss 2006).

SUMMARY OF FINDINGS

This is a great building—the BMW of office building design (the ultimate working machine). However, translation of the concept of transparency is questionable. Users miss green plants and objects made out of natural materials, such as wood. Also, the annual specific energy use claim has not been substantiated. Why is the building owner unwilling to provide historical data on actual energy use?

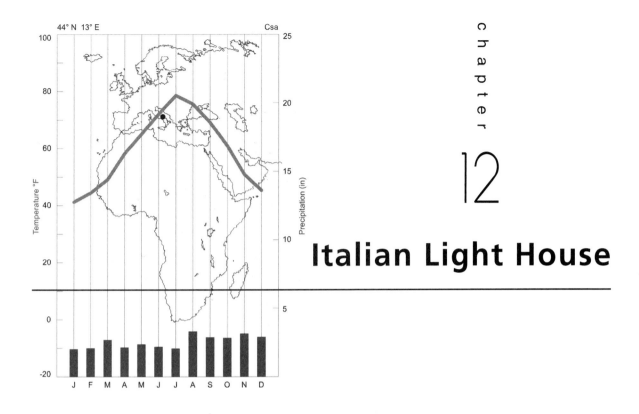

Italian Light House

iGuzzini Headquarters by Mario Cucinella Architects

Building Type:	Office
Location:	Recanati, Italy
Coordinates:	44°N, 13°E
Interviews:	Mario Cucinella, architect
	Catia Giaccaglia, owner and users representative
Site Visit:	May 2006

The addition to the iGuzzini headquarters by Mario Cucinella Architects (MCA) is a truly elegant gem of a building located inland from Ancona near the Adriatic coast of Italy (see Figure 12.1). The building features shading devices, a covered atrium, and an abundance of glass and light. The architect worked with a research institute at the École Polytechnique Fédérale de Lausanne (EPFL) to analyze daylight conditions at various times of the year, using a scale model placed under an artificial sky. The building is designed with a natural ventilation system tuned to seasonal variations in the local climate.

Fig. 12.1 The iGuzzini headquarters.

BUILDING AND SITE

The new headquarters of the lighting company iGuzzini is located in a broad valley below the hill town of Recanati near Italy's Adriatic coast. The building exemplifies current energy-efficient office design in a rational yet elegant way.

> Through its research into lighting, iGuzzini had evolved an awareness of energy use and was eager to promote the notion of energy efficiency in its new headquarters. MCA were commissioned to design a low-energy office building that maximizes daylight and permits natural ventilation for most of the year. (Slessor 1999)

The new headquarters building for the light fixture manufacturer iGuzzini is located on the main campus at Recanati. The four-story building sits just south of the old headquarters building and is connected to the old building on the three lower floors.

The structure is built around a rectangular plan measuring approximately 40 by 20 m. The three main floors contain open-plan offices and a few enclosed meeting rooms organized around a central atrium. The executive areas are situated on the top floor and have access to a roof deck. A louvered shading canopy made out of steel and aluminum protects the fully glazed south façade and extends to cover the exterior emergency stairs located on the outside of the opaque end walls on the east and west sides.

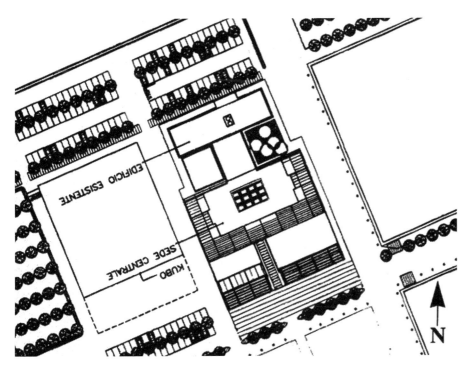

Fig. 12.2 Site plan.

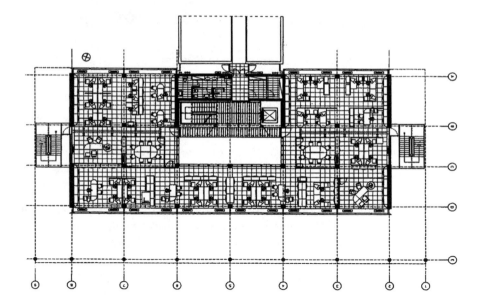

Fig. 12.3 Typical floor plan.

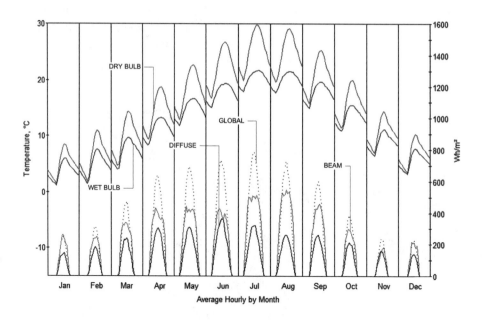

Fig. 12.4 Temperatures and solar radiation for a typical day per month, from Weather Maker.

LOCATION AND CLIMATE

A climate file for Ancona, Italy, was created with the computer program Meteonorm, version 5.1. This weather file was then converted into a format that can be read by the computer program Weather Maker. Weather Maker version 1.0.4 was used to analyze the climate (see Figure 12.4).

As a first step toward understanding the climate and how the characteristics of the seasons could influence the building design, four typical weeks were identified, representing typical seasonal weather events. Graphical representations of

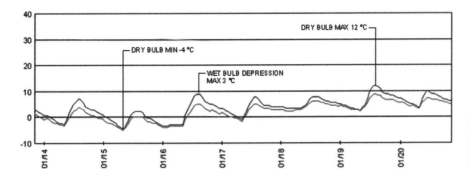

Fig. 12.5 Ambient temperature fluctuations in a typical winter week, from Weather Maker.

these four typical weeks were generated from hour-by-hour weather data, typically based on 30 years of weather data acquisition.

Winter

According to the travel site InfoRoma (InfoRoma 2006), "January is generally cold, with the freezing *tramontana* wind sweeping down from the north. January 29, 30, and 31 are known as the *giornate della merla* (days of the blackbird) and are supposed to be the coldest of the year."

As shown in Figure 12.5, the week of January 14 through January 21 in a typical meteorological year (TMY) is representative of winter conditions. The ambient air temperature may drop below freezing during the night, while the day temperatures typically fluctuate around 10°C. Most buildings will require heating during conditions like these. In a sunny location, passive solar heating may be used to condition spaces as a supplement to mechanical heating. The use of solar radiation for space heating will require that a significant amount of thermal mass be exposed to the interior of the building.

Late Spring

"May is the month of roses in Italy, with weather that is warm but not too hot for sightseeing" (InfoRoma 2006).

As shown in Figure 12.6, the week from May 7 through May 14 is representative of this transitional season between late spring and early summer in Recanati. Day temperatures typically reach 20°C in the early afternoon, with night temper-

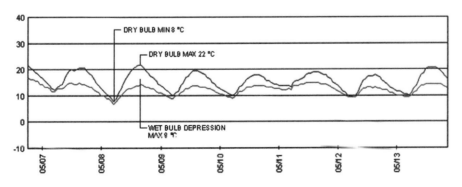

Fig. 12.6 Ambient temperature fluctuations during the second week of May in a typical meteorological year, from Weather Maker.

atures fluctuating around 10°C. The wet bulb depression may reach 8°C during this season.

Temperatures were recorded at the site on May 10 and May 11, 2006. The ambient air temperature dipped below 10°C at 6 A.M. and reached above 20°C by noon the same day. When compared to the graph in Figure 12.6, the measured data are in agreement with the TMY weather file.

Most office buildings will need some cooling during conditions like these. Since the ambient temperature is below the comfort zone most of the time, natural ventilation can be used to condition interior spaces in a work environment. Evaporative cooling may also work, since there is a significant temperature difference between the dry bulb temperature (DBT) and the wet bulb temperature (WBT).

Early Summer

"Early June is like May, but later in the month the temperature can rise steeply, particularly in the south"(InfoRoma 2006).

Figure 12.7 is a graph of the climate conditions for a week from June 7 through June 14 showing how temperatures are rising during the early summer season. On a day in a typical meteorological year toward the end of this week, the ambient temperature reaches 30°C in the early afternoon. The temperatures at night drop below 20°C and average 15°C.

A typical office building will need cooling to remove heat gain during climate conditions like these. With temperatures approaching 30°C in the early afternoon, instantaneous natural ventilation cannot be used for cooling unless it is combined with mechanical cooling. If the building has enough thermal mass and there is sufficient ventilation at high airflow rates, night ventilation cooling with high mass may work as a low-energy strategy. For this strategy to be effective, an automated system would need to be in place so that the airflow rate can be increased significantly during the night, while being limited to a minimum during the day.

Late Summer

"July and August are too hot for comfortable sightseeing. Although it is no longer true that everything shuts down in August, the cities are best avoided at this time" (InfoRoma 2006).

A seven-day period from July 20 through July 28 shown in Figure 12.8 exemplifies the climate conditions during the hot summer months of July and August.

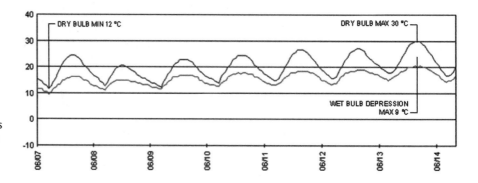

Fig. 12.7 Ambient temperature fluctuations during the second week in June, from Weather Maker.

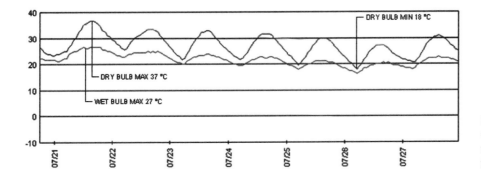

Fig. 12.8 Ambient temperature fluctuations toward the end of July, from Weather Maker.

The daytime temperatures now range in the lower thirties, with a maximum ambient air temperature of 37°C. Night temperatures drop significantly relative to the souring afternoon heat, with dry bulb temperatures below 20°C. With temperatures mostly in the range of 20°C through almost 40°C, there is no longer any significant, useful cooling effect in the ambient air. Wet bulb temperatures typically range between 18°C and 27°C. This is an indication of the relative high humidity levels in the ambient air. Even with a wet bulb depression of 10°C, the high humidity does not allow for evaporative cooling to work. Therefore, no passive, low-energy cooling strategies are available. For these two months, mechanical cooling will be needed to condition interior spaces.

Seasonal Strategies

Figure 12.9, based on the psychrometric chart, summarizes the climate analysis for the region where the iGuzzini headquarters is located. The comfort zone on

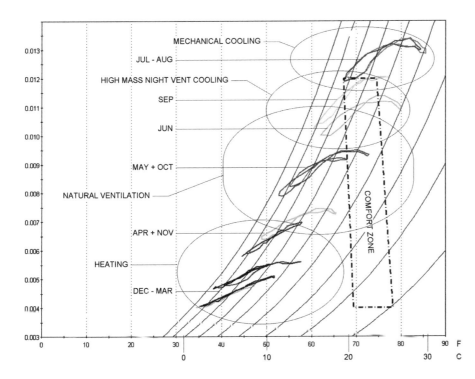

Fig. 12.9 Average-day ambient temperatures, by month, plotted on a psychrometric chart, from Weather Maker, with predominant seasonal heating and cooling strategies.

this diagram is marked according to the ASHRAE-recommended lower and upper limits for dry bulb temperature and relative humidity in order to achieve a comfortable environment for human activity.

During the summer season, July and August clearly stand out as periods when both the temperatures and the humidity levels are above the comfort zone for most of the time. Figure 12.9 shows how temperature and relative humidity change over the 24 hours in a typical day for each of these two months. During July and August there is hardly any hour where the ambient temperature or the relative humidity outside the building is suitable for natural ventilation or night vent cooling.

At the other end of the scale, December, January, February, and March stand out as winter months when heating is needed. In this sunny climate location, building designs can take advantage of solar radiation for heating when combined with the right type of glazing and interior thermal mass. Passive solar heating as a low-energy strategy still needs to be supplemented with mechanical heating.

In between the hot and humid summer and the chilly winter lie two shoulder seasons. For four to six months, natural ventilation and night vent cooling are low-energy strategies that can produce energy savings when the design is tuned to take advantage of natural sources of free energy in the environment.

PERFORMANCE BY DESIGN

"The building is designed to house the administrative, commercial and management offices of the iGuzzini company, and seeks to optimize the control of natural light, exploitation of natural ventilation, and use of thermal mass" (Cucinella 2004).

In an article in the journal *l'arca*, Mario Cucinella discusses architecture and sustainability under the title "More with Less": "We keep on producing more using less manpower, without bearing in mind the consequences this has on both the natural and social environments"(Cucinella 2000).

> The lack of any global vision has turned buildings into deaf and dumb actors on the contemporary scene, completely cut off from both the historical and the environmental context. It is as if for decades we have kept buildings attached to an artificial respiration machine. What happens if the machine cannot work? And how much does it cost to keep the machine running? The energy savings accumulated (in well designed buildings) are comparable to the way weight reduces fuel consumption in a car. Using natural light along with artificial light allows a considerable reduction and has immediate effect on the building form and well-being of its occupants. (Cucinella 2000)

During the interview with the architect in Bologna on May 9, 2006, Mario Cucinella (MC) discussed the design philosophy behind his work (Lerum and Cucinella 2006):

MC: There are two different philosophies. We must come back to the idea that we can use the natural sources of energy first and then use technology to add that small extra quality. We should not forget completely any support by the wind, the

Fig. 12.10 View of the atrium at the ground-floor level.

sun, the shape of the building, the exposition of the building—we should not completely forget about the potential of this approach and we should not only use technology. We must know that the architect can play a very fundamental role because more than 50 percent of the energy is consumed by buildings. If I tell you that your building can be much more efficient so that your building can prevent a serious problem with increasing energy consumption, then maybe you think that you can design a better building in harmony with the environment and also produce a chain effect on reducing energy demand—by architecture! It is a very simple answer.

Architects have in their hands the power to reduce energy consumption. It is not only a question about solar power, wind power, photovoltaic power—that's technology, something external. You can buy a washing machine that runs on solar power, but the point for me is that the building itself can solve a series of problems. If you translate that approach into design, then you will see that more than 50 percent of the problems can be solved by design: design philosophy, the way you make the building, the way you shape your building, the way you put your building on the solar path, the way you use shading, the way you use certain materials.

The feeling of thermal comfort in any room is to a great extent accounted for by the radiation of the surfaces, which means that your building is active. It's not passive. I try to push the idea that the architect is very important. We can change the history about energy, we don't need to wait for petrol to run out. The power of making buildings better is in the hands of the architect. Energy can be an incredible opportunity for creativity—a fantastic opportunity for the architect.

Design Methodology

MC: I think it would be interesting to work in a micro scale like a virus—a positive virus. Architects can put out a few small ideas and then we must be able to create a chain effect.

You will not find a solution with only one technology. You need to add the different strategies, and then you can solve a little bit in terms of daylight, you optimize natural ventilation, you have a strategy for the façade. It is a combination of strategies. It is important to know that it is a process of work. It is not like you can use photovoltaics and that solves the problem. No, that is one part of the combined strategies. It is important to know that technology is not something that solves the problem for you, it is something that can help you solve the problem—it is about how you design a building. So, shift the attention not to energy as something that exists or technology solving the problems, but thinking about the way you are designing the building, the shape of your building, the choice of materials. I think it is the most interesting lesson to bring to students of architecture.

Technology

MC: I am not an artist—I mean, I do something that is artistic, but to do that I need to do so much more. There is a lot of scientific work involved in designing a building. There are strong relations between shape and technology. In the history of our work we build things. If you keep it on your computer, you don't build, so you don't care about technology or material. Innovation comes from the culture of our country. It is strange that it sometimes seems like we lost completely this background. Technology, shape, innovation: they are all profoundly related to the way we design buildings.

There are many levels of technology. One level of technology is the way we organize our buildings around a sewage system in order to make our lives so much better. We do not always need to invent such an incredible technological system. Sometimes the solution is very simple. I think we can design buildings that are related not only to the climate. It is too simple to say that "it relates to the climate," context is much more wide of a definition. We have a great creative opportunity to design our buildings different, more complex—better buildings, no?

Figure 12.11 is showing how technology can be friendly. This is a doctor with a camel with a GPS satellite antenna mounted to its head for geographic positioning—it's like a hat on the camel—and a photovoltaic panel to produce energy to a battery to supply a refrigerator with medicine. Technology can be very friendly—it can improve our lives.

The Beijing Project

MC: The idea is that the building is like a leaf [see Figure 12.12]. The building is facing south to get to the most energy possible but also optimizing daylight design because electricity in China is made mainly from coal. The less we use electricity in buildings, the more we contribute to reducing carbon emissions. The title of this project is "Less CO_2" because, especially in a country where the growth is so tremendous, the building needs to address the CO_2 problem. That is in a way the panorama of why architects need to be involved in this story.

Fig. 12.11 High tech meets low tech.

Fig. 12.12 "The building is like a leaf."

iGuzzini Design Concepts

MC: The iGuzzini building is a small building located in a valley below the hill town of Recanati. The valley is turning into an industrial zone, but it is still a very interesting valley because of its east and west direction. That is also the direction of the wind: from the seaside to the inland and from the inland to the seaside. Italian regulation regarding emissions by industry is severe, so the quality of air is still quite good. So we realized the potential for using fresh air from the outside. The climate in this part of Italy brings a long middle season. During late spring and early summer, the outside temperature corresponds to the comfort zone. The idea was to apply three strategies—very, very simple.

Light and Shade

MC: We would like to use natural light, but the problem with natural light is the control of the light. What happens in many buildings is that you can have transparency, but if you don't have a strategy for controlling the daylight, people will close the blinds and switch on the electric lights. That is what happens in many buildings. So the main idea was to make a building with more light because there is also a very nice panorama of the hills so it is nice to be inside looking out—but we needed to find a strategy to protect the building.

In order to control the light entering the interior, we designed a canopy for shading. [See Figure 12.14.] A model of the building, with this shading roof included, was studied in a lighting laboratory at the EPFL. We did quite a lot of work in Lausanne to analyze the quality and the quantity of light. This laboratory has an artificial sky—it is only a sixth of the entire sky—and you place your model and turn the model six times with sensors placed inside it. The sensors record numbers and they give you results about quality and quantity of light—its two different properties of light. [See Figure 12.15.]

Then we could see how much colors influence light. If you change a color on the floor—or you make it shinier or more matte—the quality of light changes. So that is an important lesson for an architect: materials have an effect on the quality of your space. We worked into great detail in choosing materials. This lab experiment was also to test the quality of the skylights—how different colors, reflectivity, and materials would influence the quality of light. We analyzed the seasons of the year: At 12 noon on June 21 there is no sun entering the space. There is light in the patio, but at the external windows there is no solar gain. In

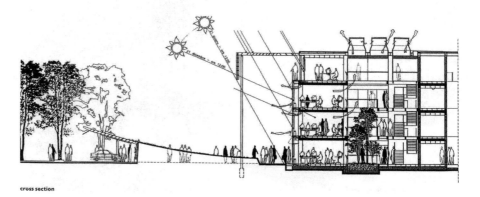

Fig. 12.13 Diagrammatic section drawing shows shading and natural ventilation strategies.

cross section

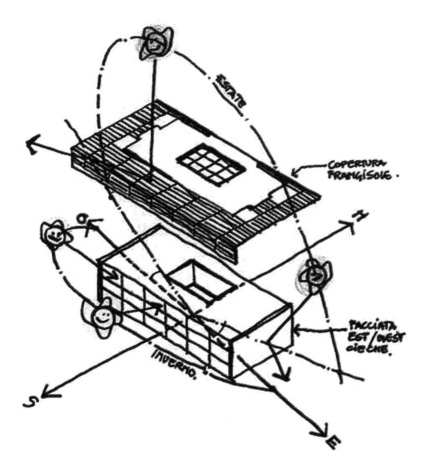

Fig. 12.14 Isometric diagram of daylight and shading strategy.

September we could see that we obtained 50 percent of solar shading by the roof [canopy]. It has an impact on the interior. An internal light shelf makes the light reflect on to the ceiling, so I can have blinds at eye level but still have diffuse natural light enter the space. In December there is a lot of sun inside the space. You can easily install Venetian blinds to avoid the glare, but you still have a very strong effect of daylight during the day. No use of artificial light is needed.

Air Movement

MC: The next strategy was about making the building breathe. So we asked ARUP to make an analysis of the external temperatures and analyze the climate. During a long period between April and June and in September and October—almost five months out of the year—the external temperatures can be good for comfort. So we wanted a building that could open up—open the windows and be comfortable. The idea was: a building can be open, but to create natural ventilation you need a strategy. You cannot do it halfway. [See Figure 12.16.]

Heating and Cooling

MC: The third strategy is about using thermal mass—it's a high-mass concrete building. Thermal mass is working by taking fresh air in during the night and absorbing heat during the day. [See Figure 12.17.]

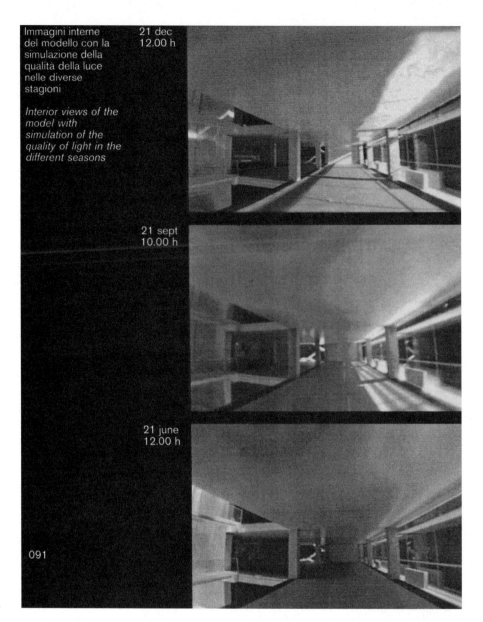

Immagini interne del modello con la simulazione della qualità della luce nelle diverse stagioni

Interior views of the model with simulation of the quality of light in the different seasons

21 dec 12.00 h

21 sept 10.00 h

21 june 12.00 h

091

Fig. 12.15 Simulating interior light conditions.

There is the relationship between the openings in the façade and the openings in the skylights, which creates a pressure differential. It is interesting to know that air movement is created by very small movement—low velocity—but also a very small temperature differential. If you have half a degree difference in air temperature between two spaces, the air is going to move. We developed the design in such a way that there will be a different temperature in the patio and a different pressure between the windows and the roof. That is enough to create a natural ventilation effect.

The fan coils are connected to a very simple control system so they switch on and off in response to internal temperatures and external temperatures. Some time during the day when the temperature outside is good and there is not too much wind, the windows open automatically and the fan coil units are switched

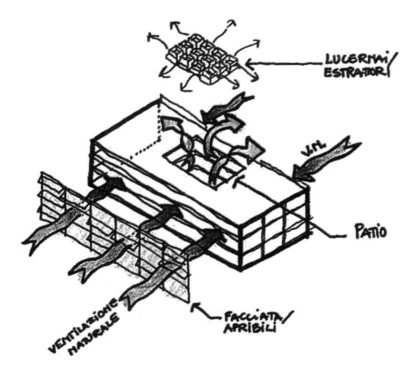

Fig. 12.16 Isometric diagram of ventilation strategy.

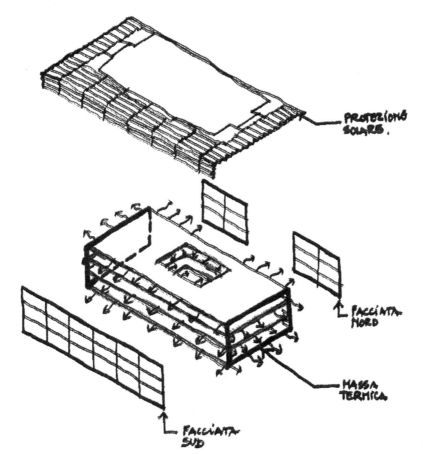

Fig. 12.17 Isometric diagram of shading and passive solar heating with thermal mass.

off. It's a very simple system that uses simple commands like temperature, humidity, and wind—they are the three factors that generate the opening and closing of the windows.

There are two operations: one is when the priority is through the control system. It is not complicated, just counting on a few numbers. You can also override the control system by a local command console so that you can open your window if you want. That is the second priority. If you don't like what the computer comes up with, you can override the system.

It is more psychological than real, because people feel that they want to decide what the building should do. Also, people are different. There are people who would like to keep a jacket on while others take their jackets off. You must create a kind of adaptive environment because people are all different. You need to provide some degree of control on the side of the user while still depending on the system.

CLAIMS

1. It has been stated that the south façade is fully shaded during the hot summer months and 80 percent shaded during the shoulder seasons. This claim can easily be substantiated by performing a simple shading analysis in a 3-D modeling program, such as SketchUp™.
2. It has been stated that natural ventilation will be sufficient to ventilate and to cool the building for 55 percent of the time. The climate analysis, along with the design strategies for a building that breathes, seems to support this claim.
3. It has been stated that the fully glazed façade, in combination with the light shelf design, creates an even distribution of daylight across the floor. This claim can be examined by measuring the light levels on a typical floor of the building as built.

AS BUILT

Light

The large areas of glass on the north and south façades, along with a light shelf, were intended to allow for daylight to enter deep into the building. On the south side, there is a shading device with horizontal louvers. The effect of these horizontal louvers on the daylight levels inside the offices was investigated in two ways: First, a three-dimensional model of the south half of the building was constructed using the SketchUp Pro computer program. Then, upon arrival at the site, photos of the shade pattern on the ground—created by the shading structure—were analyzed.

The effect of the light shelf could not be investigated, simply because this device was not installed. According to the building owner, the light shelves were "too expensive and not so necessary" (Lerum and Giaccaglia 2006). The distribution of daylight levels across a typical office floor was investigated by the use of a handheld light meter. Twelve skylights at the top of the atrium distribute daylight deep down into the space. The light distribution vertically in the atrium was tested using the same handheld light meter. Light levels were recorded and plotted on diagrams superimposed on a cross-section of the atrium and a cross-section of a typical office floor.

The placement of electric light fixtures relative to the daylight apertures is apparent in photos shot at the site. According to the building owner, the main open-plan offices are equipped with light fixtures that are controlled by continuous dimming. In response to increasing daylight levels, the system will decrease the electric lighting by a maximum of 80 percent. A more recent dimming system developed by iGuzzini allows for continuous dimming of the lighting intensity by a maximum of 90 percent (Lerum and Giaccaglia, 2006). No evidence was found of any possibility for the users to override automatic light fixture controls.

A diagrammatic wall section has been published in the magazine *Intelligent Architecture* (IA 1998). This wall section diagram shows sun angles at 8 and 10 A.M. on June 21. It is obvious from the shading analysis that no sun is permitted on the south façade on June 21. The south façade of the building is in total shade during the peak summer months. Anyone who examines the building as built will therefore understand that a drawing showing June 21 sun rays hitting the light shelf is meaningless.

Light on a Typical Office Floor

Light levels were measured on the first office floor on the south side of the building at 11 A.M. on Wednesday, May 10. The blinds were open in the midsection of the windows and there were no blinds at the lower section of the windows. The blinds at the upper section of the windows (the clerestory windows) were closed. The lower line in Figure 12.18 shows the results from measurements with the blinds closed. The blinds on the clerestory windows were then opened and the same measurements were repeated. The upper line shows the resulting light levels with the blinds open.

The light shelf shown on the architectural section drawing was not installed. It is therefore unclear what effect the light shelf would have had on the light distribution in a typical south-facing office. Even with no light shelf in place, the results obtained from this simple experiment show that the light levels and the light distribution improved significantly when the blinds on the clerestory windows were pulled up.

During the site visit all clerestory windows on the south side of the first floor

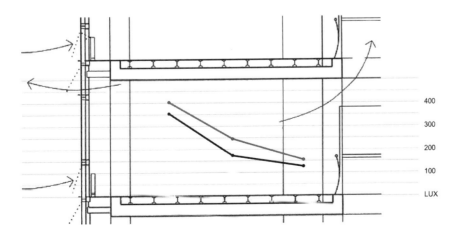

Fig. 12.18 Light levels as measured in a typical south-facing office.

were covered with blinds. This prevented the clerestory windows from performing their expected function as daylight apertures. The users explained that the blinds were closed in order to reduce discomfort due to glare. Blinds at the windows in the midsection were also closed.

Light in the Atrium

All the electric lights in the offices as well as in the atrium were on during the site visit. It was not possible to detect any changes in the electric light levels due to changes in the daylight levels in the atrium. Light levels in the atrium were measured with a handheld light meter at 11 A.M. on Wednesday, May 10. The results are shown in Figure 12.19. Readings from the meter were recorded in the unit foot candles (fc) and then converted into lux by multiplying by the constant 10.76. Light levels range from 26 fc or 280 lux at the bottom of the atrium to 76 fc or 818 lux at top of the atrium. It is worth noticing that the numbers recorded at the top level range from 452 lux directly under the skylights to 818 lux directly under electric light fixtures. The light levels at the first floor and the second floor were measured at the same position: the top of the handrails. The difference in the light levels between these two floors is most likely due to the fact that the handrail at the first floor is shaded by the floor above. The floors are made of opaque glass, but the light transmission through the glass is obviously very low.

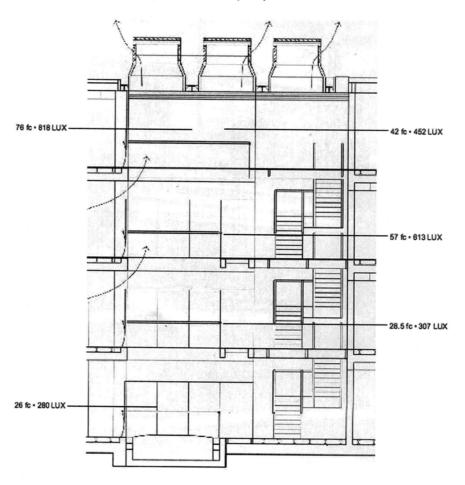

Fig. 12.19 Light levels in the atrium, as measured on May 10, 2006, at 11 A.M.

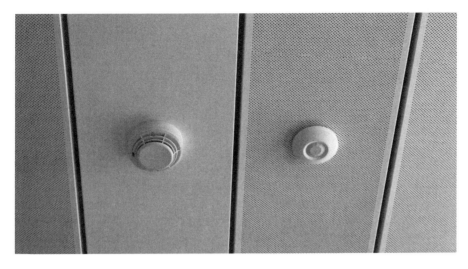

Fig. 12.20 Smoke detector (left) and light sensor in a typical meeting room on the ground floor.

The electric lights were on all the time during this experiment. It was not possible to find a maintenance person who could turn the lights off. One sees from the measurements that the light at the top of the atrium is mainly dominated by the electric light fixtures. It is unclear whether the light levels at the bottom of the garden are mainly dominated by electric lights or daylight from the skylights.

There are many light fixtures in the atrium, each including halogen lamps. Surface temperatures on the light fixtures were measured with a handheld infrared thermometer. The readings show temperatures near 200°F, or around 90°C. Since there is no mechanical cooling in the atrium, the added internal heat gain from lamps can only be removed by air moving out through the dampers in the skylights.

Lighting Controls

The lights in the meeting rooms are controlled by motion sensors. The lights would come on as soon as a person entered the room and stay on until a certain time delay after the room was evacuated. The electric lights did not respond to changes in daylight levels, and there was no way for the user of the meeting room to switch the lights off.

Automatic dimming was not installed in the small meeting rooms because they are used infrequently and intermittently, not for a continuing job. There is only a sensor for presence that turns the lights off when the room is unoccupied.

Figure 12.20 shows sensors installed in the ceiling in one of the conference rooms on the ground floor. The sensor to the left is a smoke detector and the sensor to the right is a light sensor.

SHADE

The photo in Figure 12.21, taken before noon, shows the shading effect on the ground at the south side of the building. While the vertical part of the shading structure provides 100 percent shading at this time, the more open spacing of the southernmost louvers of the horizontal part of the shading structure allows for

Fig. 12.21 Light and shade at the foot of the south-facing glazed façade.

some sunlight to pass through. Except for these narrow bands of sunlight, the entire south façade is in shade.

Figure 12.22 shows that the horizontal louvers are spaced approximately as designed. The vertical rotation of each of the louvers, however, is oriented at the same tilt angle. This differs from the design, as the louvers closest to the fourth-floor south-facing façade were designed with a different rotation.

Although observations at the building and measurements during the site visit played a crucial role in the investigation of how this building works, computer simulations were used to clarify and examine phenomena that cannot be documented at a short point in time. One such phenomenon is the shading of the south façade, which will change from day to day as the sun angle changes through the seasons.

A three-dimensional model of the south side of the building was created in SketchUp. The building was rotated 22.5 degrees toward the east, as shown in the site plan published in the German architecture magazine *Architektur Wettbewerbe* (AW 1998, pp. 8–9). A white layer was placed behind the transparent façade in order to create a clear pattern of light and shade on the glass. Studies of light and shade were carried out for the winter solstice (December 21), the summer solstice (June 21), and the fall equinox (September 21).

This shading analysis shows clearly how the three lower floors of the building are exposed to the winter sun in order to take advantage of solar radiation for space heating (Figure 12.23a). It is also clearly shown how the entire south façade is protected from heat gain from solar radiation around summer solstice (Figure 12.23c), but since the entire south façade over four floors is protected by one large overhang, the amount of light and shade is not evenly distributed during the shoulder seasons. The shading analysis for September 21 (Figure 12.23b) shows how the lower floor is in full sun while the second and third floor both are fully protected from the sun. It also seems like the south-facing glass on the fourth floor is exposed to direct sunlight around the fall and spring equinox.

Fig. 12.22 Louvered shading canopy protecting the south-facing glazed façade.

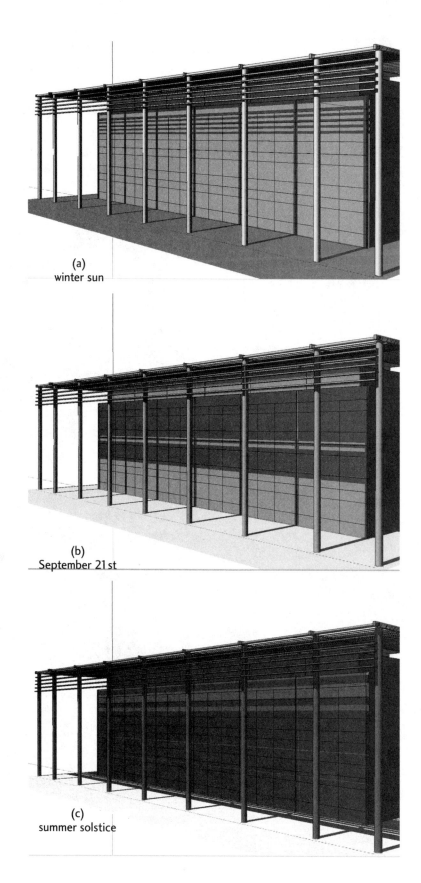

(a)
winter sun

(b)
September 21st

(c)
summer solstice

Fig. 12.23 Analysis of the shading effect of the louvered canopy on the south-facing glazed façade.

DOES IT BREATHE?

In order to understand how the air systems work, it is first necessary to separate ventilation requirements from the need for cooling. When analyzing how air moves through the building, we should look at the ventilation requirement first and then consider how cooling is added to the natural system in order to remove heat from the building interior.

Air movement through the building is described as cross ventilation across the floor plates where the offices and meeting rooms are located. The air then moves into the atrium, where it is exhausted by utilizing stack ventilation. The specially designed skylights move air out of the atrium, thus pulling air from the offices.

Aside from the operable, motorized dampers, no fans or any other mechanical equipment assist in moving the air out through the skylights. When the dampers are open, air moves out of the top of the atrium as a result of pressure differences (stack effect).

There is a row of operable windows near the floor in the offices. These windows have low-E glazing. There are also operable windows high up in the space. This configuration of operable windows near the floor and near the ceiling allows the air to move in and out of the offices, thus ventilating the office spaces even without making use of stack ventilation in the atrium.

According to the building owner, natural ventilation works during the night. The control system opens the windows only when the ambient air temperature falls within a specified range. During the summer the ambient night temperature has to be below 22°C for the night ventilation system to engage. In the winter the ambient air temperature needs to be higher than 18°C before the windows open. It is not clear whether the users are allowed to override the automatic controls.

Fan coils assist with mechanical cooling when the ambient temperatures do not allow for natural cooling. These fan coil units also provide heating when passive solar heating is not sufficient to condition the space during the winter. The fan coil units do not pull outside air directly through the exterior walls. They mainly recirculate the air inside the space, but since they are located near operable windows, fresh air will be supplied across a fan coil unit when the window next to it is open.

Electrically powered, compressor-based chillers produce the chilled water for the fan coil units. The chilled water is supplied at 9°C and returns at 12°C. Electric energy to the building is supplied from the national grid.

Smoke Test

A smoke test was performed on Wednesday, May 10, 2006, during the lunch hour, starting at 12:45 P.M. The purpose of the test was to see how the air would flow through the interior when the building was in natural ventilation mode. May 10 was a cloudy day with ambient temperatures below 20°C. There was a slight breeze in the air, coming from the northwest. This wind pattern created a positive pressure on the outside of the building on the northwest side, and similarly, a negative pressure on the south side of the building.

A smoke candle was placed in a typical open office configuration near the south-facing window wall. Immediately after the smoke candle was lit, the clerestory windows both on the south side and the north side of the building were opened. It was our intent to open all the dampers in the skylights above the atrium, as well. As it turned out, this was not possible. For some reason, the facilities person was unable to override the control system and open the dampers. Of the 24 dampers in the 12 skylights, only 2 dampers, both facing south, were open during the experiment.

The experiment was documented on videotape. The video shows clearly how the smoke escaped from the building through the clerestory windows on the south side (see Figure 12.24). At the same time, fresh air was coming in through the clerestory windows on the north side. The cross-ventilation that occurred due to wind pressure and open windows cleared the first floor of smoke in a few minutes. There was no sign of any air moving from the office area on the first floor into the atrium (see Figure 12.25).

The fact that we did not detect any air movement due to stack ventilation in the atrium does not necessarily mean that the building is not working as designed. The problem seems to lie with the control system. Manual override buttons were installed at each desk. This enables the people that work on the office floors to close and open the windows manually. However, there does not seem to be any control over the dampers in the skylights. During the site visit, only two dampers were open all the time. The other 22 dampers remained closed.

The wind rose in Figure 12.26 was produced from wind data in the Ancona weather file. Wind patterns at the iGuzzini site may differ significantly, since Ancona is a coastal city and the iGuzzini buildings are located at the floor of a wide inland valley running east to west. The wind data still indicate that the northwest–southeast wind pattern experienced during the site visit represents typical conditions.

Fig. 12.24 A cloud of white smoke developing near the south-facing façade during the lunch-hour smoke test.

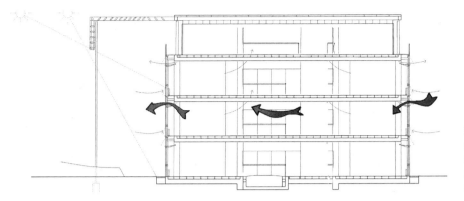

Fig. 12.25 Sectional diagram shows how wind-driven cross-ventilation occurred during the smoke test.

Natural Ventilation

Individual controls are installed at each workspace on the main office floors. These controls allow the users to manually open and close the clerestory windows for ventilation. The smoke test proved that these windows are very effective in allowing for air to move across the floor plates (cross-ventilation). It is assumed that these windows are also quite effective in providing a way for the users to individually control natural ventilation at each workplace.

The lower row of operable windows (near the floor), used in tandem with the operable dampers in the skylights, are designed to allow for natural ventilation

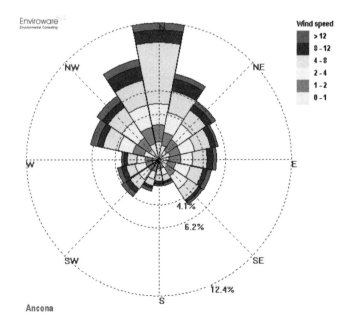

Fig. 12.26 Wind rose for Ancona, Italy, created in Wind Rose by Enviroware slr (Italy).

Fig. 12.27 Close-up view of one of the operable windows on the south-facing façade.

and night vent cooling by allowing fresh air to move in through the windows, while warmer, used air escapes through the skylight dampers. The smoke test proved that the maintenance people were unable to control the skylight dampers.

Temperature measurements during the night indicated that night-vent cooling was not functioning as designed, but the building owner claims that the automated control of the dampers and the lower windows for natural ventilation is functional (Lerum and Giaccaglia 2006).

HEATING AND COOLING

It has been stated that the building needs heating 35 percent of the time. Assuming that solar radiation is used for passive space conditioning, is a fully glazed façade on the north and south sides of the building optimal?

Two boilers produce hot water for the fan coil units and the lavatories. The hot-water temperature for space heating depends on the season. In the winter, the water is supplied at 60°C and returns at 50°C. The supply water temperature in the spring is 40°C and the return temperature is 35°C. Historical data on annual energy use by monthly distribution was not available for this building, since it is metered along with the older parts of the headquarters offices for iGuzzini.

Heat Flow

A study of the heat balance through the south-facing fully glazed walls was performed in the computer program HEED. A weather file for Ancona, Italy, was

Fig. 12.28 Close-up view of the louvered shading canopies.

used for this simulation—obtained from the EnergyPlus Weather Data Web site (USDOE 2006).

The resulting graphical representation of the balance between heat gain and heat loss through the south-glazed façade is shown in Figure 12.29. The image on the left side shows an hour-by-hour simulation for 12 days in September and October. The image on the right side shows the entire year, using monthly average temperature and solar radiation values. This study shows clearly how the heat gain through the south façade is shifted toward the late summer and early fall. This phenomenon is explained by lower sun angles, less protection of the

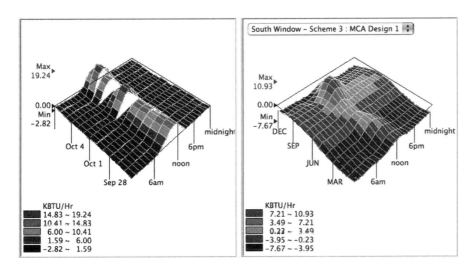

Fig. 12.29 Simulating heat gain and heat loss, using HEED.

façade, and higher ambient temperatures during the months of August, September, October, and even into November.

In order to further investigate the heat balance across the south-facing glazed façade, a model was set up in the energy simulation program ENERGY-10. A 6-meter-deep zone along the south side of one intermediate floor was studied. A weather file for Ancona, Italy, was used for this study.

A graph representing seven days in early January (Figure 12.30) shows how one can expect both heat gains and heat losses during a typical winter week. Typically, heating is needed at night and cooling may be needed during the day. The average ambient temperature during this week in a typical meteorological year is just above freezing. Although the temperature during the day may reach 10°C or 12°C, freezing temperatures are not uncommon during the night.

A graphical analysis of the image created by ENERGY-10 shows how heat gain and heat losses can be balanced. Since the ambient temperatures are below the comfort zone for 24 hours of the day, natural ventilation can be used to cool the interiors, as needed.

During the second week of May, shown in Figure 12.31, the zone along the south-facing glazed façade will see heat gains predominantly. The ambient temperatures are now fluctuating around an average of 15°C. Although day temperatures may reach above the comfort zone, nights are still cool. The environmental conditions and the resulting heat balance of the interior lend themselves to a low-energy space conditioning strategy by combining high thermal mass with natural ventilation at night.

During the third week of July (shown in Figure 12.32), the south zone sees heat gains for almost all the hours of the day. The ambient temperatures now fluctuate around an average of almost 30°C. Daytime temperatures may reach the upper 30s or even 40°C. Although the temperatures drop significantly during the night, the outside night air is seldom cold enough to represent a source of night vent cooling. Mechanical cooling is therefore needed as the main conditioning strategy at this time.

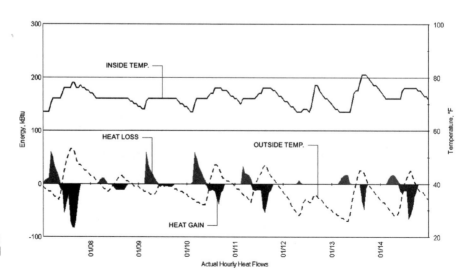

Fig. 12.30 Actual hourly heat flow during a winter week, as simulated in ENERGY-10.

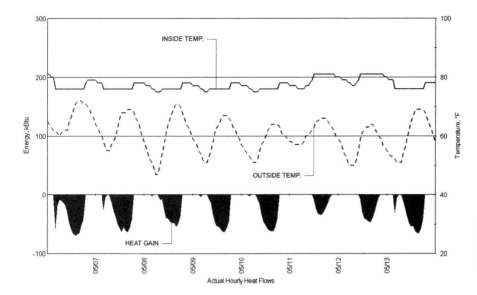

Fig. 12.31 Actual hourly heat flow during the second week of May, as simulated in ENERGY-10.

Night-Ventilation Cooling

Figure 12.33 summarizes the findings from the temperature recordings using HOBO data loggers, starting at noon on Wednesday, May 10, and continuing into Thursday, May 11. One data logger was placed at desk level in the south side office area on the first floor. A second data logger was placed inside the atrium on the top floor. A third data logger was placed on the terrace outside the top floor. This third data logger was protected from direct sunlight by one of the exterior steel columns.

The outdoor temperature on May 10 increased from 14.5°C at noon to about 18°C between 4 P.M. and 6 P.M. A minimum outdoor temperature of 9.3°C occurred at 5:20 the next morning.

When the smoke test was performed immediately after noon on May 10, the air temperature inside the office dropped 1.3°C in less than 15 minutes. The graph shows clearly how the interior temperature on the office floor dropped as

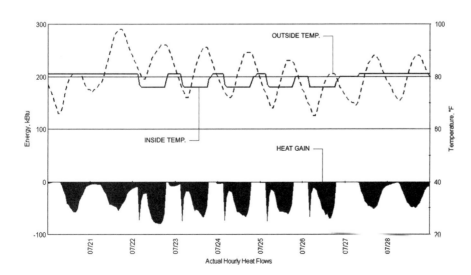

Fig. 12.32 Actual hourly heat flow toward the end of July, as simulated in ENERGY-10.

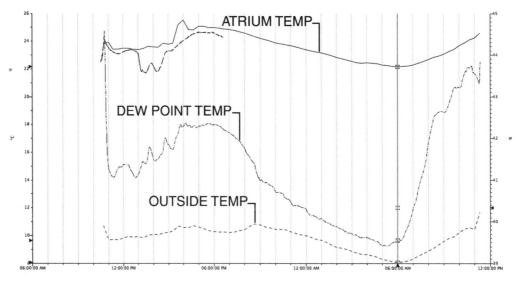

Fig. 12.33 Actual indoor and outdoor air temperatures on May 10 to 11, 2006. Graph from HOBOware.

a result of the cross-ventilation that occurred when the clerestory windows were opened. The temperatures recorded by the data logger at the top of the atrium did not record a similar pattern. Here, the temperature remained fairly constant. These findings support the conclusions from the smoke video recordings. Fresh air was moving across the floor plate but did not enter the atrium.

While the ambient temperature dropped almost 10°C during the night, the minimum temperature at the top of the atrium was recorded at 22.2°C. These findings indicate that the building did not operate in the night ventilation mode as designed. If all 24 dampers at the skylights had opened, and the windows in the exterior wall were also open during the night, we would have expected to see a more significant drop in the air temperature at the top of the atrium.

MECHANICAL COOLING

When mechanical cooling is needed, the fan coil units will either cool the air inside the building or cool fresh air coming in through the lower row of operable windows. A minimum airflow rate of fresh air is needed in order to maintain indoor air quality.

The diagram in Figure 12.34 illustrates design conditions on July 21 in a typical meteorological year (TMY weather file for Ancona) when the ambient (outside) air reaches 37°C dry bulb and 27°C wet bulb. During conditions like these, condensation would form on the cooling coil at around 23°C. Chilled water enters the coil at 9°C and returns at around 12°C. Significant condensation will therefore occur when outside air is pulled in through the fan coil units. A condensation pan inside each fan coil unit addresses this problem. Condensing water drains were also installed.

A separate forced-air system is in place on the top floor. Air-handling units are located on the roof of the old building (Lerum and Giaccaglia, 2006).

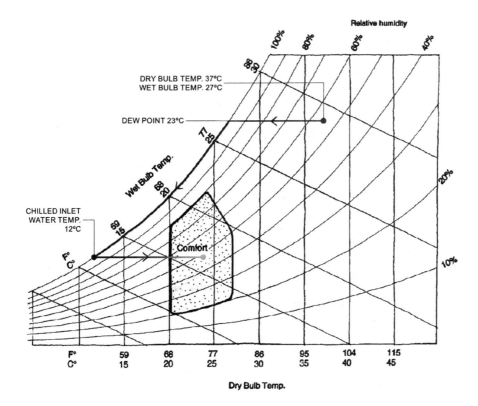

Relative humidity

DRY BULB TEMP. 37°C
WET BULB TEMP. 27°C

DEW POINT 23°C

CHILLED INLET
WATER TEMP.
12°C

Comfort

F°		59	68	77	86	95	104	115
C°		15	20	25	30	35	40	45

Dry Bulb Temp.

Fig. 12.34 Design conditions on July 21 in a typical meteorological year, plotted on a psychrometric chart.

MECHANICAL HEATING

There are two boilers and two air-cooled chillers in a central mechanical plant outside the building. A four-pipe system feeds the fan coil units, allowing each individual unit to deliver heating or cooling on demand. This system allows a fan coil unit on the north side to deliver heating while another unit on the south side delivers cooling. The hot water temperature depends on the season: It is warmer in the winter than in the fall, for example. In winter the water is supplied at 60°C and returns at 50°C. In spring the supply temperature is 40°C and the return temperature is 35°C (Lerum and Giaccaglia 2006).

WHAT IF?

Simulations carried out by the tools already mentioned may be used to test a few what-if scenarios. A what-if scenario takes the analysis of the building performance one step further: From asking the question "How does this building work?" we can now ask the question, "How could the building work in other ways?"

For this particular building what-if scenarios could be used to investigate the following:

- The fully glazed north and south façades, testing the implications of introducing highly insulated opaque panels
- The large shading device, possibly distributing the device into one section for each floor

Fig. 12.35 The iGuzzini headquarters building by Mario Cucinella Architects, main façade.

SUMMARY OF FINDINGS

The architect Mario Cucinella outlined three clearly defined design strategies for this project. These strategies reflect seasonal variations in the local climate. The three strategies, which address light and shade, natural ventilation, and passive heating and cooling using thermal mass, seem very appropriate for this particular building type and location.

The design concepts were carried over into the building as it was constructed at the site. With one exception, the missing light shelf, the major design goals are reflected in the built object. The missing light shelf seems to have created a comfort issue with the users. Venetian blinds have been installed on the inside of the clerestory windows in order to reduce glare. When the blinds are closed, the daylight levels at the workspaces decrease.

Light sensors and motion sensors are installed in some parts of the building. This system allows for the electric lights to be dimmed or switched off when there is enough daylight available or if the room is not occupied. A similar daylight responsive control system dims the electric lights on the main office floors, but all the lights remain on at minimum 20 percent effect during the entire day.

User control consoles for the operable windows were installed as an afterthought. It seems like the possibility for the user to override the automatic control system is permanent and that it may prevent the building from operating as intended in natural ventilation mode.

Historical data on annual energy use are not yet available. It is therefore not possible to evaluate the actual energy performance of the building relative to a benchmark for this type of building in this type of climate.

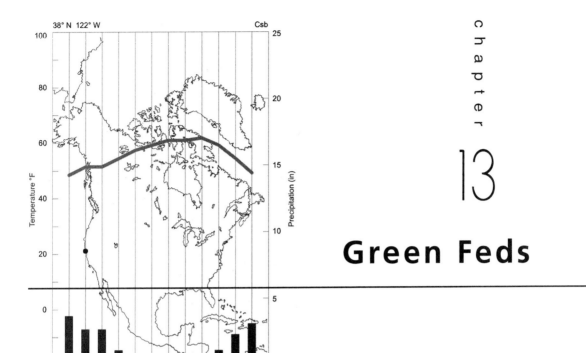

13

Green Feds

San Francisco Federal Building by Morphosis

Building Type:	Office
Location:	San Francisco, California
Coordinates:	38°N, 122°W
Interview:	Tim Christ, architect
Site Visit:	June 2006

The San Francisco Federal Building is an innovative office building for the federal government meant to become a prototype for the public services building of the future.

BUILDING AND SITE

The San Francisco Federal Building is located on a central block in downtown San Francisco, where the urban street grid is rotated about 45 degrees off of the east–west axis. This rotation provides both an advantage and a challenge to a low-energy, high-performance design. With the building rotated along the grid, more solar radiation can hit the northwest façade in the afternoon and early evening on a warm summer day.

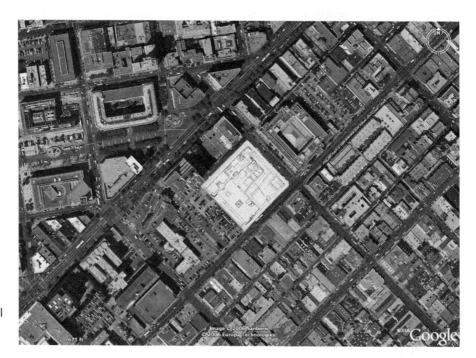

Fig. 13.1 Site plan for the San Francisco Federal Building, from Google Earth.

The rotation also happens to align with the prevailing wind direction in San Francisco (see Figure 13.1). For the entire summer, from April through October, the wind will come in off the Pacific Ocean from the west and northwest orientations, perpendicular to the long side of the building. This fairly stable and reliable wind pattern offers an opportunity to utilize wind pressure to drive a natural ventilation system based on cross-ventilation (see Figure 13.2).

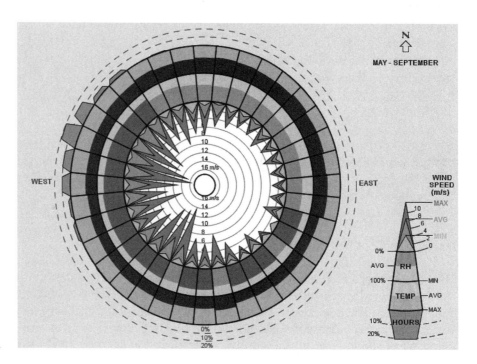

Fig. 13.2 Wind wheel, from Climate Consultant.

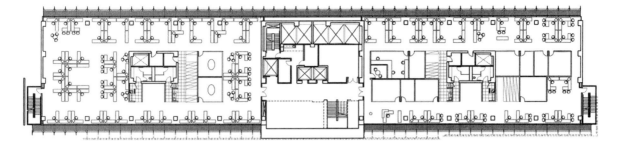

Fig. 13.3 Typical floor plan, by Morphosis.

The 18-floor building houses general office space for federal agencies. Most of the general office spaces are housed in the upper 12 to 15 floors of the tall and thin slab that is pushed up against the northwest edge of the site. A typical floor plate of 106 by 18 meters provides workspaces for up to 110 people (see Figure 13.3). The gross area of a typical floor plate is about 1,900 square meters, including stairs, elevators, and elevator lobby. Restrooms, storage rooms, and small kitchens are also included in this number. With more than 100 persons per floor, each person has about 17.5 square meters of gross floor area allocated.

The tall and thin office slab has no windows to the short ends on the east and west orientations. The two long sides have floor-to-ceiling glazed walls. The northwest-facing wall is protected from the low afternoon sun by vertical fins made of laminated glass. The southeast-facing wall is protected from intense sunlight by a screen made from perforated stainless steel. The perforation of the stainless steel screen provides for a 58 percent openness factor. Catwalks at each floor are located between the glass wall and the shading devices, providing easy access for maintenance and window cleaning.

LOCATION AND CLIMATE

A TMY climate file was used to analyze the climate of San Francisco. This file was converted to a format that could be read by the computer program Weather Maker. Weather Maker was used to generate graphical representations of temperature, humidity, and solar radiation (see Figure 13.4). The computer program Climate Consultant 3 was used to create a wind wheel diagram for San Francisco.

Located between the San Francisco Bay and the Pacific Ocean, San Francisco has a climate with characteristics that are different from other locations in California. The prevailing winds are predominantly from the north-northeast. The temperatures are cool, with few variations among the seasons. One could argue that the climate of San Francisco is easy to use as a design parameter, but it requires a thorough understanding of all of the specific parameters of this unique climate.

Figure 13.5 shows temperature variations during a typical winter week toward the middle of January. Although the temperatures during winter may go as low as 0°C, they rarely reach above 18°C. Average ambient air temperature is below 10°C (50°F). During this season, the temperature is always low enough to allow for natural ventilation to be used as a low-energy method of removing heat from the interior, if necessary. When the wet bulb temperature and dry bulb temperature

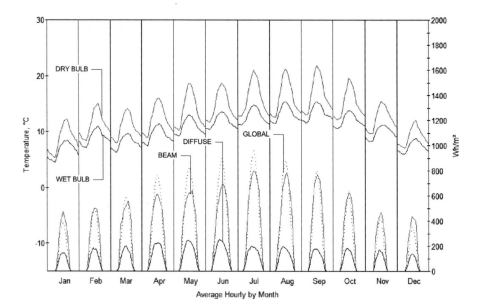

Fig. 13.4 Temperatures and solar radiation for a typical day per month, from Weather Maker.

converge, which happens quite often, the relative humidity is 100 percent. This is a reflection of the well-known fact that San Francisco quite frequently experiences fog that comes in from the Pacific Ocean.

In a thermal simulation model, one typical office floor was set up in the computer program ENERGY-10. This floor was assumed to be sandwiched between other similar office floors. The roof and floor for this section of the building were therefore assumed to be thermally neutral. Figure 13.6 shows heat flow during the same period that was analyzed for temperatures. It shows the heat transfer to and from the interior of a reference case building that was built automatically by the ENERGY-10 program. This reference building is assumed to be designed without applying any particular low-energy strategies. Figure 13.6 shows that heating will be required for most days during this period. But cooling would also be required for several days during the same week. Both heating and cooling may be needed during the same day.

A second model was automatically built by ENERGY-10, for comparison with the reference case. This second model pretends to represent the building as built with the shading fins on the northwest side and the perforated screen on the

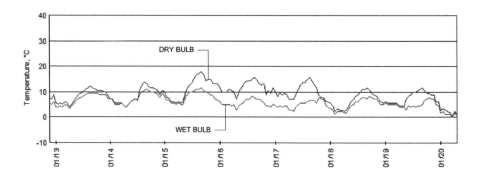

Fig. 13.5 The winter week of January 13 to 20.

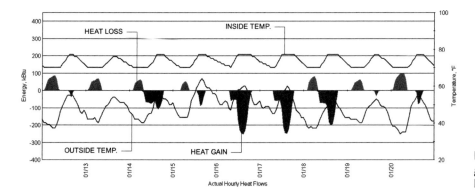

Fig. 13.6 Heat-flow graph, ENERGY-10 auto-build reference building.

southeast side. The heat-flow graph in Figure 13.7 now shows that heating is eliminated. This is possible because a number of low-energy strategies have been applied, such as correct orientation of the windows, appropriate window sizing, improved glazing properties, added thermal mass exposed to the interior, and appropriate shading. The graph also shows that heat needs to be removed every day of this relatively cold winter week. The amount of cooling varies greatly, depending on the sky cover. On clear days with abundant solar radiation, more heat needs to be removed from the interior. Since the ambient temperatures do not reach above 65°F during this period, all the heat removal can be taken care of by natural ventilation.

As shown in Figure 13.8, temperature and solar radiation data for a week from May 15 through May 19 was used to analyze the climate conditions during the late spring or early summer. The daytime high temperatures now reach 26°C, while lows frequently dip below 10°C. The relative humidity is near 100 percent in the early morning hours.

The heat-flow graph in Figure 13.9 for the low-energy building shows that heat needs to be removed from the space every day of this week, but to a varying degree. Since the ambient air temperature is below 18°C most of the time, heat may be removed from the interior by means of natural ventilation. But daytime highs go toward the upper 20s (°C) for a few days. Therefore, night vent cooling with thermal mass needs to be explored for the summer.

Analysis of a week in early July shows that the ambient temperatures are still

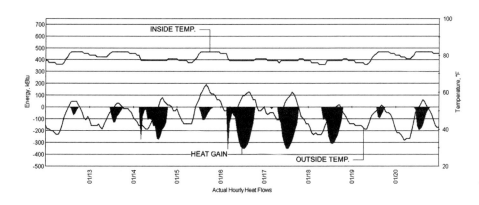

Fig. 13.7 Heat-flow graph, ENERGY-10 auto-build low-E building.

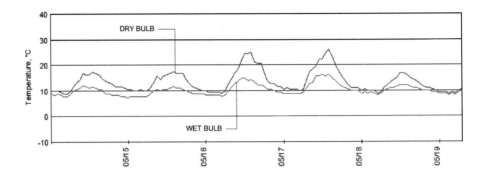

Fig. 13.8 Dry bulb and wet bulb temperatures, May 15 to 19.

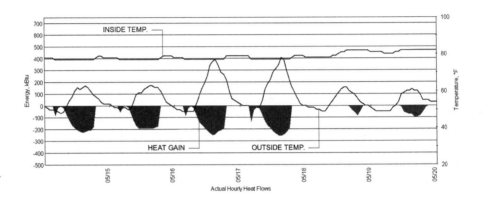

Fig. 13.9 Heat-flow graph, ENERGY-10 auto-build low-E building.

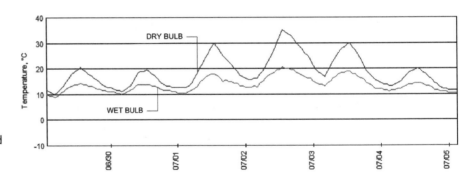

Fig. 13.10 Dry bulb and wet bulb temperatures, June 30 to July 5.

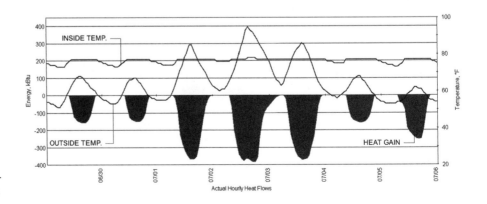

Fig. 13.11 Heat-flow graph, ENERGY-10 auto-build reference building.

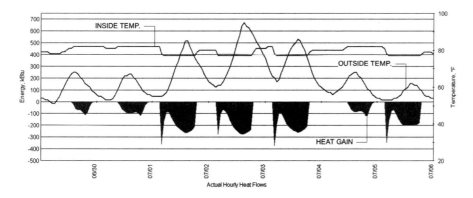

Fig. 13.12 Heat-flow graph, building as designed.

quite moderate (see Figure 13.10). The outdoor temperatures now swing comfortably between 10°C and 20°C for most days. But on three days of this week, the ambient high temperatures reach well above normal. The outdoor air temperature peaks at 35°C in the afternoon on the middle of the three hot days in a typical meteorological year.

A comparison of the heat-flow graphs of the reference case building in Figure 13.11 and the existing building in Figure 13.12 shows that heat needs to be removed from the interior every day of the typical summer week. Since the existing building was designed with low-energy strategies in mind, the surplus heat of this building is significantly less than the reference case building. Since the nighttime low temperatures still go below 18°C, cooling with high mass is theoretically still a viable strategy. But due to the high daytime temperatures and a short number of hours when the nighttime temperature reaches below 18°C, the application of night ventilation cooling with high thermal mass needs to be tested for extreme summer conditions like the three hot days of this week. This testing will be discussed in another section, "Listen to the Baby Kick."

THE DESIGN AS SEEN BY THE DESIGNER

The following are Tim Christ's (TC) responses in an interview in San Francisco, June 16, 2006 (Lerum and Christ 2006).

Design Philosophy

TC: The idea of sustainability itself is not an explicit focus of the office. But what we are interested in at Morphosis is an approach that is performance-based to most of our projects, which is to say, within the given parameters of a program for a building, whether it is an office building or a courthouse or a campus recreation center, there are latent opportunities that are derived from climate, from patterns of use, selections that have to do with the materials palette of the building—and what we are interested in is increasing or enhancing the performance of the building so that the technology that is available is applied judiciously to try to create high-performance buildings in general—and buildings that actually become emblematic, in the way they look, of some of their deep engineering principles.

Fig. 13.13 Sun Tower in Seoul, Korea, by Morphosis.

We have been interested in the office for many years in this idea of enclosure and envelope, which is now become very, very hot for a lot of architects—and we have been looking for many years at ways of creating layering in façades of buildings starting with the Sun Tower in Seoul, Korea [see Figure 13.13], the Hypo Bank Complex in Klagenfurt, Austria, and the CalTrans District 7 Headquarters building in Los Angeles, California. These projects are about screening and scrimming and layering of the façade in order to actually modulate the relationship between the interior and exterior. Now, the buildings have a kind of particular appearance— some of them—as a consequence of that material choice, but one of the things that is very important is that it's very attached now to performance criteria: to increase sun shading, for example, in this project as you have seen in the field. We don't see sustainability as a kind of interest being separated from any of the other interests that we have in technology—it is just another one of the things that we use to explore and develop a design.

As a rule we are very skeptical and I would say not particularly interested at all in the idea of marketing ourselves as "green architects" because it is really quite a fetish right now and there are certain awards or rewards that accrue to speaking that language—but if you look across the board at commercial buildings, in particular, in the United States, you see a very low level of performance even with buildings that are considered to be sustainable in their solutions.

A High-Performance Building

TC: When we received the contract to begin design on this project, we were asked to design a model building. The federal government's contact said specifically to design a model office building. It did not say *design a building that pursues energy conservation or natural resources as a kind of baseline interest.* We chose to interpret it that way in the case of the San Francisco Federal Building because we had an advantageous client, we are in a fairly progressive environment politically here in this city, and we felt that through any number of ways we could begin to push really hard on some key concepts. As a consequence we do have a high-performance building, we believe.

There are other aspects of performance than energy. We are very interested in workplace-quality issues, which are all performance issues. When we began the design of this particular project some of the other office buildings that we have done in Austria, in Italy, various places in the United States, we are looking really closely at how to enhance the quality of the workplace, and it is done usually through fairly simple means—in this case through a very aggressive attitude toward the use of daylight and the connection of the interior environment to the exterior climate through the operable windows that are occupant controlled, for example. Some of these concepts are very simple.

It is very easy to get up in front of the client and say, "Well, your project is all about the health and happiness of the worker through daylight and fresh air." Nobody can fight or argue against this, because it is just a basic principle about human metabolic response. But the difficult thing is to implement these concepts and to gain and to win the trust of the people who are responsible for paying for, constructing, and actually ultimately using the infrastructure of the building.

We are interested in this project also in the 75- to 100-year effective lifespan of

Fig. 13.14 View from a typical floor through the perforated screen (left) and through curtain wall with vertical fins (right).

the building, and so one of the key concepts is in the flexible reuse of the floor-plate so as technology changes—computers go to wireless and infrared—as different modes of work begin to evolve, we believe what we have created here is something that is a kind of universal space to a certain extent within the office environment that can support many different ways of functional interpretation and how people communicate. So [in] our initial studies along with studying climate and orientation for the site, we were looking very hard at social science research about how people work and the modes of their working environment and how those are changing in the USA—and this impacts things like furniture, impacts the space planning and all the ways that offices are organized. We think of that as performance also.

Design Strategies

TC: What we are after in these projects is a kind of inevitability, which is to say that the sun screen exists where it does on the building physically for a reason, which has to do with the interior—and there is a very direct relationship between the inside and the outside of the building. Often in architecture we work in a world now, especially with the computer, where a lot of sculptural and developed formal ideas can be made that are absolutely disconnected from the function of the building, for example—or any of the systems that are allowing the building to stand up and actually to work.

What we are interested in is diagramming these things in a very legible way, so that the fins at the north side of the building [see Figure 13.15] are very clearly about the space conditioning idea of sun shading for the building, but they also are the exterior expression. The structural moves in the building are expressed in a very honest way and a straightforward way because we are not playing games with the structure—we are simply building it and we are trying to engineer it in such a way as to be efficient and durable and kind of real—we are interested in a kind of realness.

I think in the project—and that's true on many levels: When you walk into the building you see that all the floors are concrete in the public areas of the building—they are ground, finished concrete—there is no marble, there is no stone, and there is no terrazzo even, which is a cheap material really for public spaces. We have a palette of materials that is very true to the original construction, and this is something that is difficult because in this country—say in class A office buildings—people have an expectation that there are all kinds of finishes—so you have the kind of structure of the building, and then you cover everything up with drywall and fabric and other kinds of elements like suspended ceilings—we have taken many of these things out and distilled the project down to something quite simple. I think that there isn't really any magic—it's just making each piece really work for you.

The other strategy that is involved here is a strategy that we use as public architects that work with tight budgets. These are not projects that have a lot of dollars associated with the constructions, unfortunately, and we have to be very careful that we spend the money in a way that we get the maximum impact. So we are paring down some of the elements in order to enhance other ones—and we are very conscious of this process because these big buildings are under enormous amount of scrutiny and enormous amount of review during the budgeting

Fig. 13.15 Vertical glass fins provide shading on the northwest side.

process. Anything that is seen to be superfluous—or "architectural" elements out there—is immediately attracting attention of people that want to reduce the cost—and so what you need to do is graft the performance aspects to the elements that you really want.

In this project you cannot value-engineer the sun screen out. If you do that, you now have to fully air-condition the tower. So you need to buy the space in the

Fig. 13.16 Perforated stainless steel screen and vertical glass fins on the southeast side.

floor plate literally from the lease calculation for the duct risers, and you need to provide the chillers to cool the tower, all the fan energy, everything that is required to make this work. The same with the concrete frame of the building, the thermal mass diagram. You cannot remove the concrete from the equation—you then have a building that does not work. So when you control the budget, you control all of the allocation of the resources in the design phase—you can protect all of these elements. And this is related to how you come to this marriage between the way the building looks and how it actually functions.

Cost Breakdown

TC: One of the first documents that we review is the cost breakdown of all the principal systems in the building, by percentage. So we have in front of us a document that they [GSA] have produced over many, many years constructing and managing federal properties that says this percentage will be spent on windows, this percentage will be spent on the interior finishes, this percentage on structure, this percentage on site development. These are all means that are developed over time and entered into a huge database. So what we do is that we analyze and take apart that document completely—and we try to challenge every assumption that is in there. So they assume we're going to be spending money on granite on the walls in the lobby, we say, actually no. We are using exposed concrete, which is the structure. So that money now does not go back to the government, we begin to reallocate and distribute it ourselves into the project through our cost estimating process.

This is true for the air conditioning in the building as well. The original target numbers of say, 16 or 17 percent, that were originally going to be allocated to HVAC—if we can reduce that number as we have in this project down to 9 percent of the total—or half of the assumed cost—that means that we have now 7 percent of $140 million, which is quite a significant amount of money, that we can then begin to redistribute to other areas where it is going to have the maximum benefit for our concept. So you specifically begin to analyze the cost, and this allows you to protect the design decisions, because you are armed with analytic knowledge that comes from them originally about how the money should be spent.

Operations and Maintenance

TC: At the same time we are developing a project like this with a cost/benefit analysis that is showing the owner stage by stage through the design process how many dollars we are going to save in terms of the kWh we are saving for electricity, and also run rough numbers, which are imprecise but still convincing on operations and maintenance. In school we never learn about things like O&M— it's just this kind of a strange thing that somebody will deal with after your design is implemented many years down the road.

Well, the fact is, in a project like this you so reduce the amount of chillers, cooling towers, fan motors, fire smoke dampers, all of the equipment that is required to make an office building work for a given people load—in this case 2,000 people are using the building every day. By the government's own calculation the building should cost something like $1.50 per square foot per year for maintenance and operations. It's a 6,000-square-foot building; you can do the math. The actual projected cost of O&M is about 90 cents. OK, so right there you have a figure, which depending on your interpretation of dollars varies between $200,000 and $325,000 per year—and those are dollars that are ascribed to 2004, so when you escalate those out, 3 percent a year for inflation over 50 years, you are talking about a huge sum of money that is going to be a benefit back to the owner for having gotten rid of the air conditioning.

Dollars and Sense

TC: This does not necessarily have anything to do with the global environmental crisis that we are facing—it is pure economics. It's a dollars and a business decision that they can look at and say, OK, if we want to own the building for 75 years, here is the consequence just for the maintenance and operations. WOW. And that money is going to end up in their pockets.

And this is also very important because we design a building like this that has motorized windows, for example. There is inevitably around a big conference table people who are responsible for taking care of those motors who are immediately going to stand up and say: Mr. Architect, we will not permit this to happen because you are creating an unfair burden on the federal government by having to replace mechanized elements of a window wall. We would prefer to have fixed glass that does not move, that does not operate because it's a cost issue for us. Well, if you turn around and say to them: Well, you are saving $300,000 a year in maintenance and operations on the equipment side. You have to spend a certain amount—a very small percentage—to take care of some of this wiring and the motors and the controls—and if you think that somehow these individuals are going to win the day with their argument, you are wrong because the proof is in the building. We can make the argument as a rational cost-based argument and win, but you have to have the data.

Our Job as Architects

TC: This was not taught in school, unfortunately. There needs to be a systematic analysis, and our job as architects now is less to be the kind of designer in the kind of classical sense and more to be organizers and deployers of data and information in order to protect the design integrity. And if you go and see your job in those terms, you become a much more effective, powerful part of the team, because you are no longer seen as being concerned with aesthetics or kind of the consequence as to how a building might look or its urban character or something, because you are embedded in the analysis, which is being done usually by others.

Three Modes of Breathing

TC: The window wall is divided into basically four or five different elements that work together [see Figure 13.18]. On the exterior of the building on the northwest side we have fixed sun shades that are glass elements—vertical in orientation—to protect the glass in the building from solar heat gain. This is a problem generated by the building being oriented on a northwest–southeast axis. We have low sun angles in the summer that would cause the space to overheat, unless we were able to develop these fixed sun shades. Then the window wall itself is divided into a number of elements: fixed glass at the top and bottom.

The second light of glass from the top is an element that is controlled by the building automation system: It opens to a maximum of about 225 millimeters to admit the bulk airflow that is used for actually cooling the structure, the kind of element in the natural ventilation controls—and then a large piece of glass, which is controlled by the occupant that only opens a very limited amount, but enough to bring air and the kind of perception of comfort because it is occupant controlled. We look at that out there as quite a big window that is going to be immediately adjacent to the workstation surface.

And then at the very bottom of the window we have a very developed set of elements, including a finned tube convector, which is the heating element, a hydronic system that runs the full length of the building, and then a trickle vent, which is an automated element that switches on and off in order to admit the air changes that we need to ventilate the space to meet the code when the building is in a sealed condition. That trickle vent is located proximate to the heater in the space so that we can condition that space in a kind of simple thermodynamic way, you know: proximity relationship rather than anything more sophisticated than that. We are taking advantage of the raised floor or cavity in the building to run all that hydronic tubing, the data and cabling to the workstations as well as the fire sprinklers that are serving the floor below. So it is a kind of very simple, very efficient use of the space.

Ten Modes of Natural Ventilation

TC: Generally speaking, there is a crossflow from north to south across the building driven by the prevailing winds. There are 10 modes in the natural ventilation system control sequences that show different configurations at the upper windows and the trickle vents opening and closing depending on the pressure, wind speed, and direction. Those 10 modes are in some ways perhaps an excessive number of variations in order to temper the interior environment, but we believe that it's better to start with 10 modes and reduce the operating to six rather than having to go the other direction. So, this is going to be the response. We asked the control specialists to write the algorithms based on the sequences that we produced.

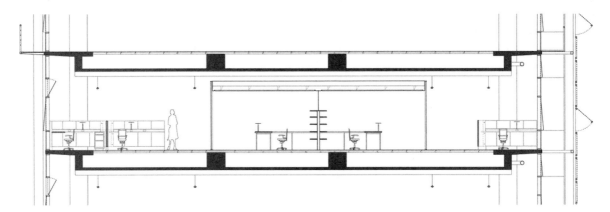

Fig. 13.18 Cross-section of typical office floor, by Morphosis.

Prevailing Winds

TC: The wind direction is predominantly from the northwest in hot weather when it is above 50°F. It's a phenomenon that has been recorded and measured. The other thing that's worth mentioning is that we looked at 50 years' worth of weather data for San Francisco based on weather tapes that are recorded at the San Francisco International Airport, which is a bit south of where we are. The airport temperatures tend to run warmer than the city by about three or four degrees F—and so we have a reasonable measure or margin of error that's built into our calculations on how the building is going to perform.

Simulations

TC: We did a lot of extensive modeling during the design phase to prove to the owner that we would be within an acceptable comfort condition. People in this country feel that they have a God-given right to 72°F plus or minus 3°F. The 72° set point is used to define thermal comfort by ASHRAE. We are going to be outside that narrow definition of human comfort in large part because we are falling under an interpretation of human comfort that has been adjusted for natural ventilation by ASHRAE. We're proud to be one of the first generations of buildings that are looking at naturally ventilated spaces as opposed to full air conditioning.

The temperature range we are working within is closer to 9°F or 10°F rather than 6°F, and we have shown through the modeling that there is a risk of the building exceeding 79 or 80°F roughly 8 hours per year, which is a very small margin. The federal government was concerned about this decision to an extent, but they also have to close buildings in Minnesota because of snow accumulation, say, and in this climate we are really not anticipating that anyone will even have to go home because it is too warm.

Dress Code

TC: In this country people tend not to dress in response to climate. When we travel in places like the United Kingdom or certainly in Asian cities that are warmer or more tropical, people dress more appropriately for the climate. This is something that used to be a learned behavior; it's going to happen as people are adjusting to the realities of diminishing natural resources in the world. When energy gets too expensive, we will be much more sensitive. We have been very lulled in the last 50 years in this country by the perception that buildings have to maintain a certain stable interior temperature no matter what happens outside.

We are not proposing a specific dress code for this building, but we do think it's very important that there are social consequences of what we design. There were many people in the early stages of this project that were trying to prohibit the use of occupant-controlled windows. And the observation was made: Well, people will not be able to remember to close the window, so if there is a wind-driven rain, the high winds are going to blow people's papers around. In essence, they were saying that you can't trust the average office worker in the federal system to close a window. And we said, this is absurd. People have opened and closed all kinds of windows for many thousands of years. I don't know how long the operable window or openings in windows have been controlled, but air conditioning was invented and fully implemented in this country in the 1920s and any buildings that predate that relied on very simple aerodynamic principles for thermal comfort.

Intelligent Systems—Intelligent Users

TC: The belief that people will use their building intelligently is true for the skip stop elevators as well. There are many people that say that the users will not learn how to walk up or down a flight of stairs to adjacent floors—it's too complicated! We have to assume a certain minimum intelligence in the population in order to accrue the benefits that are going to happen.

A User's Manual

TC: We are currently working on a kind of user's manual. If you look at a car and you go out to buy an automobile, the amount of sensing technology and the amount of smart technology in an average automobile outstrips any building that is built today in the United States. It's just a typical automobile, which is a very discrete object that cost a discrete amount of money as compared to millions and millions of dollars spent to build large construction projects. And that car comes with a manual—it comes with many pages of documentation that tells you how to optimize the performance of that vehicle. And people presumably read the manual that comes with their phone or their digital camera.

A building is no different. There are certain rules about how it's going to be used over its life span, certain rules that have to do with remodeling the building, for example, or how to optimize the use of the thermal system that we design into it, rules that will be presumably read and studied and utilized by the building occupants. It's shocking to me sometimes to consider how little heed is paid to that. It is assumed walking through a space that there is a thermostat on the wall and that we have some sort of reliable source of refrigerated air. This is a kind of an assumption. Well, we are changing that. And with that comes a certain responsibility for the tenants.

A Didactic Building

TC: We are interested in looking back. The whole notion of thermal mass in buildings is something that is timeless, and it is as old as architecture itself. It's a very simple idea and it is easy for people to grasp, and I think going back to the San Francisco Federal Building: Some of the things that we are doing here—we are trying to make the concepts very legible and comprehensible to people so when they walk in they see the ceiling and they understand that if they are in direct communication with that slab, they are going to feel cool. It's a very simple idea for people to grasp. And if we were somehow cleverly able to conceal the reality that the concrete is there, we would really not be doing our job, because we want the building to be didactic to a certain extent, to explain to people how it is working.

The Concrete and the Slag

TC: One of the things that has been discovered and widely talked about through the discussions about sustainability in architecture is that Portland cement is a filthy material during production. Portland cement is the principal component of any concrete mix design, and especially in the developing world like China and India there are tremendous air-quality issues that have emerged because of the particulates that are coming out of these concrete batch plants. There is also a tremendous amount of energy required to produce the Portland cement. You go to a city like Shanghai and you can sit down and you can have your drink and look out over an incredible panorama of neon signs, and then look hard down at the river at midnight and it's filled with barges that are filled with coal. The coal barges are filling the river 24 hours a day, and what they are doing is, they are powering this beautiful dream of this Asian kind of miracle which is Shanghai.

We need to get away from these heavy first uses of energy as part of our approach to sustainability. So one of the innovations that is happening in the concrete industry is that we are looking for materials to displace the percentage of Portland cement. The most common one is fly ash, which is a by-product of coal burning. The fly ash tends to bring the concrete up into a very dark color. It's many shades darker than the conventional concrete mix design. The benefit is that fly ash tends to be very workable in the concrete, and it is a waste material.

In rough terms, every ton of Portland cement that is created introduces one ton of the greenhouse gas CO_2 into the atmosphere. So that's equivalent to 600 pounds of carbon. Now, when you have a project like the San Francisco Federal Building that is 46,000-plus cubic yards of material—it's a lot of concrete. We were looking hard early on at what are the other alternatives. The slag that we are using is typically used in engineering applications, not in "architectural" concrete. Concrete contractors are afraid of it because they have not used it very often. We have a lot of exposed concrete in our building, and they were concerned that it was going to be flowable, that it was going to be workable, that it would not add unduly to the time it takes for the concrete to set up. We did a lot of early mockups and testing of the material, and one of the things that we discovered, among others, is that the color was coming up to a very beautiful off-white.

Many architects that have visited the building question me closely and ask whether we are using some white-pigmented cement in the mix, or "How do you afford to do this?" White cements are available, but they are very expensive and they don't tend to be easy to use for a contractor. We replaced 50 percent of the Portland cement with slag in our building. We have done some calculations that show that it would be equivalent to taking something like 12,000 cars off the road for a year because of the amount of carbon they are putting into the environment—it's really quite significant. That's an example of how we try to lower the first environmental impact of the building. The other benefit—of course—is the structural benefit. We have a shear wall–only building, which uses no moment frames. The shear walls and the columns are holding the building up. The concrete is a high-strength mix for the most part—in all the vertical elements—it's about 8,000 PSI concrete. With 50 percent slag material it is testing out anywhere between 10,500 and 12,000 PSI, which means that we are getting higher strength performance out of the same material, which is obviously a benefit. So, again, a combination of performance and sustainability and then the appearance—it's all tied together.

Bolted Hot Dipped Galvanized Steel Frames

TC: The idea of a maintenance-free building is a myth, but to a certain extent—if you look at intelligent uses of materials that you have in front of you—it is possible to create a building that has great longevity for the owners without a lot of regular maintenance. We looked at industrial type materials. In this project we have exposed concrete, we have the glass with high quality anodized aluminum frames, and for all the secondary metal structures—the roof trusses and then the sun screen itself—we looked to material that had great longevity because they had been carefully specified in the original documents. So what we did in case of the primary and secondary steel, which is attached to the concrete, were hot-dipped galvanized coatings. Wherever possible we bolted together all of the frames.

Bolting means that we don't have field welding, which would require periodic retouching and maintenance to keep the rust from happening. Over a course of maybe 20 to 25 years, the galvanizing is going to provide a completely weatherproof surface against an environment in San Francisco, which is a peninsula that has a lot of salt in the air, which is coming off the ocean. Similarly we have specified a 316-alloy stainless steel for the sun screen. There are other alloys: stainless 302 and 304 with lesser purity—they have a different compositional makeup. The 316 is a very high quality, probably the highest-quality architectural metals that you can do. The benefit again being that it will never need to be painted or treated in any way. It's going to continue to patina but the rust will not be a problem. We really firmly believe that there is an argument to be made about these materials so that people are not out there repainting or putting individuals at risk from the standpoint of having scaffolding up 18 floors off the ground.

Integrally Colored Fiber Cement Board

TC: We make a very serious effort to look at each material in the building in terms of the maximum benefit that it can pay. The same holds true for the interior of the building. As opposed to having lots of drywall and gypsum board, which will be damaged and painted over and over again, we specified an integrally colored fiber cement board, which is a very simple industrial material from Europe that is maintenance free. It is a very tough and durable material that will never need to be treated in any way other than being routinely cleaned.

Screen Transparency at 58 Percent

TC: We look at different percentages of transparency for different functions in the buildings we design—and play with these perforated metals. The material that was used in this project is a 16-gage sheet metal. We were looking for maximum openness that we could achieve through the punching of the material to create this veil or this screenlike appearance, Any percentage above 60 or 62 will cause the material to begin to deform during the process of punching the sheets so that they become very unworkable to fabricate.

We do a lot of primary research into materials in our office. We don't rely on systems that are out there, things you can find in the Sweets catalog or some other source. Nor do we rely on other people to design the components for us. We tend to work directly with the manufacturers. The first phone call that we made on this project was directly to the steel mill. We said, "Look, we want to get some pricing from the very beginning. What is it going to cost to buy 130,000 square feet of 316 stainless on a coil? What does the raw material really cost you?" This is very important because it starts to guide the cost estimators, the value engineering people, the construction manager and the owner from looking at this as being very exotic and hence unaffordable. When you begin your discussion with a steel mill, you have good data to start with that is not encumbered by all of the middlemen. You are just working with the pure material and then start taking the material through these various industrial processes to get to where you are in the building.

The way the process ran is very close to where we had mapped it out. Some of the sources that we had discovered really became the appropriate source for the actual building. We thought that was very interesting, actually.

Operable Screen Elements

TC: In retrospect, we would have preferred that the screen could be just fixed, but when we proposed a multitenant office building with the sun screen on the outside, even though we do a lot of mockups and testing of the optical qualities and light transmission of the material, people are overly concerned about the sense that they are going to be in a cage, shut in by having this exterior element that they cannot control. So at every level of the building—basically at the eye level for a sitting person—is a series of operable elements in that screen that will allow the panels to open 90 degrees so you have a completely unobstructed view. The operable elements then form a horizontal shelf in the sunscreen that will basically shade the glass. It's not going to create a heat gain problem. But again, there is a lot of wiring and motors and complications that are related to this solution—this is not ideal.

Shading Optimization

TC: We are not compromising the view or the amount of daylight entering the space. There is not really any passive solar design that is being accounted for in the modeling—it has not been looked at. If there is a passive solar benefit, it's going to be something that just accrues to the building energy performance, allowing it to run less of the hydronics heating in the winter. But the engineering side has not been formally studied. Most of the modeling and the predictions that we are doing are really on the low-energy cooling side, because that's really where the benefits accrue and where you will find the greatest risk. Heating the building in a climate like San Francisco is really not that big of a challenge. Cooling it without air conditioning is a challenge anywhere.

Source of Energy for Heating

TC: Down the street is a district heating, steam-generation plant, which serves a lot of the big buildings that are in this part of the city including City Hall and some of the state buildings. We tap into steam lines that are carried within the streets. We have future capacity to put gas-fired boilers into the building in any event that the steam generation is no longer viable—in 20 or 30 years.

Source of Energy for Cooling

TC: The chilled water comes from compressor-driven chillers that decimate the heat into the environment through cooling towers on the roof of the building. The building is fully air conditioned from levels 1 through 5 plus the basement areas. The natural ventilation scheme, supplemented with some under-floor displacement ventilation where required, is in the tower on levels 6 through 18.

Glazing

TC: We specified a high-performing insulating glass with a low-E coating on the number 2 surface. We feel that we have achieved a very high level of visible light transmittance in the glazing itself with the maximum low-E benefit in terms of performance. We are very pleased actually with the way the building feels from the interior condition right now.

Daylight and Electric Light Controls

TC: We have fully dimmable ballasts on the light fixtures. We were able to specify a well-designed fixture. We were very fortunate to be able to use this. It's 95 percent uplit with perforations on the bottom of the fixture, which are able to permit 5 percent light down—and so it is relying on reflected light off of the curved concrete ceiling. There are twin high-output T5 lamps within each fixture. They are fully dimmable. So we have a very low-cost sensing technology along the core of the building that's going to be constantly measuring the available light. It is what we call a daylight harvesting system—or that is actually a misnomer since daylight does not need to be harvested—we would rather call it a daylight utilization system. Our observation is that in a typical working day those lights will rarely be on. They are more available for people working late in the afternoon in the wintertime or anybody that's in there at night or in the very early morning.

We are supplementing the overhead lights with task lights that are attached to the workstation, which is to be very standard although it is often not in what's called systems furniture. Those task lights are going to be a supplement to any requirements that people have above and beyond the utilization of daylight. We are hoping that motion sensors will be incorporated with the task lighting. We have been working very closely on a performance spec for the furniture. The furniture in the building will have a lot to do with achieving the performance goals in respect to the ventilation and also daylight utilization.

A Loftlike Building

TC: Thom Mayne, the principal at Morphosis, has been thinking a lot about loftlike spaces. He has been spending a lot of time in New York, walking into these great buildings. Architects like them because they are simple and they are pleasing in their proportions. I don't think the federal government really would be comfortable with the idea that we would design a loft-type space. They are too kind of formal in their working environments that they set up.

This building in general represents a real departure for them in terms of what the interior environment is going to feel like. And there were efforts to transform the design into something more conventional by different interior architects who were involved. I think we managed to preserve the feeling of it as more open and maybe more industrial. I don't know if *industrial* is the right word here, but the concrete is what it is: a very honest simple material—it does not pretend to be something that it isn't. And we took great pains not to cover up all these surfaces. It is just not our aesthetic or our interest. We are good modernists in the sense that we think that materials should be true to what they are and not hide behind some cloak of something else.

The Architecture of the Well-Tempered Environment

TC: Reyner Banham wrote this beautiful book about the architecture of the well-tempered environment, and it really was about that sense of freedom. We live in a very different world now. We live in a world where we have much more available tools for analysis both of the global climate, energy resources, politics. It is now possible to say that it is irresponsible to build buildings conventionally the way they have been done in the United States for the last 75 years and then pursue an energy policy that involves chasing foreign sources of oil at the cost of many, many lives. That is just fundamentally irresponsible. Architects and engineers are somehow complicit if they continue to design buildings that overrely on fossil fuel in times when we really don't need to do so.

We now have tools that allow us to make structural connections between the decisions that we make as we design and specify materials and the consequences of those things. We should really start with a baseline, which says: We want to be responsible citizens of the planet—and I don't mean that in a kind of lofty or sanctimonious way. We have a fundamental primary responsibility because we can control many of these decisions about where the materials come from, who produces them, at what cost—and we can have a huge impact,

This is a single building designed for only 2,000 people here in San Francisco. What we are really firmly pushing now is that this building should stand something like a model to other developers and other people in this region, for example, who are looking at doing large capital-intensive or say commercial office buildings—or even residential buildings. What they really should be doing and what I think is starting to happen is that people will look at the example of this building and look at what the federal government has done and say, "Well, now why can't I do that in my 10-story office building, which I am doing across town from here, since it seems to have some good environmental exposures and things and will work?"

They could be coming up against building code and fire code issues that are going to prohibit them from having windows that can open because that is just the way it exists in San Francisco and people have labored under this regime for many years. Well, the fact that this building was able to be built by the federal government using their own reviewers and their own fire officials—not the locals—means that the building as standing becomes an emblem of an alternate path. We are achieving a higher level of fire safety for the occupants in the event of a fire than in buildings that have been approved by the local building authorities. So what we really are trying to do is to change the whole framework in which buildings are designed and approved and built. If we have done our job, we will start to see examples of how the methodology that we have used here can be applied widely.

Pigeons and Falcons

TC: Could the screen and the catwalks at each level become a gigantic bird cage? The answer: Make a pair of peregrine falcons nest up on the roof of the building. Protect the falcons' nest and let them feast on the pigeons. That will keep them away from the building—nature's own way.

LISTEN TO THE BABY KICK: NIGHT-VENTILATION COOLING WITH HIGH THERMAL MASS

In order to test the applicability of night-ventilation cooling for the three hottest days in the weather file, a night-vent cooling simulation was performed using the computer program ENERGY-10. ENERGY-10 does not perform real night-vent cooling simulations, but there is a way to trick the program into simulating the effect of high airflow rates with 100 percent outside air during the night. Doug Balcomb describes this procedure in greater detail in the ENERGY-10 help files.

The first week in July was used for this night-vent cooling exercise. There are three hot days in this week. The outdoor temperature peaks at around 95°F on the middle of the three hot days in the afternoon at around 3 P.M [see Figure

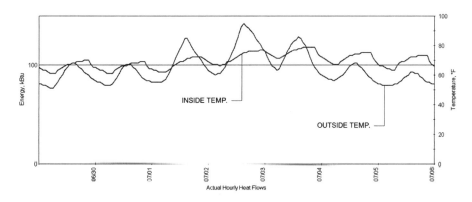

Fig. 13.19 Graph from ENERGY-10 shows how night-ventilation cooling causes the indoor temperatures to peak below the maximum ambient air temperature.

13.19]. The three hot days are followed by two cooler days. Night-vent cooling was simulated by applying a schedule where the fans would move air through the building at high airflow rates during the night and then all the systems would be shut off during the day. It was assumed that significant amounts of high thermal mass would be exposed to the interior. ENERGY-10 then calculated the predicted indoor air temperature fluctuations hour by hour due to the absorption of heat by the thermal mass during the day and the release of heat from the thermal mass to the cooler air during the night. Figure 13.19 shows how remarkably well this low-energy strategy could work in a well-designed building placed in a moderate climate, such as that of San Francisco.

The outdoor temperatures peaks at 95°F after 3 P.M., and the indoor temperature peaks at around 75°F after 9 P.M. The temperature peaks are cut and also shifted toward the time when the building is no longer occupied. Figure 13.19 shows how the building is able to coast through a series of three very hot days without overheating, even when there is no air-conditioning system. On the following two cooler days, the indoor temperatures swing above ambient temperatures, but still within the comfort zone.

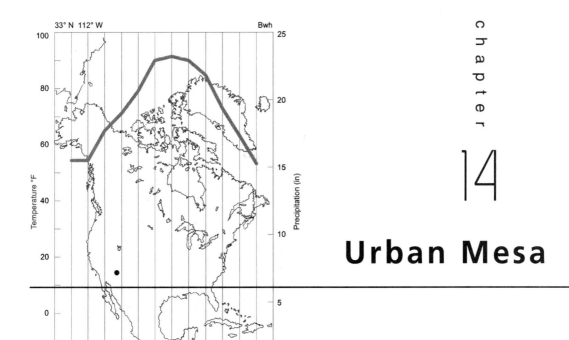

14

Urban Mesa

Burton Barr Central Library by Will Bruder

Building Type:	Library
Location:	Phoenix, Arizona
Coordinates:	33°N, 112°W
Interviews:	Will Bruder, architect
	Rosemary Nelson, head librarian
	Bill Ruehle, building operations
Site Visits:	Several, 1996–2006

This showcase building in the Phoenix public library system is located along Central Avenue in downtown Phoenix, Arizona. A high-profile building that has been widely published, it still holds some secrets that have not yet been fully explored. As claimed by the architect, this building is "near perfect," utilizing all the basic design strategies of a climate-responsive building in a hot and dry place (see Figure 14.1).

Fig. 14.1 Burton Barr Central Library by Will Bruder: Saddlebags, shade sails, and a roof that floats on light.

BUILDING AND SITE

The Burton Barr Central Library is located on Grand Avenue in Phoenix (see Figure 14.2). The five-story building is aligned with the north–south axis, with large glazed walls facing north and south. The long east and west sides of the building are protected by *saddlebags,* which are unconditioned spaces clad in a perforated copper screen.

The Great Public Reading Room on the fifth floor receives daylight from the north and south glass walls and also from circular skylights in the roof. This large room with its tall ceiling height has a raised floor with a displacement ventilation

Fig. 14.2 Aerial view of the site, from Google Earth.

system that also provides heating, ventilation, and cooling to the space. Two long east- and west-facing walls are constructed from large 12-inch-thick prefabricated concrete panels with no thermal insulation other than the concrete itself. The lower floors are conditioned by a conventional forced air heating and cooling system. Gas-fired absorption chillers deliver chilled water to the many air handling units, which are located in the saddlebags (see Figure 14.3).

The Burton Barr Central Library in Phoenix was included as a case study in the Vital Signs program (Burrelsman, Villers, et al. 1996) and was also the case study building for the Agents of Change workshop in 2004. Additional information on the Agents of Change Phoenix Workshop is posted ataoc.uoregon.edu/workshops/phoenix2004.shtml.

LOCATION AND CLIMATE

The Sonoran Desert

Phoenix is located in the Valley of the Sun at the northern edge of the Sonoran Desert (see Figure 14.4). The climate is hot and dry, with average summer day temperatures reaching the upper 100s and lower 110s (°F). The summer design-day temperatures extracted from a typical meteorological year weather file are a dry bulb temperature 107°F, with a wet bulb temperature of 70°F. An average winter day sees dry bulb temperatures in the range of 45°F to 65°F, with wet bulb temperatures ranging from 40°F to 48°F, as shown in Figure 14.5.

An average day in the early spring in March sees dry bulb temperatures from 55°F to 75°F. This is a time of year when a high mass building can float comfort-

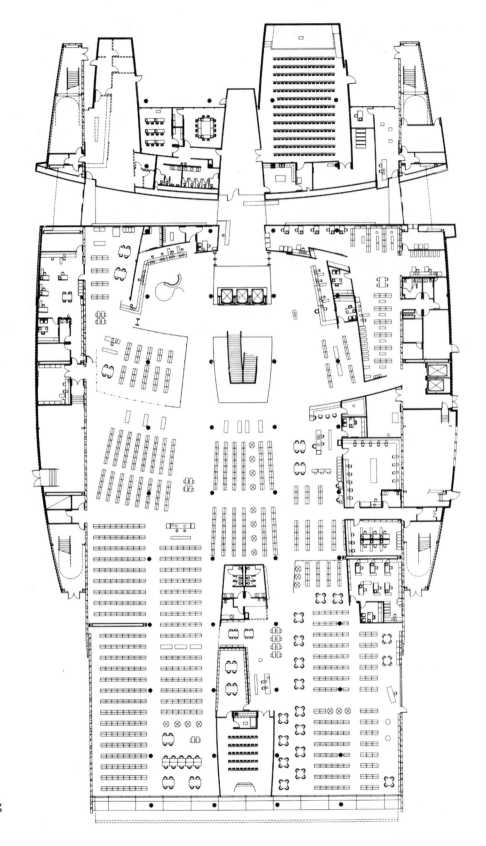

Fig. 14.3 Plan drawing of the ground floor.

Fig. 14.4 Ocotillo buds after a rainstorm in the Sonoran Desert.

ably without applying any energy for heating or cooling. Average dry bulb temperatures in the early summer month of May range from 62°F to 92°F, with average wet bulb temperatures ranging from 55°F to 65°F. A hot summer day in July typically sees dry bulb temperatures from 80°F to 105°F, with wet bulb temperatures around 65°F to 70°F.

Phoenix enjoys an abundance of clear sunny days all year-round. The beam solar radiation ranges from 200 to 250 Btu/ft² and is fairly even through all the months of the year.

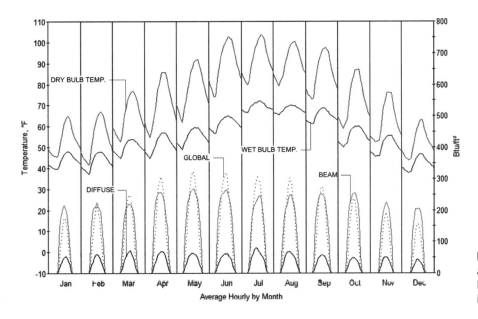

Fig. 14.5 Temperature and solar radiation for Phoenix, from Weather Maker.

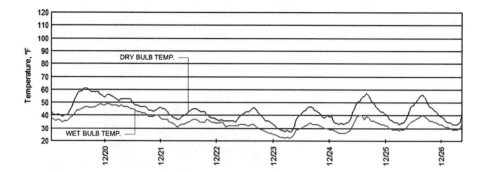

Fig. 14.6 Extreme winter week: December 20 to 26, from Weather Maker.

The coldest days in a typical meteorological year occur just before Christmas. During a week from December 20 through December 26 (Figure 14.6), the extreme minimum temperature is 28°F. The average high temperatures range from 45°F to 60°F. With most days being sunny and clear, passive solar heating is an appropriate low-energy strategy.

Average daytime temperatures during a week from January 5 through January 12 range from 60°F to 70°F dry bulb (Figure 14.7). The lows are in the 40s and 50s with a minimum low of 42°F dry bulb temperature. Again, passive solar heating is an appropriate strategy for a high-performance building design.

In the early spring week of February 26 through March 4 (Figure 14.8), the maximum dry bulb temperature reaches 84°F, with averages from 75°F to 84°F. The lows range from 45°F to 55°F. Taking the solar radiation into account, this period of the year allows for comfortable indoor temperatures without any use of heating or cooling in a well-designed building.

In the late spring week from April 26 through May 2 (Figure 14.9), highs now average 90°F with nighttime lows around 60°F dry bulb. Most buildings will now need a form of cooling system to remove heat from the interior. A well-designed building with high thermal mass can utilize night ventilation as a low-energy cooling strategy.

An early summer week, from June 7 to June 13 (Figure 14.10), illustrates a typical early summer situation with daytime high temperatures now reaching above 100°F and sometimes above 110°F dry bulb. With lows ranging from 75°F to 80°F, nighttime ventilation for cooling is no longer a viable strategy. However, with wet bulb temperatures at or below 70°F, evaporative cooling could be used as a low-energy strategy during these early summer weeks.

Phoenix has a monsoon season where the wet bulb temperature hovers around 70°F with a maximum wet bulb temperature at 74°F in a typical meteoro-

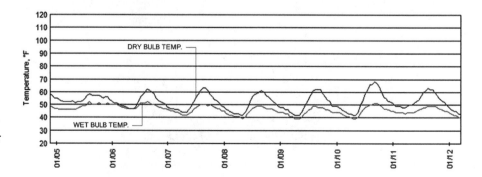

Fig. 14.7 Typical winter week January 5 to 12, from Weather Maker.

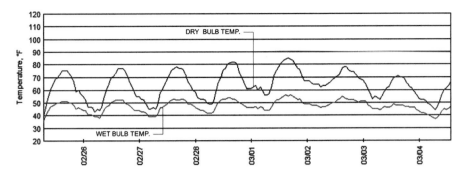

Fig. 14.8 A week in early spring: February 26 to March 4, from Weather Maker.

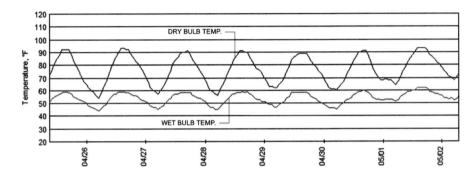

Fig. 14.9 A week in late spring: April 26 to May 2, from Weather Maker.

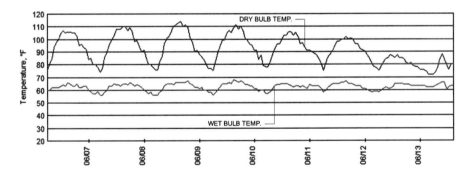

Fig. 14.10 A week in early summer: June 6 to 13, from Weather Maker.

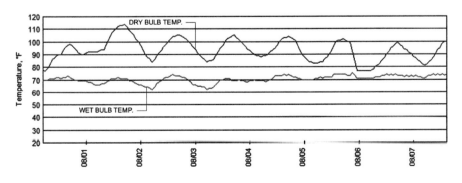

Fig. 14.11 A week during the monsoon season: August 1 to 7, from Weather Maker.

logical year. In a week from August 1 through August 7 (Figure 14.11), the dry bulb temperature reaches a maximum of 114°F. A maximum wet bulb temperature of 74°F occurs on a day when the simultaneous dry bulb temperature is 90°F. These conditions translate to a relative humidity of 50 percent and a dew point temperature of 69°F. During these extreme monsoon days evaporative cooling is no longer viable. Some sort of mechanical cooling is required, and the most predominant cooling system is the forced air system with compressor-driven chillers. Radiant cooling systems may be a more efficient and also more comfortable alternative to the forced air system, but a dehumidification system, such as a low-flow air-conditioning system, must support the radiant systems in order to avoid the risk of condensation with rising dew point.

THE DESIGN AS SEEN BY THE DESIGNER

The following are excerpts from a lecture that Will Bruder (WB) presented at the Agents of Change meeting at the Burton Barr Central Library on January 8, 2004 (Bruder and Nelson 2004).

A Green Agenda

WB: The Burton Barr Central Library speaks to an agenda that is about the future, not the past—and toward that end I could give you a foundation on how this building came to be. This building was designed from the inside out and the outside in—and that is a very important pair of phrases because most buildings are designed in different ways and for us to be talking about buildings that are compatible with this world, they have to be designed from the outside in without compromising the inside-out. That's quite important.

Now, as we look at this building from a pragmatic side of it being a library, a significant, major cultural building in the fifth largest city in America, there were certain agenda issues that had to be first and foremost. And one of those agenda items was that for Rosemary Nelson [the head librarian], she wanted a building that would work and be functional, that would allow them to serve their public and allow minimum of cost to be undertaken each year to serve that public. It had to be a very serviceable and functional building. Towards that end, we did research about the library. We wrote a 650-page document after talking to them and their peers, everybody involved in the library process. After going to five major cities and looking at recent libraries that had been accomplished and critiquing them, we had 28 citizen meetings. We empowered the community to own this building. We listened to that community.

There was not too much talking about energy and green building or any of that stuff, but again, you have to remember in 1990 when we conceived this building, *green* was not the common nomenclature—we just did it. We made it green. It was part of our agenda before we got the commission—we talked about it a little bit in getting it—it wasn't the key to our getting it—but it wasn't on everybody's lips as it is starting to be now. We have had everybody from kids to the literally challenged to historic preservation groups and community leaders. As we took input from them, a lot of the successes of what has become of this building are the results of people seeing themselves reflected in the buildings and the

Fig. 14.12 South façade, as seen from the deck park, with lower floors projecting out over the roof of the I-10 freeway tunnel.

ideas and the design. So we are doing all these things, we are trying to create a good library and a good civic building and understand that. While we are doing all this on the left side of the playing field, on the right side of the playing field—over here—we have our agenda of creating this energy-efficient, smart building, this really integrated building responding to its place.

Regionalism

WB: When we started doing this building, we wanted to design a building that literally would not fit anywhere else, a building that was site-specific to this latitude and this set of conditions and climate that you could not take it away. If you see a slide of this building somewhere and it doesn't have the name Phoenix underneath it, if you have knowledge of what a good green building would be, there would be all kinds of clues that would tell you at least the latitude, and maybe the climate and why it was the way it was. And as a detective, you could play Sherlock Holmes and you could nail the building. I think that's important. It took on another metaphorical or abstract quality that was about placemaking.

But on the other side of the playing field, we started a whole series of analyses prior to any conceptual thinking about an idea. With a group of very, very fine engineers (and that was the ARUP group in Los Angeles, California), we sat down with them while all these other meetings were going on in one area, and we said: "OK, guys, let's talk in the abstract. How can this be the best building ever built in our time? What does that mean in this desert place? How do we have to conceive it? What becomes the materiality? What is the right attitude about exposures of buildings and the things we have to think about and do? What's that all about?" So we started there equally to this other side of being a library. So it wasn't that we designed a building and then we brought this green agenda to it.

You don't do that. You start from the beginning together, in sync, to make a building that's whole and has integrity. As we start asking those questions, one of the things, obviously, that came into the diagram was issues of mass, the issues of exposure, the issues of heat and thermal swing.

And as we started understanding what mass meant, we looked back at our forebears and we looked at things like the massive mud walls, if you will, at Casa Grande. We looked at primitive cultures here that built in stone and we looked at the more primitive, but recent cultures of wonderful old adobes off the main street of Phoenix and we remembered going to a dinner party in the middle of summer and how the thermal swing was working with it. We remembered my own efforts early on, because I had been working in this town for about twenty years when this building came about. We looked at everything we were seeing happening globally, because again, you know we talk about regionalism, and regionalism is very important to the understanding of place and yet, in the world we live in today—that entire globe is our region. Global regionalism is where we've arrived at. You think about desert cities and what has happened in desert cities and what are the strategies that have made things that we can borrow and steal from and learn and modify to get there. [See Figure 14.13.]

Fig. 14.13 Massive concrete walls, here acting as side fins protecting the south façade.

A Hundred Dollars

WB: As we were getting all this information together and looking at what might have to happen, we had another little bug in the soup, and that bug was always floating on the top; it never really went away no matter how hard we stirred the pot. We had to build for a hundred dollars a square foot. So this was a bit different than ARUP being the fine engineers working with Lord Norman Foster on the Hong Kong/Shanghai Bank at a thousand dollars a square foot. We made the engineers work as hard as they worked for him, and they rose to the occasion, but for the fees for a hundred-dollars-a-square-foot building rather than a thousand-dollars-a-square-foot building. They got into the zone of understanding that we weren't kidding. This was real, there wasn't another contingency that was going to come from the federal government or the city or somebody to pay some more.

We came in at ninety-eight dollars a foot with the building that stands here today. That was always there, so strategies had to be captured that would not only be perfect, but would be perfect within the realm of reality. We wanted to build our building, we just didn't want to remember it as models and drawings and great printouts of where it might all go.

Concrete

WB: So we started again, as I often do, of trying to identify early on, again without any preconceptions, what are the possibilities of systems. As we looked at this building, and started to understand the code implications of this building, the cost implications, the constructability implications, we came across the idea that it was going to really want to be made out of concrete. And not just concrete, but at that time in this marketplace, poured concrete was not an option for an affordable building. Precast was the answer. You built precast freeway bridges, you built precast tilt-up warehouses, you built all kinds of structures out of concrete Ts, you build prisons, you build hospitals, you build all kinds of things. As we looked at that system of tinker toys, of precast construction, of columns, of beams, of Ts, of floor systems and things like that as well as wall systems on our perimeter, it seemed to be a feasible way to pursue our budget and our attention to mass. It would also be a way that we could create a building of basic honest integrity. It's a building that reveals itself.

The sandblasted finishes, and polished finishes, and rough-textured finishes of this concrete, which again wasn't just this concrete, again here we're talking about a regionally appropriate building so you would assume you build again looking at energy and where it comes from and the materials equation—all this. We have a concrete plant up in Cottonwood and one down in Tucson. We went a little farther, not much, but we went to San Diego, because the concrete in Arizona is of a tonality that's probably a 6-gray to 7-gray on scale of 1 to 10, whereas the concrete in this building is about a 3-gray. And it is the same source for cement that Louis Kahn used for the Salk Institute. So it's about finesse, it's about sophistication, it's about thinking. Is it easy? No. Is it fun? Yes. Are there bad days? Definitely. Is it a long journey? Sure, but it's all about that sort of integration. [See Figure 14.14.]

Fig. 14.14 Steel forms for the precast concrete columns, as public art.

Craft

WB: There was a day in America—Eero Saarinen was at the heart of that day—when *vision* and *invention* were not dirty words—they were common words for the practice of architecture. It was beyond what you would find at a Web site or Sweets Catalog (Web sites didn't exist back then), it just became part of doing architecture. Not too many architects are interested in or willing to pursue that, but it still happens and it can happen, and it has to happen if you want to achieve these sorts of results. We made a full bay mock-up of this building in a warehouse downtown with everything being real except we made a Styrofoam column and beam. Everything else was real.

Uninsulated Walls

WB: Now that we made this decision about precast as a key element to where we might be for the main guts of the building holding up the big loads, we decided to look back at the thermal mass question. ARUP had done enough calculations at that point to know what that meant. In their ideal world they were coming up with this very peculiar idea that at first blush you would say: "You're crazy." But it's a 12-inch-thick uninsulated solid thermal mass wall. The perimeter walls on the east and west of this building are full-blown concrete, not some sort of magic insulation inside, not some sort of magic lightweight aggregate that makes it thermally.

It's just about the situation that ARUP calculated, analyzed, looked at with the whole swings and everything based on areas and things that were starting to come into play as we understood the greater sense of the building. If everything was run properly, you would throw off the heat from about 1:32 A.M. until dawn and the whole cycle of building up heat in these walls would displace itself later, when nobody was in the building. So consequently, we have uninsulated walls. It works very well. [See Figure 14.15.]

Site Analysis

WB: We had five-plus acres of site here. It was a hodgepodge of about six different property ownerships. We have a freeway just south of us, and the reason our building drops down to two stories is that the southern edge of the building is actually carried on the freeway tunnel, which runs under the building, which we built our building on top of and created a whole system of separated beams that slide and slip because this building has no control joint. The freeway moves a quarter-inch a day, but we stay still.

Fig. 14.15 Daylight washes the smooth concrete surfaces in the Great Reading Room.

We oriented the box, if you will, north to south. This is the main street of Phoenix, Arizona, on the west side of this building. Its Main Street—its Central Avenue. We wanted an aspect of prominence on that street, and yet because of the way the little bridge comes across the park, on the southern edge we could not enter a parking lot, we could not drop people off in a bus easily, we had to come to the north and come in on the axis and enter this parking garden that surrounds it totally with desert landscape. Part of the diagram, from being sustainable and green, is looking at that landscape around our building. You can talk about the city and this building and you can define the edge because these are all desert trees. We created a desert piece that was dropped into the setting.

Design Strategy

WB: So we have a box with its long axis north–south. We have the east–west exposure, and part of what the client wanted at the time was a building that was functional and simple and orderly on a grid. What is unique about this building conceptually, there is not a left or right or emphasis heavily on one or the other, there is a total emphasis. As part of the energy diagram for one reason, but also as part of a functional diagram of how the building would work, we decided that we take the box, we move all the core functions of the box that would normally be around the elevators and the main stair—the restrooms, the mechanical support, the janitor's closet, all those things you see in any building up and down the street—and we pushed them outside the box. They live in the saddlebags of service. [See Figure 14.16.]

The saddlebags of service are covered in copper on one side; they contain emergency staircases and mechanical rooms and IT riser situations and restrooms and things like that. They do not clog up the clarity of the interior diagram, which is about books and people. It's all out there. It's also the lateral bracing system for the building because under those elements are 80-foot caissons into the foundations of this building and the huge bridge trusses that rise up to the top of the building that provide for lateral bracing, because there are no lateral bracing elements in floors 2 through 5. There had to be a couple at the joint of the deck park down there, which is an anomaly. But again, total flexibility for the owner. So as an architect you're not just thinking about energy, you're not just thinking about books, you're not just thinking about architecture, you're thinking about all these things together.

As we moved those saddlebags of service out, they provided great assistance to ARUP's diagram of thermal mass and what it means. We have essentially covered the entire thermal mass component of the building in shade. Well, in many portions of it it's in an unconditioned situation, so we're not wasting energy out there, it is shaded. And shade is a very valuable tool in the desert. It has great implications to it.

Copper

WB: The skin is copper. It is the grain elevator silo. As we look at Figure 14.17, we have fire escapes on the four corners. They are totally open, they're open by virtue of the perforations in the copper. That wall is 90 percent solid copper, 10

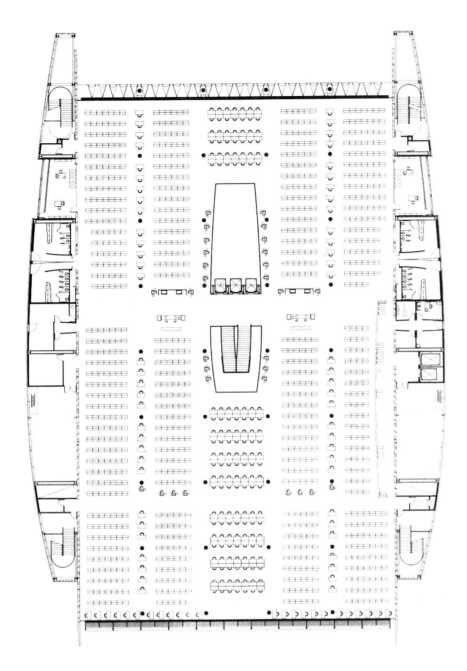

Fig. 14.16 Plan drawing of the top floor with Great Reading Room.

percent open. It's a rather phenomenal statistic. As we opened things up, we didn't want any windows to read in the saddlebags at all. So over any glass (the windows are operable for maintenance) we have the perforated skin so you can see through the transparency at night. It's very dramatic. You need 10 percent outside air for a healthy building, and we gave the skin a 10 percent perforation. It has this permeability, and it happens that way.

I wanted to do copper, so I called some very sophisticated wall-system contractors and subcontractors because we're in the big leagues—and we got absurdly obscene answers back. I called them up and said: "You know, I got these

Fig. 14.17 Perforated copper skin protects the unconditioned saddlebags.

copper sides on my building, I think they're about as big as two football fields." Then we got their attention. Now they were listening, but they weren't listening real well. They were quoting prices of over a hundred dollars a square foot—and that was a day when a square foot of copper on the open market was about four dollars, or three dollars and something a square foot.

So I remember a building down in Tempe that went up about 1974 behind the old Hayden Flour Mill, which was two big cylinders of steel. And it just looks like our building here. I tracked the company down, we called Nebraska, found out that obviously they've never done copper, but they had a spark of interest. We shipped them some copper sheets—we went out there and saw it rolled on their equipment that one hour was making grain elevators, the next hour was making experiments for some weird architect in the desert. They did fabricate it, just enough for us to make samples. A mock-up wall that was delivered here for everybody's perusal, as well as technical perusal, and we then shipped it to Florida for destructive wind testing, which did happen. But through that destructive wind testing, we understood a lot more about expansion, about fasteners, about all these things. We had about three different patterns of the sample, so we could test them and determine what was really there.

Shade Sails

WB: As we look at the north and south, there were great challenges to be dealt with there. North, we say what's the challenge there? Well, at this latitude you find from about May until about September for about three or four hours a day because of the high-rise of sun and setting of sun we have full sun across the north elevation. So the shade sails on the north side create a filtered light across this elevation. They do their real work for about three to four months out of a year. They are perforated and open weave, they are acrylic-coated Teflon fabric; they are sailboat technology. [See Figure 14.18.]

Any one person who comes from sailboat culture or sea culture will recognize the fittings of a sail top and bottom. They are standard components. It's a shading device that does not move. It is not kinetic. It's very important that it's there, because again along with this diagram of the building, as an architect conceptually I wanted anybody that drove down Central Avenue in this city to be able to look up at this building and have no doubt it was the library. And by these windows on the north and south on the main street people look up all the time, day or night and they see transparency. That was very important to the diagram.

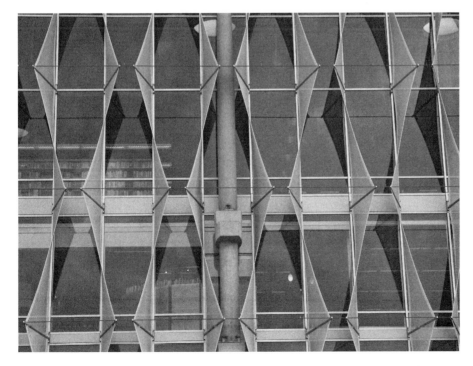

Fig. 14.18 Shade sails on the north façade.

Louvers

WB: The south side is where it really becomes outrageous. Because during the winter, during the low sun angle of this latitude the sun just comes hurling itself through this building potentially—or it would if we allowed it to. And so what we developed and devised on that side of the building was a system of standard louvers.

It was very interesting because the model for us at the time was a building at Niagara Falls, which was sort of epic at the time. We knew about a research office building there, it was four sided. It was a rather elegant building, but it was a double-walled system and we looked at that for a bit. It had louvers inside of it and we thought this was interesting and cool, but all of a sudden we discovered through our calculations that we didn't need the second skin. We didn't really need the extra layer in a hot and dry climate, but that Niagara building was an influence to where we were going with this building.

So we talked to a bunch of people in schematic design and design development and we proceeded with this idea of setting up a system of louvers with access for maintenance. We thought we were totally fine with the louvers, but by the time we had bid the building a year and a half later, all the louver companies in America had gone out of business, because postmodern architects weren't really interested in the agenda we're talking about today. And the idea of louvers on a building was a pretty questionable one. [See Figure 14.19.]

We have a computer program that reaches out to 2040 at this point that plots the sun from dawn to dusk. There's no inflection if there's a cloudy day or rainy day or anything, it was programmed to move on any day. There's a gap of approximately one-half inch between the louvers, so you get this wonderful filtered light that comes through it. It's never totally black—it manipulates the light.

Fig. 14.19 Southwest corner with copper-clad saddlebag, high mass concrete wall (vertical fin), and louvers protecting the south-facing glass.

A Global Building

WB: It is a global building. The fabric for our shade sails is from Paris, France. The louvers for the south side of the building came from Germany. Fabrication of our sails took place outside Portland, Maine, by a sail manufacturer. The idea of using copper for the cladding of the skin of this building started because Arizona was the copper state—on our license plates. Perfect, ideal, poetic, right? Value, beautiful, precious. We could not find anybody with a four-foot coil to fabricate that corrugated profile, which was done on grain-elevator equipment in Nebraska. So we went to Eastern Europe for all the copper for this building. It's a strange diagram and web we weave to how these things are built. Somebody found a four-foot coiler in Buffalo, New York, a year after this building was done.

The Great Reading Room

WB: As we move up into the great room on the top—again, it gives the building its character, it's a destination. [See Figure 14.20.] In our city nobody had, other than lawyers and bankers and wealthy people, the opportunity to go in a building and stand and look at their city from a window. The common man in Phoenix had no place like this. They could climb a mountain at one of our wonderful parks and that was cool, but it's quite different to walk to a window and stand before the proportion and scale of something like the Great Reading Room and look across your world.

We felt it very important, as illogical as it seemed for a brief flash, that we put the entire nonfiction collection-public room—the largest public reading room in America—at the top of this building. Rather than storage or boardrooms or administrative offices. It's a very special room you go up into. As we got to that room, again it was part of one level of the diagram of light and daylighting efficiency, but also the spirit of this building.

Playing with Light

WB: I've been playing with light since day one, at one level. It's interesting how things happen. A funny story of learning about light is tied to being a young man here in 1971, having worked on a gymnasium in a suburb of the community near the university. Going there one day when this big tall basketball court gymnasium had just placed the concrete tees on and I'd go there at lunchtime of course. And at lunchtime, as the sun was high in the sky, it was like a cathedral. I thought, this is the coolest thing I'd ever imagined, because there was a seep along the edge of the wall and the roof. It was really beautiful. When I came there two days later, they had put the roof on. It died. But I always remember that one day and that one moment that was magic and I'll never forget it. That was the seminal point of this detail that one can see up on the roof of this building.

As we ascend to the top of the building, the musculature of the concrete floors go from one to five. The roof could not be about that musculature because we weren't talking about similar loads. We wanted to do exposed steel. My directive to ARUP was: "I would like it to appear light and be light. I would like it to be detached at both walls on the perimeter. And wherever there's a column, I want

Fig. 14.20 The Great Reading Room, Phoenix Central Library.

a skylight. Make it happen." And the engineers came after two weeks with a fax through the machine—one 8.5 × 11 piece of paper. That is the roof one can now see. There were two and a half years more work and modal analysis to make that simplicity exist just like the sketch said it would.

Suddenly the roof floats on light at solar noon everyday through approximately six-inch edges that are 300 feet long. And then, above each column, there is a skylight because we wanted the clarity of light and not the interference of light. Each of the lenses has a film within the laminated glass over the columns. That film is blue—there's always a blue sky over the library even though Arizona doesn't always have a blue sky. It's the color of glacial ice, so there's coolness about the room that plays with your mind, psychologically. In each one of those seven-foot dishes is one small oculus that sits just south of center, and it's aligned perfectly for the summer solstice event, at solar noon. Not only does the roof float, which it does every day, but at the moment of the solstice a beam of light hits the joint of the steel connector at the top of each column and there's a dagger of light over every column and again: the dagger at Chaco Canyon, the solar observatory at Chichén Itzá. [See Figure 14.21.] We wanted to make a space that sort of placed you in the universe.

Systems Integration

WB: We looked at the mechanical system being a gas-fired system for energy efficiency. We were trying to do what was right all the time, as much as we could con-

trol and do. And in the eleventh hour, we almost had the decision to go with gas-fired chillers thrown out by the politics of the city because the electrical utilities finally found out we were doing this. They thought it would be a bad example to everybody else they were selling energy. They almost brought us down, but we prevailed.

So again, it's important to understand that it wasn't only a $98-a-square-foot budget for this building, it was a sensibility about what it would take to operate this building, and the intelligence of the systems that were conceived and executed and calculated and drawn and detailed complement that goal. I've been known as an energy master supposedly for a long time because it wasn't that my buildings were masterful in their energy consumption, but people didn't know how to deal with the strangeness or the peculiarity of these buildings. People would rationalize away the aesthetic because they didn't know how to deal with it and then classify it. "Well, must be, you know—green." I've never achieved the perfection that I've wanted to achieve in that realm. This building probably comes as close to anything I've ever done in my life to approaching excellence under that category. You can always work harder, but that's very much what it's about.

As we look at the systems again, there's a simplicity, a logic that's inherent from the saddlebags, where the main units live for the air-handling into the ceiling system, that's integrated coming from the east and west. The fifth floor has a raised computer floor, where everything comes out of the floor. At one level it is about exposed and honest. The other level is very carefully integrated. And again as we look through the whole diagram of the building there's this simplicity.

Fig. 14.22 Northwest corner with shade sails and copper-clad saddlebag.

Lessons Learned

WB: Architecturally it's there. I mean I cannot tell you: "If I had another four dollars and twelve cents a square foot to do the building, I would have done this." I think it is unfortunate that the software doesn't always make the motors over the crystal canyon work. That's been a frustration because only a few times did we get those puppies working. And occasionally a panel or a bay of the louvers on the south will not work. Those are technological glitches. The interesting thing about marking the solstice is that it's pure static geometry. We never have to worry that people are going to come and the computer's not going to work and we aren't going to have a solstice. It's a static moment that just happens with the sun.

We solved our pigeon problem with cables and nets. We did not envision the pigeon problem as we should when we started. They loved our stairwells. It would be nice if we could occupy those stairwells as reading spaces, but that's not part of our culture in our time.

I wish Parks and Recreation would really respect the desert landscape that's around this site because they've pretty well tortured it and butchered it at this point. It's irresponsible beyond irresponsible because it should be like the botanical garden at Papago Park—it should be a model.

I must say that the mechanical systems have worked out. We've had many changes within the building. We've been active as architects in rearranging several things. We just rearranged the children's area. So the building lived up to all the things we envisioned for the flexibility. That's cool. It isn't static. If you look at the map of the building when we opened, you're going to find a whole bunch of things that have moved on the chessboard just like we said they would.

It's still one killer party building. That's another plus we had envisioned when we built the building, that it would be the best place in town to have a party. A lot of people think so. So there are a lot of fundraisers that happen in our building and a lot of other things that happen in our building. It's the preferred venue for urban events that make a great city great.

The Canyon and the Mesa

WB: You go through a lot of phases of the project. As you enter the site from First Street, that alignment was at the time being studied as an art walk. I proposed to make a subterranean canyon along this alignment, eight stories deep with the top two stories being shops and boutiques and galleries, and six stories of underground parking on an open canyon. So you would have the canyon against the metaphor of the mesa. And again this metaphor of a mesa comes from the fact that as we're looking for images that will enable us to communicate.

This building was a big, bold step, and I learned a lot on this one. The biggest building I had done before this was one-tenth as big as this one. The reality is that people are scared of forms and shapes that are different, they are scared of change and the tools that you have as architects are not going to be your printouts from your computers, they're not going to be your renderings or your models, they're going to continue to be your ability to communicate with words and talk to them. Give them comfort and visualization through words and metaphors and ideas: a crystal canyon, a saddlebag of service, a mesa. In Arizona we don't talk about buildings like they do in Chicago or Manhattan. It's not talking about the Empire

Fig. 14.23 Urban mesa: View of the Phoenix Central Library from Interstate 10.

State Building or talking about the Sears Tower. We talk about the desert landscape, we talk about our mountain ranges. Those are the names we give things.

I wanted to bring an illusion of abstraction from the landscape rather than from a built nomenclature of this place. So it becomes an abstract mesa, its scale is on the edges. Its scale was defined for the building to be viewed from the freeway stacks about two miles out on both the east and west flanks of the freeway that goes under the building [see Figure 14.23]. You see it at one scale of abstraction there or you come up close to it—it's still abstract. And yet then there's the ribbing and the scale and the truck siding on the bottom and the top, the grain elevator siding. You can feel the ribs and there's a whole set about it.

You can't whine about what you can't do—everybody wants your best. A good architect will not sign a contract document that says: "As an architect we will like you to only perform at 72 percent of your best—that's what we will pay for, that's what we want. Any more, you're in trouble."

Learning from Soleri

WB: This building would not be here without Paolo Soleri's Cosanti. I worked with Paolo in 1967 to 1968 at Cosanti and Arcosanti. Cosanti is a place built from nothingness; it's the ultimate statement of the ordinary becoming the extraordinary, what you can do and dream of. When you are building for this kind of budget you have to have the vision that Paolo had. Paolo Soleri had just completed his drawings for a city on the mesa—the first Arcosanti project below the rim where he is actually building right now. It's about the big ideas.

LISTEN TO THE BABY KICK: ANNUAL ENERGY USE

Historical data on annual energy use was provided by the city of Phoenix. The graph in Figure 14.24 shows monthly values in kWh/m² for the total energy

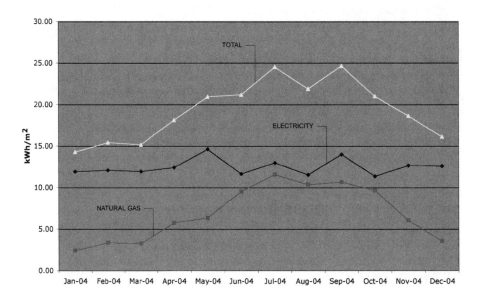

Fig. 14.24 Energy use for the year 2004, by month and by energy source (electric and natural gas).

used, with breakdowns into electricity and natural gas. Natural gas is mainly used for cooling, since the building is equipped with gas-fired absorption chillers. Gas is also used for the boilers that deliver hot water for lavatories and for heating. Figure 14.24 is based on actual energy-use data for 2004, and the numbers were converted into SI units for comparison. The total specific energy-use average is 225 kWh/m^2 per year, based on data for 2004 (232 kWh/m^2 per year) and 2005 (221 kWh/m^2 per year). This is quite good for a building that is more than 10 years old, considering the extended hours of operation for a central library and the severe desert climate. The number corresponds to the actual annual energy use for education buildings in the United States (refer back to Figure 1.3), which one can assume have a different load profile and significantly fewer hours of operation.

According to Rosemary Nelson, the head librarian, the building uses roughly half the energy per unit of floor area as compared to the building that it replaced.

The curve in Figure 14.24 reflects the relative significance of air conditioning as a major end use. While the use of electricity (lights, plug loads, fans, elevators) is relatively constant throughout the entire year, the use of natural gas follows a curve that is comparable to the monthly distribution of cooling degree-days.

EXPERIMENTAL EVALUATION

This section reports on findings from analyzing a data set generated by HOBO™ data loggers that were placed at various locations inside the library during 2005.

Instrumentation and data acquisition started in March 2005 and continued until early January 2006. Two data loggers and four external sensors were used to monitor temperatures resulting from heat transfer through the 12-inch-thick concrete wall between a corridor and an air handler room on the west side at the third floor. Two additional data loggers and five external sensors were used to monitor air temperature stratification at the northeast corner of the elevator tower in the fifth-floor Great Reading Room.

The wall heat transfer data set is complete from March until November. One of the loggers (on the saddlebag side) stopped working in November, while the other (on the corridor side) recorded data until January 2006. The sensor that was placed into the core of the concrete wall was accidentally pulled out during a few summer weeks. The data for this short summer period are therefore unreliable.

One of the data loggers at the tower was lost to vandalism some time during the summer. The four external sensors from this logger were retrieved, but the data from the end of June until the end of year 2005 were permanently lost. We therefore have a complete data set for the tower location for three months: from March 19 until June 19. In the desert climate of Phoenix, weather data from mid-March to mid-June serve well as recordings of conditions changing from the end of winter to the early summer. With these limitations in mind, the data set is still sufficient to analyze the performance of the concrete wall and the stratification in the Great Reading Room.

The 12-Inch Concrete Wall

The instrumentation was limited to a section of the wall on the third floor (west side) where the wall forms a thermal barrier between an air-conditioned corridor (inside) and an unconditioned air handler room (outside). The air handler room is protected by the perforated copper screen as the only exterior wall.

Although this experimental setup represents a typical condition, one should also note that the 12-inch-thick concrete wall acts as an interior wall in some cases, where the lavatories project out into the saddlebags. In other cases, like the south end of the Great Reading Room, the uninsulated concrete wall is actually the (unprotected) exterior wall, as seen in Figure 14.16 and Figure 14.19.

West Concrete Wall—March 16

March 16 was the coldest day in March 2005 and therefore can be seen as a typical early spring day in Phoenix. Although the average outside temperatures (on the saddlebag side) are below the indoor temperatures (Figure 14.25), the maximum outside air temperature is equal to the indoor air temperature (on the corridor side) at the peak around 6 P.M. The minimum outside air temperature is about 53.7°F at 7 A.M. The core temperature of the concrete wall is fairly stable and fluctuates between 66°F and 69°F. The greatest temperature difference between the core and the inside air is approximately 5 to 6 °F.

It is worth noticing that the minimum ambient air temperature on this day was 46°F, according to the data obtained from the Climate Vault for Phoenix. At this time of the day (on the coldest day in March 2005), the core temperature of the wall was 21°F to 22°F above the ambient air temperature outside the saddlebag screen.

In this "early spring" state, the heat transfer is directed outward. The building is losing heat to the saddlebag zone at a fairly constant rate. Further analysis is needed to determine the scale and significance of this heat loss relative to other heat loss components of the building, but the small number for the average temperature difference between the indoor air temperature and the concrete wall

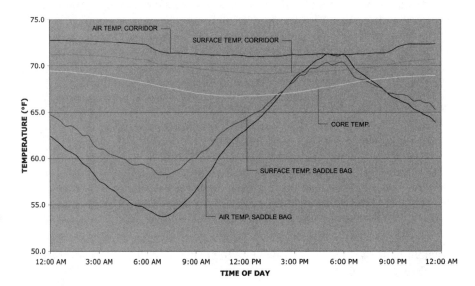

Fig. 14.25 A 24-hour snapshot of temperature fluctuations in and adjacent to the 12-inch-thick concrete wall on March 16, 2005.

core temperature (approximately 3°F) indicates that the heat loss through the wall is minimal.

West Concrete Wall—July 15

July 15 was the warmest day in July 2005 and can therefore be seen as a typical summer day in Phoenix. Although the average outside temperatures (on the saddlebag side) are well above the indoor temperatures, the minimum outside air temperature approaches the indoor air temperature (on the corridor side) at around 7 A.M. (Figure 14.26). The maximum outside air temperature (inside the air handler room) reaches 100°F at 6 P.M. The core temperature of the concrete wall is fairly stable and fluctuates between 83°F and 85°F. The greatest temperature difference between the core and the inside air is approximately 4°F—at midnight.

It is worth noticing that the maximum ambient air temperature on this day was 116°F. At this time of day (the warmest day in July 2005), the core temperature of the wall was 32°F below the ambient air temperature outside the saddlebag screen.

In this state, the heat transfer is directed inward. The building is gaining heat from the saddlebag zone at a fairly constant rate. Further analysis is needed to determine the scale and significance of this heat gain relative to other heat transfer components of the building. As noted earlier, the heat loss through the wall seems rather small, since the average temperature difference between the core and the inside air is only 3°F to 4°F.

West Concrete Wall—Seasonal Performance

Figure 14.27 illustrates the seasonal variations from March through November. If one defines the turning points between winter and summer as the points in time where the average ambient air temperature balances with the average indoor air temperature, the summer in Phoenix can be described as a six-month season starting on April 15 and ending on October 15. Coincidentally, this is also the sea-

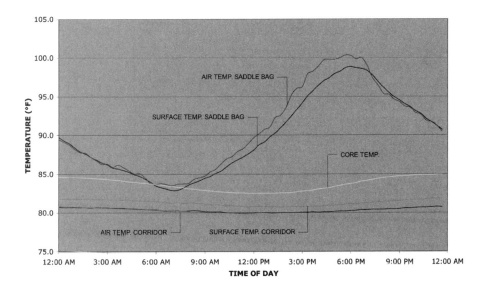

Fig. 14.26 A 24-hour snapshot of temperature fluctuations in and adjacent to the 12-inch-thick concrete wall on July 15, 2005.

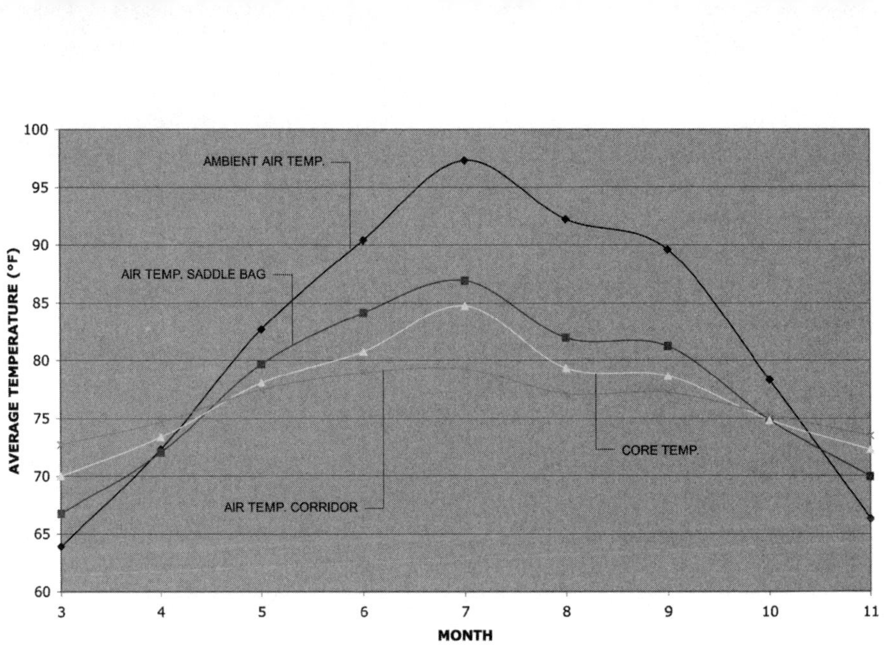

Fig. 14.27 A visualization of the average monthly temperature fluctuations in and adjacent to the wall. The average monthly ambient (outside) air temperature is from the Climate Vault page at the National Weather Service Web site for Phoenix.

son when the water temperature in an unheated outdoor pool is comfortable for swimming.

The July data for the core temperature may not be reliable, since the sensor accidentally dropped out from the wall for a couple of weeks during this time. That taken into consideration, we see that the difference between the average core temperature of the 12-inch-thick concrete wall and the average indoor air temperature fluctuates between zero at the turning points and plus or minus 3 to 4°F during the summer and the winter.

It is worth noticing that the monthly average air temperature on the saddlebag side of the wall is about 10°F lower than the monthly average ambient air temperature during the hottest summer months. This phenomenon results from the fact that the perforated copper screen renders the outside of the concrete wall in full shade. Without the unconditioned, but shaded saddlebag, the wall performance would have been quite different. Therefore, the results from this specific investigation are only valid for this particular building and cannot be seen as evidence that uninsulated west-facing concrete walls work well in the Sonoran Desert.

STRATIFICATION

Great Reading Room—March 19

The purpose of monitoring the Great Reading Room with instruments was to analyze potential air temperature stratification in the space as an indicator of the performance of the displacement ventilation system that is also used for heating and cooling. The air enters the room through diffusers located in the raised floor and leaves the space at about 10 feet above finished floor level through the saddlebags.

Figure 14.28 shows that there is little or no significant stratification in the space during the winter season. There is a slight increase in air temperatures from T2 to T6, but the air temperature near the floor (T1) is less than 1°F below the air temperature at the top (T6). This is a reflection of the fact that heat is delivered to the space as warm air coming out of the floor vents at this time.

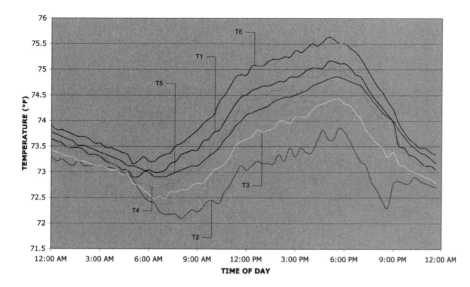

Fig. 14.28 A 24-hour snapshot of air-temperature fluctuations in the Great Reading Room on March 19, measured at the northeast corner and at the top of the elevator tower. T1 through T6 are air temperatures registered at vertical increments starting at 3 feet above the finished floor (T1) and ending at the top of the railing above the tower (T6).

The lowest registered air temperature at the top of the tower railing was 58°F at 1:20 A.M. on December 18, 2005. This is probably well below the night setback. If so, the data indicate that the air temperature in the upper zone of the Great Reading Room (above the occupied zone) fluctuates quite significantly.

Great Reading Room—July 19

The graph in Figure 14.29 shows that there is significant stratification in the space during the summer season. The increase in air temperatures from T1 to T6 reaches 10°F in the late afternoon. In this mode, heat is removed from the space as cool air is coming out of the floor vents.

The highest registered air temperature at the top of the tower railing was 92.5°F at 7:20 P.M. on July 22, 2005. This is well above the set-point temperature in the occupied zone. Again, the data indicate that the air temperature in the upper

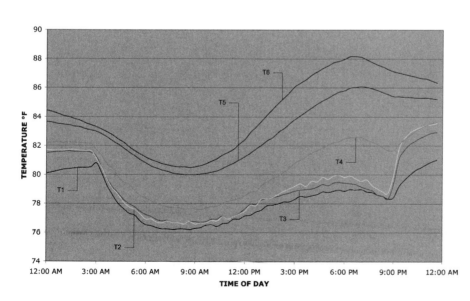

Fig. 14.29 A 24-hour snapshot of air-temperature fluctuations in the Great Reading Room on July 19, measured at the northeast corner and at the top of the elevator tower. T1 through T6 are air temperatures registered at vertical increments starting at 3 feet above the finished floor (T1) and ending at the top of the railing above the tower (T6).

Fig. 14.30 View of the Great Reading Room with the external louvers closed.

zone of the Great Reading Room (above the occupied zone) fluctuates quite significantly, both in the winter (below the comfort zone) and in the summer (above the comfort zone).

The fact that the air temperatures in the upper regions of the Great Reading Room (above the "occupied" zone) is allowed to fluctuate greatly is often seen as a proof of energy efficiency. This is an important feature of the displacement ventilation principle. If the Great Reading Room had been conditioned with a conventional forced-air system based on mixing of the air in the entire volume, more energy would be spent for heating and cooling the space. Another advantage of the displacement ventilation system is that it leaves the floating roof clear of any clutter from ductwork needed for mechanical systems.

The high maximum air temperatures recorded at the top of the elevator tower in the summer (and likewise, the low minimum air temperatures in the winter) could also be seen as an indicator that the building energy performance could benefit greatly from added roof insulation.

USER SATISFACTION

The following is a client's statement that the head librarian Rosemary Nelson (RN) presented at the Agents of Change meeting at the Burton Barr Central Library on January 8, 2004 (Bruder and Nelson 2004):

RN: I do about 50 tours a year of this building for architects and engineers from all over the world. I can attest that it's a world-class building. It's been recognized as one, and it will be for many years to come. I tell young architects that I think the key to a successful project is listening to your clients. If they are not articulate, make them articulate and then listen to them. I have seen many libraries that don't work and it's because the staff was not articulate enough to get the ideas and the concepts across to the architects. Will (Bruder) not only brought his experience from building us some branch libraries prior to designing the central library, but he also brought a team that was willing to listen to us. The other key to the success of the functionality of this building is that we involved staff at all levels. Everybody got to see their piece, everybody got to talk about how their workflow should go and as a result, when the director of the Los Angeles Public Libraries brings her clients here for one of my fabulous tours, she tells them it is not only a building of its place, it is the most functional central library that's been built in this country. I think it's all about everybody dropping their ego and just sitting down and really communicating to make a project happen with a goal to satisfy not only the architect, but to satisfy the client as well.

chapter 5

Summary of Part Two

This short summary describes how the method presented in Part Two was used as a guide to the investigation of seven buildings from around the Northern Hemisphere. The method was developed as a theory of how one can learn from real, contemporary buildings. The analyses of the seven buildings are not complete in the sense that each and every one of the 15 steps described in Part One of this book was fully explored. The investigation of the seven buildings is, however, a valuable volume of knowledge that has provided insight into how these buildings work and how they perform.

Here follows a summary of some of the findings from Part Two:

NOT BUILT AS DESIGNED

Upon arrival at the building, one will sometimes find that there are features of the design that do not make it into the built object. This was true for the light shelves at the iGuzzini building, which were a significant part of the daylight design concept. The predicted performance of the light shelf design was studied extensively under an artificial sky in a test conducted at the École Polytechnique Fédérale de Lausanne (EPFL). This feature of the design did not make it into construction, but it has still been included in several publications. This finding not only underscores the importance for the architect to make sure that important energy-saving and performance-enhancing features make it into construction, but also underscores the importance of the site visit as crucial to understanding how buildings work.

NOT PERFORMING AS PREDICTED

The site visits that were organized as part of the research for this book also revealed examples of performance features that deviated from the design as published. These findings are not necessarily negative or disappointing. As for the wall vents at the Nature Institute in Nuuk, Greenland (Chapter 8), it was found that indoor air quality and user comfort did not suffer significantly. In terms of energy efficiency, the building performs quite well considering the severe (arctic) climate conditions at the site. There are indications in the finding from this investigation that the low airflow rates may be one of the most important contributors to the high performance of this particular building.

Other findings may be seen as indications of unrealized potentials for energy savings. One example is the Aasen Centre (Chapter 9), where constant indoor air temperature and relative humidity was a determining design premise for the mechanical systems. Significant differences in the indoor surface and air temperatures were found on a summer day in 2005, while no evidence was found that the exhibited artifacts were suffering from these deviations from the predicted performance. Sergio Fox, who was the main climate engineer on the Pihl & Søn building (Chapter 10), and also on the Winter Palace restoration project, explained in our interview how artifacts react differently to fluctuations in temperature and relative humidity, depending on the time scale. Greater temperature swings may be allowed in slow-acting museum buildings stabilized by high thermal mass. This realization may be used as an encouragement to employ methods of passive heating and cooling strategies in high-performance buildings designed to house artifacts.

ANNUAL SPECIFIC ENERGY USE

Actual historic energy-use data based on utility records were obtained for four of the seven buildings that were investigated. Partial data were presented for the Post Tower (Chapter 11), but these numbers were generated from estimates based on actual data. The building owner refused to provide historic data for the total energy use of this building. For the iGuzzini building (Chapter 12), no actual data could be produced since the new building is an addition to an older office building and the two buildings sections are measured by one meter. There are no data available for the San Francisco Federal Building (Chapter 13) because it was not yet occupied at the time of writing.

Three of the four buildings where data are available show quite promising results. The two office buildings described in Chapters 8 and 10, both designed by KHR, use from 160 to 180 kWh/m² per year. These are numbers that are very close to new proposed energy standards for Northern Europe, a result that is quite impressive considering that the two buildings are more than 10 years old. The public library building (Chapter 14) checks in at 225 kWh/m² per year, which is also impressive, considering that this building was designed in the early 1990s and also taking into account the extended hours of operation and the severe (hot and dry) climate. These three buildings benefit from innovative features of their design, such as natural ventilation combined with passive cooling (Chapter 8 and

10), or gas-fired absorption chillers combined with displacement ventilation (Chapter 14). The last building where measured data were available (Chapter 9) exhibits an innovative and highly acclaimed architectural design combined with very conventional mechanical systems, which in turn may be seen as an indication of a potential for significant energy savings that could be realized through a more innovative approach to the environmental control systems design.

COMPARING APPLES TO ORANGES

The process of analyzing and understanding why condensation in the fan coil units at the Post Tower was not a great concern led to a preliminary study of the same issue as it pertains to the fan coil units at the iGuzzini building. In both cases, design-day data were used to generate graphs of the dew point fluctuations under extreme climate conditions at each unique location.

The lesson learned here is that once a workable method of investigation is developed, comparative studies may be carried out with little additional effort. These comparative analyses then generate insight into how and why some features work perfectly in one location and may fail severely if uncritically transferred to another building at a different place. This underscores the importance of the message that the performance of each building can only be understood fully after a site visit and a careful investigation of the generated data.

The condensation study led to a deeper understanding of the relationship between the climate and the type of systems used in a high-performance building. The application of passive cooling at the San Francisco Federal Building cannot be disconnected from the office floor layout, the orientation of the building, the prevailing winds, and the generally cool ambient air. The avoidance of condensation in the fan coil units at the Post Tower cannot be disconnected from the use of groundwater for cooling (16°C supply temperature) combined with radiant cooling embedded in the exposed concrete ceilings. The fact that the fan coil units at the iGuzzini building required condensing water drains cannot be isolated from the local climate conditions with high summer dew point temperatures—and the fact that the forced-air system requires chilled water supply temperatures below at 12°C.

It is important to realize that the strength of a comparative analysis of high-performance buildings lies in the fact that each building, if successful, is uniquely designed for its location and climate. Only when this is fully understood is it possible to learn from comparing apples and oranges.

TRANSPARENCY

In modern architecture, transparency is often used as a metaphor for democracy. Deutsche Post World Net sees transparency as a vehicle in the transformation and modernization of the German postal system into a self-governed organization that aims at being one of the top players in the worldwide business of shipping. The translation of the concept of transparency into the architectural design, as a major metaphor for democracy or as a vehicle for competitiveness in the global marketplace, still demands contemplation. Transparency, as it is often interpreted in contemporary (modern) architectural design, appears on three levels:

1. There is transparency from the outside in. Since many buildings now use an envelope that is completely made out of glass, there is (at least theoretically) an opportunity for the greater community (the public) to look into their inner workings by peaking in through the façade.
2. There is transparency from the inside out, which provides the users with the opportunity to enjoy an outside patio or garden as an extension of the interior, or enjoy wide views of the surrounding landscape.
3. With the widespread use of interior walls made entirely of glass, there is also an inner transparency. In an office building of the future, this type of transparency may be seen as promoting cooperation and communication, but it may also be experienced as a mild form of surveillance.

In an office layout with transparent walls to the corridor and opaque walls defining each workstation, the office worker may experience that the opaque partition walls prevent visual communication with fellow workers, while any person passing by in the corridor can look into each individual workstation. This particular arrangement exhibits a certain affiliation with J. Bentham's Panopticon, as a

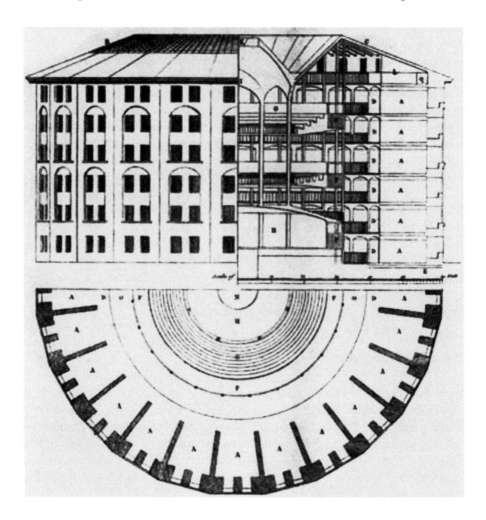

Fig. 15.1 J. Bentham. Plan of the Panopticon.

Fig. 15.2 Danish architecture firm C. F. Møller's contribution to an international competition for the most energy-efficient office building in Europe, with a predicted annual specific energy use of 64 kWh/m² per year.

prison described by the French philosopher Michel Foucault (Foucault 1995; see Figure 15.1).

One of the characteristics of the Panopticon, which was seen as an improvement at the time, was that one inmate could not see the inmates next door, while one guard could see all the inmates from one location. In his discussion of the Panopticon, Foucault writes:

> Each individual, in his place, is securely confined to a cell from which he is seen from the front by the supervisor; but the side walls prevent him from coming into contact with his companions. He is seen, but he does not see; he is the object of information, but never the subject in communication (Foucault 1995, p. 200).

The purpose of introducing Foucault's description of Bantham's designs here is not to suggest that the "office of the future" is a modern version of the Panopticon. It is, however, necessary to make an attempt to understand the concept of transparency in modern architecture and the many ways this concept may be trasferred to the built object. This is particularly important because excessive use of glass as the main component of the exterior wall will often contribute to the building performing below the optimum. There is therefore a need to develop new additions to the contemporary architectural language that deal with the size and shape of the apertures that transfer heat, light, and solar radiation. When the fully glazed façade, free from its load-bearing function, was introduced in modern architecture, it was a revolutionary move. Today, the architect should revisit this move in a critical and creative exploration of the appropriate form for each building type in its climate and location.

References

CHAPTER 1

ASHRAE (1999). *Applications handbook* (IP edition).

ASHRAE (2006). "Building sector unites to confront global climate change." Retrieved 12/1/06, from www.ashrae.org/pressroom/detail/16042.

Banham, R. (1962). "The environmentalist." *Program*: 57–64.

Banham, R. (1966). "Frank Lloyd Wright as environmentalist." *Arts and Architecture* 83: 26–30.

Robinson, N. A., UNCED, et al. (1992). *Agenda 21 & the UNCED proceedings*. New York: Oceana.

CHAPTER 2

Brown, G. Z., and M. DeKay (2001). *Sun, wind & light: Architectural design strategies*. New York: John Wiley & Sons.

McKnight, T. L. (2000). *Physical geography: A landscape appreciation*. Upper Saddle River, NJ: Prentice Hall.

Moore, F. (1993). *Environmental control systems*. New York: McGraw-Hill.

Olgyay, V. (1963). *Design with climate: A bioclimatic approach to architectural regionalism*. Princeton: Princeton University Press.

Stein, B., J. S. Reynolds, et al. (2006). *Mechanical and electrical equipment for buildings*. Hoboken, NJ: John Wiley & Sons.

CHAPTER 3

Ahnfeldt-Mollerup, M. (1998). "Grønlands Naturinstitut [Greenland's Nature Institute]." *Arkitektur DK* 42(6): 332–342.

Neumann, O. (2004). "Greenland's Nature Institute, Siaqqinneq, Nuuk—KHR arkitekter AS." *On Site* (11): 60–61.

SketchUp (2006). "Three-dimensional model of a city." Retrieved 10/15/06, from sketchup.google.com.

CHAPTER 4

Lawson, M. (2004). *Front row: Norman Foster.* United Kingdom, BBC Radio 4.

Lerum, V., and R. Harrison (2004). Interview. London.

Powell, K., S. Dawson, et al. (2004). "Sterling Prize 04." *Architects' Journal* 220(20): 28–72.

CHAPTER 5

Banham, R. (1966). "Frank Lloyd Wright as environmentalist." *Arts and Architecture* 83: 26–30.

Fehn, S. (1999). "Interview with Sverre Fehn." *A + U: Architecture and Urbanism* (1): 14–19.

Foucault, M. (1982). *The archaeology of knowledge and the discourse on language.* New York: Pantheon Books.

Gutsa, T. (1998). *Listening to the baby kick,* 1998—Opal Stone." http://www.artthrob.co.za/01mar/news.html.

Møller, H. S., and S. Fehn (1997). "Sverre Fehn—an interview with the Norwegian architect." *Living Architecture* (15): 211–213.

CHAPTER 6

Halvorsen, K. (1987). *A forske pa samfunnet—En innforing i samfunnsvitenskapelig metod.* Oslo: Bedriftsokonomens Forlag.

Lave, L. A., and J. G. March (1993). An introduction to models in the social sciences. Lanham, MD: University Press of America.

Robinson, K. S. (2002). *The Years of Rice and Salt.* New York: Bantam Books.

Sundt, E. (1865). "Norlandsbaadea." Folkeveunen:40.

CHAPTER 8

Forskrift om endringer i forskrift 22.1.1997 (2007). nr. 33 til Plan—og bygningsloven om krav til byggverk og produkter til byggverk (TEK): 9.

Lerum, V. (1996). "Energy-efficient office buildings at high latitudes." *Architecture.* Trondheim, Norwegian University of Science and Technology. Dr. Ing: 281.

Lerum, V. and O. Neumann (2005). Interview. Nuuk.

Lerum, V. and K. Nygaard (2005). Interview. Nuuk.

Siewertsen, B. (2007). "Vejrarkiv." Retrieved 3/20/07, from http://www.dmi.dk/dmi/vejrarkiv-gl?region=7&year=2006&month=3.

CHAPTER 9

Fehn, S. (1993). "Maison expérimentale, Mauritzberg." *Architecture d'Aujourd'hui* (287): 104–107.

Fehn, S. (1999a). "Interview with Sverre Fehn." *A + U: Architecture and Urbanism* (1): 14–19.

Fehn, S. (1999b). "The primitive architecture of Morocco." *A + U: Architecture and Urbanism* (1): 40–43.

Fehn, S. (2001a). "Aukrustsenteret: Sverre Fehn, sivilarkitekt MNAL." *Byggekunst: The Norwegian Review of Architecture* 83(2): 72.

Fehn, S. (2001b). "Ivar Aasen-tunet: Sverre Fehn, sivilarkitekt MNAL." *Byggekunst: The Norwegian Review of Architecture* 83(2): 73.

Lerum, V., and O. Hegge (2006). Interview. Grorud.

Møller, H. S., and S. Fehn (1997). "Sverre Fehn—an interview with the Norwegian architect." *Living Architecture* (15): 211–213.

Statsbygg (2001). "Ivar Aasen-tunet." Oslo, Statsbygg: 19.

Statsbygg (2005). "Energiforbruk i statens bygninger 2004." Oslo, Statsbygg: 55.

Tournier, M. (1982). *The four wise men*. Garden City, NY: Doubleday.

Tussa (2007). "Welcome to Tussa." Retrieved 3/20/07, from http://www.tussa.no/default.asp?menu=464&id=.

Wiggers, L. (1994). "Erklaerede uøkologer." *Arkitekten* 96(17): 596–598.

Wikipedia (2007). "Pegasus." Retrieved 3/20/07, from http://en.wikipedia.org/wiki/Pegasus.

Wolleng, T. (1979). *Håndbok 33: VVS-tekniske klimadata for Norge.* Oslo: Norges Byggforskningsinstitutt.

CHAPTER 10

Bergsøe, N. C. (2001). "Detailed monitoring report." *NatVent work package 2: Performance of naturally ventilated buildings.* Copenhagen: Danish Building Research Institute (SBI): 19.

Christoffersen, J., E. Petersen, et al. (2001). *Architecture, energy, and daylight. By og Byg Resultater.* Copenhagen: Danish Building Research Institute: 64.

Encyclopaedia Britannica (2006). "Diffusion." Online edition, retrieved 10/22/06, at www.britannica.com.

Lerum, V. (1996). "Energy-efficient office buildings at high latitudes."
Architecture. Trondheim, Norwegian University of Science and
Technology. Dr. Ing: 281.

Lerum, V., and S. Fox (2006). Interview. Copenhagen.

Lerum, V., and J. Søndergaard (2005). Interview. Copenhagen.

Wikipedia (2006). "Dilution." Retrieved 10/22/06, from http://en.wikipedia.org/
wiki/Dilution.

CHAPTER 11

Blaser, W. (2004). *Post Tower: Helmut Jahn, Werner Sobek, Matthias
Schuler/Werner Blaser*. Basel: Birkhäuser.

KA (2004). Architektur macht flessig: Angenehme Räume verändern die
Menschen. Rhein-Zeitung. Koblenz: 1.

Lerum, V., G. R. Beckman, et al. (2005). Interview. Chicago.

Lerum, V., S. Reuss, et al. (2005). Interview. Bonn.

Reuss, S. (2006). Bonn Weather File. V. Lerum: 2.

CHAPTER 12

AW (1998). "Hauptverwaltung der Firma iGuzzini in Recanati, Italien."
Architektur + Wettbewerbe (176): 8–9.

Cucinella, M. (2000). "Architettura e sostenibilita: More with Less."
Arca (149): 2–3.

Cucinella, M. (2004). *Works at MCA (buildings and projects)*. Bologna.

IA (1998). "Auf der Sonnenseite: iGuzzini Hauptverweltung in Recanati, Italien."
Intelligente Architektur (14): 58–63.

InfoRoma (2006). "Weather." Retrieved 6/15/06, from http://www.inforoma.it/
weather.php.

Lerum, V., and M. Cucinella (2006). Interview. Bologna.

Lerum, V., and C. Giaccaglia (2006). Interview. Recanati.

Slessor, C. (1999). "Light canopy." *Architectural Review* 205 (1224): 66–69.

USDOE. (2006). "EnergyPlus Weather Data." Retrieved 6/15/06, from
http://www.eere.energy.gov/buildings/energyplus/cfm/
weather_data.cfm.

CHAPTER 13

Lerum, V., and T. Christ (2006). Interview. San Francisco.

CHAPTER 14

Bruder, W., and R. Nelson (2004). Agents of Change Workshop. Phoenix, Arizona State University: 15.

Burrelsman, T., B. D. Villers, et al. (1996). "Phoenix Central Library: Thermal performance of a desert monument." Retrieved 3/17/07, from http://arch.ced.berkeley.edu/vitalsigns/workup/phoenix_lib/phoenix_home.html.

CHAPTER 15

Foucault, M. (1995). *Discipline and punish: The birth of the prison.* New York: Vintage Books.

Photography and Illustration Credits

Figure 1.1	Peter Barfoed
Figure 1.3	"HVAC Applications," *ASHRAE Handbook,* IP edition (1999), Table 2, p. 34.8.
Figure 1.4	Vidar Lerum
Figure 2.1	U.S.A.F. climate zone map from the Map and Geography Library at the University of Illinois at Urbana–Champaign.
Figure 2.2	Olgyay, Victor; *Design with Climate.* © 1963 Princeton University Press, 1991 renewed PUP. Reprinted by permission of Princeton University Press.
Figure 2.3	National Atlas of the United States, http://nationalatlas.gov
Figure 2.5	Meteonorm Version 5.1 (www.meteonorm.com). Meteotest, Fabrikstrasse 12, 3012 Bern, Switzerland
Figure 2.6	Google Earth™ mapping service
Figure 3.1	Google SketchUp (www.sketchup.google.com).
Figure 3.2	Meteonorm Version 5.1 (www.meteonorm.com). Meteotest, Fabrikstrasse 12, 3012 Bern, Switzerland
Figure 3.3	Mario Cucinella Architects
Figure 4.1	Mario Cucinella Architects
Figure 5.1	"Listen to the Baby," drawing by Vidar Lerum, based on the sculpture by Tapfuma Gutsa, "Listen to the Baby Kick, 1998—Opal Stone," image available at: http://www.artthrob.co.za/01mar/news.html.
Figure 5.2	© Transsolar
Figure 6.1	Photo credit: Håvard Dahl Bratrein. Tromsø Museum by permission.
Figure 7.1	© 2007 The Thomson Corporation. All rights reserved. Republication or redistribution of Thomson content, including by framing or similar means, is prohibited without the prior written consent of Thomson. EndNote® is a registered trademark of The Thomson Corporation.

Figure 8.3	Photograph courtesy of Therma-Stor LLC (www.ThermaStor.com)
Figure 8.4	Danish Meteorological Institute
Figures 8.5–8.7	The Midwest Research Institute (MRI), management and operating contractor for the National Renewable Energy Laboratory (NREL), developed ENERGY-10 Version 1.8 and holds certain intellectual property rights, including trademark and copyright rights related to ENERGY-10 Version 1.8 software, that it has licensed to the Sustainable Buildings Industry Council (SBIC) for the purpose of commercialization. SBIC is an independent nonprofit organization whose mission is to advance the design, affordability, energy performance, and environmental soundness of America's buildings. NREL is the nation's primary laboratory for renewable energy and energy efficiency R&D. NREL is the principal research laboratory for the DOE Office of Energy Efficiency and Renewable Energy.
Figure 8.8	KHR Architects
Figure 8.12	Danish Meteorological Institute
Figure 8.16	Copyright 1996–2006 Onset Computer Corporation, 470 MacArthur Blvd., Bourne, MA 02532 USA. All rights reserved.
Figure 8.22	Copyright 1996–2006 Onset Computer Corporation, 470 MacArthur Blvd., Bourne, MA 02532 USA. All rights reserved.
Figure 8.24	The Midwest Research Institute (MRI), management and operating contractor for the National Renewable Energy Laboratory (NREL), developed ENERGY-10 Version 1.8 and holds certain intellectual property rights, including trademark and copyright rights related to ENERGY-10 Version 1.8 software, that it has licensed to the Sustainable Buildings Industry Council (SBIC) for the purpose of commercialization. SBIC is an independent nonprofit organization whose mission is to advance the design, affordability, energy performance, and environmental soundness of America's buildings. NREL is the nation's primary laboratory for renewable energy and energy efficiency R&D. NREL is the principal research laboratory for the DOE Office of Energy Efficiency and Renewable Energy.
Figure 9.3	Architect Sverre Fehn MNAL
Figures 9.7–9.11	The Midwest Research Institute (MRI), management and operating contractor for the National Renewable Energy Laboratory (NREL), developed ENERGY-10 Version 1.8 and holds certain intellectual property rights, including trademark and copyright rights related to ENERGY-10

Version 1.8 software, that it has licensed to the Sustainable Buildings Industry Council (SBIC) for the purpose of commercialization. SBIC is an independent nonprofit organization whose mission is to advance the design, affordability, energy performance, and environmental soundness of America's buildings. NREL is the nation's primary laboratory for renewable energy and energy efficiency R&D. NREL is the principal research laboratory for the DOE Office of Energy Efficiency and Renewable Energy.

Figure 9.12	Architect Sverre Fehn MNAL
Figures 9.13–9.14	Drawing by Lone Wiggers
Figure 9.15	Drawing by Sverre Fehn, photographed by Vidar Lerum
Figure 9.16	Drawing by Lone Wiggers
Figure 9.17	Architect Sverre Fehn MNAL
Figure 9.24	Architect Sverre Fehn MNAL
Figure 9.25	© Tussa Kraft AS, www.tussa.no
Figure 9.26	Source: Statsbygg
Figures 9.27–9.31	Drawing reprinted from Statsbygg report 602/2001 by permission.
Figures 9.37–9.38	Drawing reprinted from Statsbygg report 602/2001 by permission.
Figure 9.39	The Midwest Research Institute (MRI), management and operating contractor for the National Renewable Energy Laboratory (NREL), developed ENERGY-10 Version 1.8 and holds certain intellectual property rights, including trademark and copyright rights related to ENERGY-10 Version 1.8 software, that it has licensed to the Sustainable Buildings Industry Council (SBIC) for the purpose of commercialization. SBIC is an independent nonprofit organization whose mission is to advance the design, affordability, energy performance, and environmental soundness of America's buildings. NREL is the nation's primary laboratory for renewable energy and energy efficiency R&D. NREL is the principal research laboratory for the DOE Office of Energy Efficiency and Renewable Energy.
Figure 10.2	KHR Architects
Figures 10.6–10.15	The Midwest Research Institute (MRI), management and operating contractor for the National Renewable Energy Laboratory (NREL), developed ENERGY-10 Version 1.8 and holds certain intellectual property rights, including trademark and copyright rights related to ENERGY-10 Version 1.8 software, that it has licensed to the Sustainable Buildings Industry Council (SBIC) for the purpose of commercialization. SBIC is an independent nonprofit organization whose mission is to advance the design,

affordability, energy performance, and environmental soundness of America's buildings. NREL is the nation's primary laboratory for renewable energy and energy efficiency R&D. NREL is the principal research laboratory for the DOE Office of Energy Efficiency and Renewable Energy.

Figure 10.19	KHR ARchitects
Figure 10.22	Danish Building Research Institute 2001
Figures 10.25–10.29	Drawing by KHR Architects
Figures 10.30–10.31	Danish Building Research Institute 2001
Figure 11.1	Murphy/Jahn
Figure 11.2	© Google Earth™ mapping service
Figure 11.3	Murphy/Jahn
Figure 11.4	Murphy/Jahn, photographed by Altenkirch
Figures 11.7–11.10	The Midwest Research Institute (MRI), management and operating contractor for the National Renewable Energy Laboratory (NREL), developed ENERGY-10 Version 1.8 and holds certain intellectual property rights, including trademark and copyright rights related to ENERGY-10 Version 1.8 software, that it has licensed to the Sustainable Buildings Industry Council (SBIC) for the purpose of commercialization. SBIC is an independent nonprofit organization whose mission is to advance the design, affordability, energy performance, and environmental soundness of America's buildings. NREL is the nation's primary laboratory for renewable energy and energy efficiency R&D. NREL is the principal research laboratory for the DOE Office of Energy Efficiency and Renewable Energy.
Figures 11.11–11.12	Murphy/Jahn, photograph by Andreas Keller
Figure 11.14	Murphy/Jahn, photograph by Andreas Keller
Figure 11.15	Murphy/Jahn
Figure 11.16	Murphy/Jahn, photograph by Andreas Keller
Figures 11.17–11.19	© Transsolar
Figure 11.21	Murphy/Jahn, photograph by Andreas Keller
Figure 11.22	Murphy/Jahn, photograph by Altenkirch
Figure 11.23	Murphy/Jahn, photograph by Andreas Keller
Figures 11.24–11.25	© Transsolar
Figure 11.26	Murphy/Jahn, photograph by Andreas Keller
Figure 11.28	© Transsolar
Figure 11.31	© Transsolar
Figure 11.32	M&M Systeme. Reprinted with permission of John Wiley & Sons, Inc.
Figure 11.33	*Mechanical and Electrical Equipment for Buildings.* Ben Stein, John S. Reynolds, Walter T. Grondzik, Alison G. Kwok.

	Copyright 2006, John Wiley & Sons Inc. Reprinted with permission of John Wiley & Sons, Inc.
Figure 11.34	The Midwest Research Institute (MRI), management and operating contractor for the National Renewable Energy Laboratory (NREL), developed ENERGY-10 Version 1.8 and holds certain intellectual property rights, including trademark and copyright rights related to ENERGY-10 Version 1.8 software, that it has licensed to the Sustainable Buildings Industry Council (SBIC) for the purpose of commercialization. SBIC is an independent nonprofit organization whose mission is to advance the design, affordability, energy performance, and environmental soundness of America's buildings. NREL is the nation's primary laboratory for renewable energy and energy efficiency R&D. NREL is the principal research laboratory for the DOE Office of Energy Efficiency and Renewable Energy.
Figure 11.35	© Transsolar
Figure 12.1	Photo by Vidar Lerum
Figures 12.4–12.9	The Midwest Research Institute (MRI), management and operating contractor for the National Renewable Energy Laboratory (NREL), developed ENERGY-10 Version 1.8 and holds certain intellectual property rights, including trademark and copyright rights related to ENERGY-10 Version 1.8 software, that it has licensed to the Sustainable Buildings Industry Council (SBIC) for the purpose of commercialization. SBIC is an independent nonprofit organization whose mission is to advance the design, affordability, energy performance, and environmental soundness of America's buildings. NREL is the nation's primary laboratory for renewable energy and energy efficiency R&D. NREL is the principal research laboratory for the DOE Office of Energy Efficiency and Renewable Energy.
Figure 12.10	Mario Cucinella Architects
Figure 12.11	Image provided by SolarWorld AG
Figure 12.12	Photo by Vidar Lerum
Figures 12.13–12.19	Mario Cucinella Architects
Figure 12.25	Mario Cucinella Architects
Figure 12.26	Enviroware, srl (Italy)
Figure 12.28	Photo by Vidar Lerum
Figure 12.29	HEED
Figures 12.30–12.32	The Midwest Research Institute (MRI), management and operating contractor for the National Renewable Energy Laboratory (NREL), developed ENERGY-10 Version 1.8 and holds certain intellectual property rights, including trademark and copyright rights related to ENERGY-10

Version 1.8 software, that it has licensed to the Sustainable Buildings Industry Council (SBIC) for the purpose of commercialization. SBIC is an independent nonprofit organization whose mission is to advance the design, affordability, energy performance, and environmental soundness of America's buildings. NREL is the nation's primary laboratory for renewable energy and energy efficiency R&D. NREL is the principal research laboratory for the DOE Office of Energy Efficiency and Renewable Energy.

Figure 12.33	Copyright 1996–2006 Onset Computer Corporation, 470 MacArthur Blvd., Bourne, MA 02532 USA. All rights reserved.
Figure 12.34	*Mechanical and Electrical Equipment for Buildings*. Ben Stein, John S. Reynolds, Walter T. Grondzik, Alison G. Kwok. Copyright 2006, John Wiley & Sons Inc. Reprinted with permission of John Wiley & Sons, Inc.
Figure 13.1	© Google Earth™ mapping service. Site plan by Morphosis
Figure 13.3	© Morphosis
Figures 13.4–13.12	The Midwest Research Institute (MRI), management and operating contractor for the National Renewable Energy Laboratory (NREL), developed ENERGY-10 Version 1.8 and holds certain intellectual property rights, including trademark and copyright rights related to ENERGY-10 Version 1.8 software, that it has licensed to the Sustainable Buildings Industry Council (SBIC) for the purpose of commercialization. SBIC is an independent nonprofit organization whose mission is to advance the design, affordability, energy performance, and environmental soundness of America's buildings. NREL is the nation's primary laboratory for renewable energy and energy efficiency R&D. NREL is the principal research laboratory for the DOE Office of Energy Efficiency and Renewable Energy.
Figure 13.13	© Morphosis, photographed by Young-II Kim.
Figure 13.18	© Morphosis
Figure 13.19	The Midwest Research Institute (MRI), management and operating contractor for the National Renewable Energy Laboratory (NREL), developed ENERGY-10 Version 1.8 and holds certain intellectual property rights, including trademark and copyright rights related to ENERGY-10 Version 1.8 software, that it has licensed to the Sustainable Buildings Industry Council (SBIC) for the purpose of commercialization. SBIC is an independent nonprofit organization whose mission is to advance the design, affordability, energy performance, and environmental soundness of America's buildings. NREL is the nation's primary laboratory for renewable energy and energy efficiency R&D. NREL is the principal research laboratory

	for the DOE Office of Energy Efficiency and Renewable Energy.
Figure 14.2	© Google Earth™ mapping service
Figure 14.3	bruder DWL architects
Figures 14.5–14.11	The Midwest Research Institute (MRI), management and operating contractor for the National Renewable Energy Laboratory (NREL), developed ENERGY-10 Version 1.8 and holds certain intellectual property rights, including trademark and copyright rights related to ENERGY-10 Version 1.8 software, that it has licensed to the Sustainable Buildings Industry Council (SBIC) for the purpose of commercialization. SBIC is an independent nonprofit organization whose mission is to advance the design, affordability, energy performance, and environmental soundness of America's buildings. NREL is the nation's primary laboratory for renewable energy and energy efficiency R&D. NREL is the principal research laboratory for the DOE Office of Energy Efficiency and Renewable Energy.
Figure 14.16	bruder DWL architects
Figure 14.20	bruder DWL architects, photographed by Bill Timmerman.
Figure 14.23	bruder DWL architects, photographed by Bill Timmerman.
Figures 14.25–14.29	Copyright 1996–2006 Onset Computer Corporation, 470 MacArthur Blvd., Bourne, MA 02532 USA. All rights reserved.
Figure 15.2	Drawing by Lone Wiggers, C. F. Møllers Tegnestue

Index

NOTES

NOTES

NOTES

NOTES

NOTES

NOTES

NOTES